《多彩中国节》丛书编委会
Editorial Committee of the Colorful Chinese Festivals Series

顾　问
史蒂文·伍德·施迈德　冯骥才　周明甫

主　编
彭新良

编　委（按姓名笔画排列）

韦荣慧　田　阡　邢　莉　刘　哲
齐勇锋　阮全友　张　刚　张　跃
张　暖　张曙光　陈　娟　徐　敏
黄忠彩　萧　放　曹雅欣　彭新良

Consultants

Steven Wood Schmader　Feng Jicai　Zhou Mingfu

Chief Editor

Peng Xinliang

Editorial Board

Wei Ronghui　Tian Qian　Xing Li　Liu Zhe

Qi Yongfeng　Ruan Quanyou　Zhang Gang　Zhang Yue

Zhang Nuan　Zhang Shuguang　Chen Juan　Xu Min

Huang Zhongcai　Xiao Fang　Cao Yaxin　Peng Xinliang

丛书主编　彭新良

The Dragon Boat Festival

汉英对照

端午节

田阡　石甜　编著
王阿秋　译

全国百佳图书出版单位
时代出版传媒股份有限公司
安徽人民出版社

图书在版编目（CIP）数据

端午节 : 汉英对照 / 田阡，石甜编著 ; 王阿秋译 . -- 合肥 : 安徽人民出版社，2018.8
（多彩中国节丛书 / 彭新良主编）

ISBN 978-7-212-10026-1

Ⅰ . ①端… Ⅱ . ①田… ②石… ③王… Ⅲ . ①端午节－风俗习惯－中国－汉、英 Ⅳ . ① K892.18

中国版本图书馆 CIP 数据核字 (2018) 第 005330 号

《多彩中国节》丛书

端午节：汉英对照
DUANWU JIE

彭新良　丛书主编

田阡　石甜　**编著**　　王阿秋　**译**

出 版 人：徐　敏	**选题策划**：刘　哲　陈　娟
出版统筹：张　旻　袁小燕	**责任编辑**：袁小燕　周　羽
责任印制：董　亮	**装帧设计**：陈　爽　宋文岚

出版发行：时代出版传媒股份有限公司 http://www.press-mart.com
　　　　　　安徽人民出版社 http://www.ahpeople.com
地　　址：合肥市政务文化新区翡翠路 1118 号出版传媒广场八楼
邮　　编：230071
电　　话：0551-63533258　0551-63533259（传真）
印　　刷：安徽联众印刷有限公司

开本：880mm×1230mm　1/32　**印张**：9.125　**字数**：270 千
版次：2018 年 8 月第 1 版　　2018 年 9 月第 1 次印刷

ISBN　978-7-212-10026-1　　　　　　　　**定价**：40.00 元

代 序

我们共同的日子

个人一年一度最重要的日子是生日，大家一年一度最重要的日子是节日。节日是大家共同的日子。

节日是一种纪念日，内涵多种多样。有民族的、国家的、宗教的，比如国庆节、圣诞节等。有某一类人的，如妇女、儿童、劳动者的，这便是妇女节、儿童节、劳动节等。也有与人们的生活生产密切相关的，这类节日历史悠久，很早就形成了一整套人们约定俗成、代代相传的节日习俗，这是一种传统的节日。传统节日也多种多样。中国是一个多民族国家，有56个民族，统称中华民族。传统节日有全民族共有的，也有某个民族特有的。比如春节、中秋节、元宵节、端午节、清明节、重阳节等，就为中华民族所共用和共享；世界文化遗产羌年就为羌族独有和独享。各民族这样的节日很多。

传统节日是在漫长的农耕时代形成的。农耕时代生产与生活、人与自然的关系十分密切。人们或为了感恩于大自然的恩赐，或为了庆祝辛勤劳作换来的收获，或为了激发生命的活力，或为了加强人际的亲情，经过长期相互认同，最终约定俗成，渐渐把一年中某一天确定为节日，并创造了十分完整又严格的节俗，如仪式、庆典、规制、禁忌，乃至特定的游艺、装饰与食品，来把节日这天演化成一个独具内涵、迷人的日子。更重要的是，人们在每一个传统的节日里，还把共同的生活理想、人间愿望与审美追求融入节日的内涵与种种仪式中。因此，它是中华民族世间理想与生活愿望极致的表现。可以说，我们的传统——精神文化传统，往往就是依靠这代代相传的一年一度的节日继承下来的。

然而，自从 20 世纪整个人类进入由农耕文明向工业文明的过渡，农耕时代形成的文化传统开始瓦解。尤其是中国，在近百年由封闭走向开放的过程中，节日文化——特别是城市的节日文化受到现代文明与外来文化的冲击。当下人们已经鲜明地感受到传统节日渐行渐远，并为此产生忧虑。传统节日的淡化必然使其中蕴含的传统精神随之涣散。然而，人们并没有坐等传统的消失，主动和积极地与之应对。这充分显示了当代中国人在文化上的自觉。

近 10 年，随着中国民间文化遗产抢救工程的全面展开，国家非物质文化遗产名录申报工作的有力推动，传统节日受到关注，一些重要的传统节日被列入了国家文化遗产名录。继而，2006 年国家将每年 6 月的第二个周六确定为"文化遗产日"，2007 年国务院决定将 3 个中华民族的重要节日——清明节、端午节和中秋节列为法定放假日。这一重大决定，表现了国家对公众的传统文化生活及其传承的重视与尊重，同时也是保护节日文化遗产十分必要的措施。

节日不放假必然直接消解了节日文化，放假则是恢复节日传统的首要条件。但放假不等于远去的节日立即就会回到身边。节日与假日的不同是因为节日有特定的文化内容与文化形式。那么，重温与恢复已经变得陌生的传统节日习俗则是必不可少的了。

千百年来，我们的祖先从生活的愿望出发，为每一个节日都创造出许许多多美丽又动人的习俗。这种愿望是理想主义的，所以节日习俗是理想的；愿望是情感化的，所以节日习俗也是情感化的；愿望是美好的，所以节日习俗是美的。人们用合家团聚的年夜饭迎接新年；把天上的明月化为手中甜甜的月饼，来象征人间的团圆；在严寒刚刚消退、万物复苏的早春，赶到野外去打扫墓地，告慰亡灵，表达心中的缅怀，同时戴花插柳，踏青春游，亲切地拥抱大地山川……这些诗意化的节日习俗，使我们一代代人的心灵获得了美好的安慰与宁静。

对于少数民族来说，他们特有的节日的意义则更加重要。节日还是他们民族集体记忆的载体、共同精神的依托、个性的表现、民族身份之所在。

谁说传统的习俗过时了？如果我们淡忘了这些习俗，就一定要去重温一下传统。重温不是表象地模仿古人的形式，而是用心去体验传统中的精神与情感。

在历史进程中，习俗是在不断变化的，但民族传统的精神实质不应变。这传统就是对美好生活的不懈追求，对大自然的感恩与敬畏，对家庭团圆与世间和谐永恒的企望。

这便是我们节日的主题，也是这套《多彩中国节》丛书编写的根由与目的。

中国 56 个民族是一个大家庭，各民族的节日文化异彩纷呈，既有春节、元宵节、中秋节这样多民族共庆的节日，也有泼水节、火把节、那达慕等少数民族特有的节日。这套丛书选取了中国最有代表性的 10 个传统节日，一节一册，图文并茂，汉英对照，旨在为海内外读者通俗、全面地呈现中国绚丽多彩的节庆文化和民俗文化；放在一起则是中华民族传统节日的一部全书，既有知识性、资料性、工具性，又有可读性和趣味性。10 本精致的小册子，以翔实的文献和生动的传说，将每个节日的源起、流布与习俗，图文并茂、有滋有味地娓娓道来，从这些节日的传统中，可以看出中国人的精神追求和文化脉络。这样一套丛书不仅是对我国传统节日的一次总结，也是对传统节日文化富于创意的弘扬。

　　我读了书稿，心生欣喜，因序之。

冯骥才

（全国政协常委、中国文联原执行副主席）

Preface

Our Common Days

The most important day for a person is his or her birthday while the most important days for all are festivals, which are our common days.

Festivals are embedded with rich connotations for remembering. There're ethnic, national, and religious ones, such as National Day and Christmas Day; festivals for a certain group of people, such as Women's Day, Children's Day, and Laborers' Day; and those closely related to people's life and production, which enjoy a long history and feature a complete set of well-established festive traditions passed on from one generation to another. These are so-called traditional festivals, which vary greatly, too.

China, consisting of 56 nationalities, is a multi-ethnic country. People in China are collectively called the Chinese nation. So it's no wonder that some of the traditional festivals are celebrated by all nationalities while others only by certain nationalities, with the representatives of the former ones being the Spring Festival, the Lantern Festival, the Dragon Boat Festival, the Tomb-Sweeping Festival, and the Double Ninth Festival, etc. and that of the latter being the Qiang New Year, a unique festival for Qiang ethnic group. Each of ethnic groups in China has quite a number of their unique traditional festivals.

The traditional festivals have taken shape in the long agrarian times when people were greatly dependent on nature and when life was closely related to production. People gradually saw eye to eye with each other in the long-term practicing sets of rituals, celebrations, taboos as well as games, embellishments, and foods in a strict way and decided to select some days of one year as festivals with a view to expressing their gratitude to nature, celebrating harvesting, stimulating vitality of life, or strengthening bonds between family members and relatives. In this way, festivals have evolved into charming days with unique connotations. More importantly, people have instilled their common aspirations and aesthetic pursuits into festive connotations and rituals. To put it simply, festivals are consummate demonstrations of Chinese people's worldly aspirations and ideals, and Chinese people's spiritual cultures are inherited for generations by them.

Nevertheless, the cultural traditions formed in the agrarian times began to collapse with human beings being in transition from agrarian civilization to industrial one, esp., in China, whose festive cultures were severely hammered by modern civilization and foreign cultures in nearly one hundred years from being closed to opening up to the world. Nowadays, people strongly feel that traditional festivals are drifting away from their lives and are deeply concerned about it owing to the fact that dilution of traditional festivals means the fall of the traditional spirit of Chinese people. Of course, we don't wait and see; instead, we cope with it in a positive way. This fully displays the contemporary Chinese people's cultural consciousness.

In recent ten years, the traditional festivals have been earning more and more attention and some significant ones are included to the list of the National Heritages with the vigorous promotion of China's Folk Heritage Rescue Program and China's intangible cultural heritage application; for example, China set the second Saturday of June as "Cultural Heritage Day" in 2006; the State Council decided to list three significant traditional festivals as legal holidays—the Tomb-Sweeping Festival, the Dragon Boat Festival, and the Mid-Autumn Festival in 2007. These measures show the state gives priority to and pay tribute to the inheritance of public traditional cultures.

Holidays are necessary for spending festivals which will be diluted otherwise; however, holidays don't necessarily bring back traditional festivals. Since festivals, different from holidays, are equipped with special cultural forms and contents, it's essential to recover those traditional festive customs which have become stranger and stranger to contemporary Chinese people.

In the past thousands of years, our ancestors, starting from their aspirations, created many fine and engaging traditions. These aspirations are ideal, emotional, and beautiful, so are the festival traditions. People usher in the New Year by having the meal together on the New Year's Eve, make moon cakes by imitating the moon in the sky, standing for family reunion, or go to sweep the tombs of ancestors or family members for commemorating or comforting in the early spring when the winter just recedes and everything wakes up while taking spring hiking and enjoying spring scenes by the way. These poetic festive customs greatly comfort souls of people for generations.

As for ethnic minority people, their special festivals mean more to them. The festivals carry the collective memory, common spirit, character of their ethnic groups as well as mark their ethnic identities.

Are the traditional festive customs really out-dated? We're compelled to review them if we really forget them. What matters for review is not imitating the forms of the ancient Chinese people's celebrations but experiencing essence and emotions embedded in them with heart and soul.

Traditions have evolved with history's evolving, but the traditional national spirit has never changed. The spirit lies in people's never-ending pursuit for beautiful life, consistent gratitude and awe for nature, constant aspiration for family reunion and world harmony.

This is also the theme of our festivals and the root-cause of compiling the series.

The Chinese nation, featuring its colorful and varieties of festive cultures, boasts the common festivals celebrated by all nationalities, such as the Spring Festival, the Lantern Festival, the Mid-Autumn Festival, and the ethnic festivals, such as the Water Splashing Festival (Thai people), the Torch Festival (Yi people), Naadam (Mongolian nationality). This series, selecting the most typical ten festivals of China, with each festival being in one volume with figures and in both English and Chinese, unfolds the colorful festive and folk cultures in an engaging and all-round way for appealing to foreign readers. If put together, they constitute a complete set of books on Chinese traditional festivals, being instructive and intriguing. The ten brochures elaborate on the origins, distribution, and customs of each festival in an engaging way with figures, tales, and rich literature. Chinese people's spiritual pursuit and cultural veining can be tracked in this series, serving as a summary of Chinese traditional festivals and innovative promotion of them.

I went over the series with delight, and with delight, wrote the preface, too.

Feng Jicai

CPPCC National Committee member

Former Vice-president of the China Federation of Literary and Art Circles

目 录

Contents

第一章

端午节的传承

每年的农历五月初五，是中国的端午节，也是中国人最为看重的传统节日之一。

端午节，有端五、重五、重午、端阳、地腊（道教节庆）、女儿节、浴兰和天中节等二十余种说法，别称数量是各传统节日之最。在中国，一些少数民族也过端午节，如彝族、傣族、土家族、纳西族、侗族、布依族等，只是过节的习俗和形式各异。在全国各地，端午时令最普遍的活动是划龙船、吃粽子、喝雄黄酒、挂菖蒲与艾草等。在南方很多地方，这些庆祝方式甚至越来越隆重。

那么，端午节是怎么来的？为什么选择在五月初五这一天？为什么要划龙船、吃粽子、喝雄黄酒、贴天师符？屈原是谁？龙舟与图腾有什么关系？诸多疑问在中华民族的历史长河中都能找到答案。

一、
端午节的起源

端午节可以说是上古风俗遗存最多的节日，形成过程也很复杂。关于端午节的起源，有很多种说法，按照影响力的大小，端午起源大致可以分为三类：一是图腾说。端午这一天是古代吴越族举行图腾祭的节日。二是纪念说。不同地区纪念不同的人物，从江汉平原到江浙一带，这些人物包括了屈原、伍子胥、介子推、越王勾践、孝女曹娥、伏波将军马援、汉苍梧太守陈临等。他们有的是历史人物，有的是传说人物，但都是老百姓祭拜的对象。三是驱毒避邪禳灾说。端午在农历五月，这一时期气温升高，蛇虫繁殖，病毒滋生，民间一直认为五月是凶月，端午有驱五毒、挂艾叶菖蒲、饮雄黄酒等习俗。通过这些习俗祛邪禳灾，保佑人们平平安安。

张正明学者认为，端午节实际上是文化事项异源合流，是人类与自然环境互约共进的结果。

（一）最常见的说法——纪念屈原

一般认为端午节是为了纪念屈原。屈原是中国历史上最伟大的诗人之一，正是由于屈原的缘故，端午节也被称为"诗人节"。唐末江南僧人文秀写过一首《端阳》诗，诗云："节分端午自谁言，万古传闻为屈原，堪笑楚江空渺渺，不能洗得直臣冤。"表达了人民大众对屈原的同情与崇敬，抒发了作者对昏君奸臣的痛恨。屈原是谁？为何后世的端午习俗都与纪念屈原有关？让我们回到距今2300多年的春秋战国时代。

○屈原

当时，中原大地的秦、楚、齐、燕、赵、韩、魏七个国家争城夺地，互相杀伐，混战不断。楚国大诗人屈原正当青年，得到楚怀王的信任，被任命为左徒官。屈原见百姓饱受战乱之苦，十分痛心。于是立志报国为民，劝楚怀王任用贤能，让百姓能安居乐业。

当时西部的秦国最强大，时常攻击其他六国。因此，屈原到各国去游说，希望各国联合起来对付秦国。后来，楚、齐、燕、赵、韩、魏六国君王齐集楚国国都——郢，结成了联盟，怀王成了联盟的领袖。联盟的力量阻止了强秦的扩张，屈原得到了怀王的重用，全面负责内政外交大事。但是，当时的楚国有一群以子兰为首的贵族，因屈原得到赏识而怀恨在心。他们常常在怀王面前说屈原独断专权，根本不把怀王放在眼里。挑拨离间的人多了，怀王也渐渐相信了这些谣言，对屈原不满起来。

秦国的间谍把这一情况报告了秦王，秦王听到这个消息，把大臣张仪召进宫商量。张仪认为，六国中齐楚两国最有力量，只要这两国不和，联盟也就解体了。张仪愿意利用楚国内部不和的机会，亲自去拆散六国联盟。秦王大喜，准备了金银财宝交给张仪，狡猾的张仪还把象征权力地位的相印交还给秦王，假装辞去秦国官职，向楚国出发。

张仪到了郢都，先拜访屈原，之后一直劝说屈原要考虑秦国的强大，秦楚联合对双方有好处，结果被屈原拒绝了。张仪看到屈原丝毫不肯退让，于是就去找子兰。张仪告诉子兰："有了六国联盟，怀王才信任屈原；拆散了联盟，屈原就没有什么可怕了。"子兰听了，十分高兴。于是，楚国的贵族和张仪沆瀣一气。子兰又引他拜见了怀王的宠妃郑袖，张仪把一双价值万金的白璧献给郑袖。郑袖非常高兴，答应帮助他们。郑袖、张仪和子兰商量后认为，要秦楚联合，必须先拆散六国联盟；而拆散联盟，先让怀王不信任屈原。子兰想了一条计策——让郑袖在怀王面前说屈原向张仪索取贿赂。

子兰向怀王引荐张仪。张仪为了劝说怀王拆散六国同盟，列举了秦楚联盟的很多好处。最后还说："只要大王愿意，秦王已经准备了六百里土地献给楚国。"怀王听说不费一兵一卒，白得六百里土地，怎么能不高兴。回到宫中，还把此事告诉了郑袖。郑袖向楚怀王道喜，但又皱起眉头："听说屈原向张仪索要一双白璧没有成功，恐怕会反对这件事吧！"怀王听了，半信半疑。第二天，怀王摆酒席招待张仪。席间讨论起秦楚友好，屈原果然激烈反对，与子兰、靳尚进行了争论。怀王想起郑袖所说，屈原果然竭力反对秦楚和好，加上自己又贪图秦国的土地，他不禁怒道："难道楚国的六百里土地抵不上你一双白璧！"说完叫武士把屈原拉出宫。

屈原回到家中，闷闷不乐，不禁长叹。姐姐女媭问明情由后，劝他不要再议论了，屈原道："我是楚国人，死也不能看到楚国遇到危险啊！"屈原写了一篇名叫《离骚》的长诗，把对楚国的忧愁和自己的怨愤都写了进去。这篇诗传到宫中，子兰、靳尚等人又有了攻击的理由，说屈原把怀王比作桀纣。怀王一怒，撤掉了屈原的官职。女媭劝屈原换个地方休养一阵，屈原搬出了郢都。

楚怀王和齐国断绝邦交、拆散联盟以后，就派人跟张仪到秦国接收土地。快要进入秦都咸阳时，张仪装作喝醉酒，下车时跌了一跤，推说跌伤了腿，就告别了楚使，先进城去了。楚使住在客栈里，天天去找张仪，张仪总是推脱腿伤未愈不能接见。一直过了三个月，张仪得到消息，证实六国联盟确实已经瓦解了，才出来接见楚使。当楚使提到交割土地时，张仪说："我说献给楚王的是自己的六里土地。秦国的土地怎么能够献给旁人呢？"楚使只得空手回来报告楚王。楚怀王气昏了，仗着这几年养精蓄锐、兵粮充足，就派了大将军带领十万大军，进攻秦国。

秦王索性联合齐国，分两路迎击楚军。楚军挡不住两国夹攻，连打几个败仗。屈原急坏了，决定赶回郢都。半路上，他接到了怀王的命令——出使齐国，恢复联盟。屈原立刻奔赴齐国。怀王违背联盟，齐国十分愤恨，但是屈原是齐王敬重的人，经过一番谈判，就答应撤回助秦攻楚的齐兵。屈原还未返国，就得到了秦楚议和的消息，便急忙赶回楚国去。子兰、靳尚听说屈原回来了，连忙来报告王后郑袖。郑袖向怀王哭诉。第二天，怀王下了命令："任屈原为三闾大夫，立刻赴任。"怀王派子兰把命令传达给屈原。屈原仰天长叹："大王，你不能再糊涂啊，楚国的江山，楚国的百姓，全在你的身上呀！"

怀王三十年，秦国占领了楚国北部的八座城池。怀王正在愁闷，忽然接到秦王的来信，请他到秦国武关地方商谈秦楚永世友好的办法。怀王左思右想，子兰首先劝怀王："秦王愿意和好，这机会可失不得。"靳尚也说："这一去，至少会让两国有几年太平。"怀王回到后宫，又听了郑袖一番劝说的话，这才同意去武关会谈。

楚怀王和靳尚带了五百人马动身出发。半个月后，只剩下靳尚一人一马逃回郢都。楚怀王和五百人马一到武关，就被秦国扣留，已经送往秦国都城咸阳了。郑袖为了安定人心，立太子熊横为顷襄王，自己掌握大权，还任命子兰做令尹，管理全国军政。屈原拼死赶到郢都，要求顷襄王恢复六国联盟，用强大的实力，向秦国讨回怀王。子兰等人不但不听屈原的主张，而且驱逐他立刻出都，不许他再回郢都。过了三年，传过来了怀王的死讯。楚怀王死后，秦国把枯骨送还楚国。怀王的灵柩到达郢都时，沿路都有人失声痛哭。屈原在怀王灵柩面前哭昏了过去，要求顷襄王利用各国都在怨恨秦国的机会，设法联络其他几国，一同抗衡秦国。顷襄王完全不听。屈原日夜在宫门前痛哭，期望能打动顷襄王。但这惹恼了郑袖，她叫顷襄王革掉屈原的三闾大夫职位，押送其流放江南，永远不准其过江。

屈原在陵阳住了九年，后来到黔中郡溆浦住下。满腹的忧愁愤恨，他都写成了诗篇。顷襄王当政的第二十一年，秦国大将军白起进攻楚国，占领了郢都，楚国的宗庙和陵墓都被毁了。楚国要亡了！屈原决定回到郢都，死在出生的土地上。屈原昏昏沉沉地走了几天，到了汨罗江边，径直投进汨罗江。

屈原投汨罗江后，人们怕他的尸体被鱼龙吃掉，每当这一天到来时都用竹筒贮米投进水中祭奠他。汉朝建武年间，

○ 追踪屈子

传所投之物被蛟龙所窃，于是人们划龙船赶走蛟龙，又用荷叶包成粽子并以五色丝带缚绑。这些为蛟龙所惮惧，投入水中方能见效。

旅游小贴士

汨罗江畔

汨罗江发源于湖南平江县，在岳阳市境内注入南洞庭湖。汨罗江两岸粉墙村舍，如今保留了屈子祠、骚坛、屈原墓群等古迹和遗迹。每逢农历五月初五，汨罗江畔的百姓总要举行盛大的龙舟竞赛活动，以纪念伟大的爱国主义诗人屈原。

屈子祠

屈子祠是为纪念我国伟大的爱国诗人屈原而修建的，伫立在玉笥山麓汨罗江边，始建于汉代，清乾隆年间重修。

交通：

飞机：从长沙黄花机场可乘大巴车或者出租车抵达汨罗市，再从汨罗市乘专线车至玉笥山屈子祠景区。

火车、汽车：由湖南省岳阳市乘火车至汨罗市车站或乘岳阳市直达汨罗市的汽车，再从汨罗市乘专线车至玉笥山屈子祠景区。

（二）文献考古者的说法——辟邪

在先秦时期，人们认为五月是一个不好的月份，灾难频繁、容易生病，五月被称作"凶月"。《史记》记载了一个故事，一个名叫田婴的人娶了很多老婆，这些老婆为他生了四十个儿子。有一次，他的一个小老婆将在五月初五这天生产。田婴知道后就对他这个小老婆说："五月是一个凶月，你不要生孩子。"可是，到了五月初五这天，他的小老婆还是生下了孩子，是个男孩，取名田文。这个孩子一直被秘密抚养。直到有一天，田婴的儿子们告诉他，他们还有个兄弟在，于是田婴非常生气，叫来田文母子二人，并生气地说："我叫你不要生，你为什么要生？"田文看见父亲发怒，心疼母亲，忙跪下给父亲磕头，并说："您为什么不要我？为什么不要五月份生的孩子呢？"田婴回答说："五月份出生的孩子，等他长大成家时，对他的父母有伤害。所以不能要。"此时，田文冷静地问他的父亲："人的生命是天给的，谁都不能剥夺，难道因为他可能有伤害，就把他给杀死么？这样天也不会答应。"这个故事表明，当时的人们认为五月初五是个很凶险的日子，需要用各种形式避邪，以保护自己的生命健康，同时为家人祈福。

　　端午跟卫生健康的关系，主要可能是跟节气有关。端午节在很多地方被称为端阳节。所谓"端阳"，是阳气之端，也就是阳气极盛的时候，即夏至。刘德谦根据《荆楚岁时记》中提到"仲夏端午"食粽，以及《玉烛宝典》把竞渡列为夏至活动的记载，认为端午节源于夏至。但是，夏至的阴历日期并不固定，据学者高丙中先生推测，民间曾把夏至"转换"成端阳节，并固定在五月十五日；在魏晋南北朝时，两节并行，"大端午"（夏至）与"小端午"（初五）两节习俗逐渐合流，最后为"小端午"兼并。

　　所以，端午节的风俗大体是原来应对夏至气候变化而形成，将瘟病虫毒祸害归结为日期的邪恶，其禁忌的产生可以追溯到夏商周三代。到了唐朝，这个"恶日"才变成大众联欢节庆之日，饮食装饰也因而变得考究起来。

（三）江浙一带的说法——纪念孝女曹娥

还有一说是端午节纪念孝女曹娥，这个故事在江浙一带流传。很久以前，江浙地区有一个小渔村，有一位曹姓渔夫，天天都在舜江上打鱼，一年到头都不休息。渔夫有个女儿叫曹娥，当时十四岁，生得非常漂亮，又很聪明孝顺。

有一年的春末夏初，舜江江水暴涨，巨浪一个接一个袭来，眼看就淹没了滩涂。洪水袭来也意味着鱼虾会很多，曹娥的父亲想去捕鱼。曹娥很担心父亲的安危，但曹娥的父亲觉得只要小心就应该不会发生意外。

曹娥的父亲走了之后，曹娥在家忐忑不安，就到江堤上去寻找父亲的身影，盼望父亲尽早回家，但一直都没有看到父亲回来。滚滚的江水卷起浊浪拍打江堤，曹娥越来越不放心，便沿着江堤到处寻找。太阳快下山的时候，跟着曹父一起打鱼的村民回来了，个个都被淋湿了，他们跟曹娥说，打鱼的时候正在结网时好几个村民就被巨浪冲走了。曹娥赶快往下游跑。村民们劝她回去，但怎么也劝不回去她。曹娥在江边来回找了三天都没有找到父亲，眼泪也哭尽了，找不到父亲就不回

○孝女曹娥

家。曹娥哭了七天七夜，最后眼泪哭干了，流出来的都是血。

到了第八天，曹娥看到江面一个巨浪托起了她父亲，便马上扑了过去。又过了三天，人们在下游的江面上看到了一男一女，是曹娥反剪双手紧抱着她的父亲。曹娥终于将父亲的尸首找到，带回江边。是曹娥的孝心感动了天地。

曹娥的孝心也让乡亲们感动，他们安葬了曹娥父女，并在江边修建了庙来祭拜曹娥，还将渔村也改名为曹娥村，舜江也改名为曹娥江。每逢曹娥救父这一天，曹娥庙就举行庙会，很多人来到曹娥庙祭拜曹娥娘娘，这一天正是五月初五。因此，很多人将端午节视作纪念曹娥的日子。

旅游小贴士

上虞曹娥庙

曹娥庙，早年又叫灵孝庙、孝女庙，是为彰扬东汉上虞孝女曹娥而建的一处纪念性建筑。曹娥庙始建于公元151年，几经迁徙、扩建、修葺，奠定了现有庙宇布局严谨、错落有致、气势恢宏的建筑基调。

每逢农历五月十五至二十二，曹娥庙里都要举行盛大的庙会，有武技、马术杂技、绍剧戏文等表演，气氛热烈。

地址：曹娥街道孝女路

交通：

飞机：坐飞机抵达杭州萧山机场，或者宁波机场，改乘长途汽车到达绍兴市下属的上虞市；再改乘旅游专线或者出租车，抵达外环南路孝女庙村。

火车、汽车：乘火车到达上虞北站，改乘公交车或出租车，到达小曹娥镇。

（四）另一种说法——纪念伍子胥

伍子胥也是楚国人，比屈原早出生两百多年。伍子胥的父亲和兄弟都被楚王所杀，为了复仇，他离开楚国，投奔吴国，帮助吴国

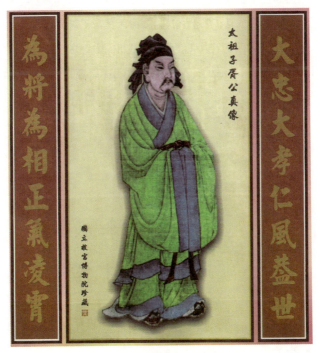

○伍子胥

攻打楚国。终于在第五次战争时，攻下了楚国的都城郢。当时杀害他父亲和兄弟的楚平王已经死了，子胥便挖了楚平王的坟墓，将平

王的尸体用鞭子狠狠地抽打了三百下，以报杀父兄之仇。

伍子胥在吴国深得吴王阖闾的信任。阖闾死后，儿子夫差继位，夫差想消灭自己的邻居越国，越国的国王勾践亲自投降请和，夫差便答应了。伍子胥凭借着丰富的政治和军事经验，建议夫差彻底消灭越国，夫差不听。吴国大臣受越国贿赂，在夫差面前说伍子胥的坏话，结果夫差相信了，并赐伍子胥宝剑要他死。伍子胥视死如归，在死前对到场的人说："我死后，将我眼睛挖出悬挂在都城的东门上，我要看着越国军队入城灭掉吴国。"说完便拔剑自杀。夫差听说了伍子胥临死前所说的话，勃然大怒，便命人把伍子胥的尸体装在皮革里在五月初五这天投入大江。后来，苏州人为纪念这位忠臣，把此江称为胥江。因此，后世相传的端午节也有了纪念伍子胥的说法。

旅游小贴士

伍子胥与苏州城

公元前514年，伍子胥奉吴王阖闾之命，"相土尝水，象天法地"，建造阖闾大城，即今之苏州城。据说伍子胥选的城址是龙穴宝地，刚刚破土动工，老天便刮起狂风，下起暴雨。原来，海龙王派出了一条孽龙来兴风作浪，要让这座城造不起来。伍子胥抽出身上的宝剑，和孽龙展开了一场恶斗。伍子胥凭着一身好本领，将孽龙斩成几段。然后又命民工造八个陆城门——"象天之八风"，八个水城门——"象地之八卦"。伍子胥还命人在西城门外挖一条大河，直通太湖，并开凿了运粮的"百尺渎"，通向长江。从此，这块龙穴宝地被镇住了，苏州再也没有水患了。据说，伍子胥自刎后，他的头颅就悬挂在西面的城门上。后人为了纪念伍子胥，便把悬挂过他头颅的城门叫胥门。胥门外通向太湖的一条大河叫胥江，入湖口叫胥口。还在太湖边上造了一座胥王庙，封他为湖神。

苏州伍子胥墓，封土高约 1 米多，加以麻石砌成，墓前碑书"吴相国伍公之墓"。近处还有二妃墓、拜将台等古迹。

地址：江苏省苏州市沧浪区念珠街 38 号

交通：

飞机：苏州没有民航机场，乘飞机要取道上海虹桥机场、浦东机场或无锡机场。

火车：目前苏州有三个客运站，分别是苏州站、苏州新区站、苏州园区站。其中苏州站最为主要站点。

汽车：苏州每天有多班高速大巴开往上海。

（五）闻一多的考证——图腾说

中国近代著名学者闻一多认为，端午节与龙图腾有关系。最明显的事例就是，端午节最重要的两项活动——龙舟竞渡和吃粽子都和龙有关，而这些主要是吴越风俗。吴越民族在五月份日照最长的这一天，举行盛大的图腾祭，距今至少有四五千年的历史。当时住在江南的吴越民族，由于受到水旱灾害和瘟疫虫害的威胁，便以有神力的"龙"作为自己民族的图腾，对其顶礼膜拜，希望得到龙的保护。在端午这天，将各种食物装在竹筒中，或裹在树叶里，一面往水里扔，献给图腾，一面自己吃。并在急鼓声中，在水面上划龙舟取悦图腾。

还有学者认为端午节肇始于中国一些少数民族。如龙文玉认为

端午起源于苗族，是苗族的节日，端午节是用苗语命名的节日，端午事件是发生在苗区的事件，端午活动是苗族纪念死者的活动，他

○龙图腾

们纪念的对象是屈原，屈原就是苗人。有学者从船棺葬、铜鼓船纹、龙舟竞渡三方面进行考证后认为，端午节本是以船为生的古代濮族人民的节日，竞渡本是濮人招魂、送魂升天的仪式。后来不知到什么时候，鸟舟发展为龙舟，招魂仪式演变成竞渡游戏，濮族的节日成为我国多个民族习俗（如濮、越、苗、楚）、多种节日内容（如端午节、三月上巳节、夏至节）的一个综合性节日。

二、
端午节的传承

　　如前所述，端午节是随着历史和环境的变迁不断添加新的内容并赋予其文化意义的节日。大体来说，先秦时期就有关于端午节与恶月有关的说法，到汉代，又增添了纪念屈原的内容。魏晋南北朝时期，端午习俗丰富起来并逐渐趋于娱乐化。隋唐时期端午习俗已在民间广为流传，成为全国节日，娱乐性进一步加强。至宋代，端午节作为庶民的传统节日已真正确立下来。

（一）雏形时期

　　早在先秦时期，五月即被视为"恶月"，而五月五日更是"恶月恶日"，民间甚至有"不举五月子"的风俗。《史记·孟尝君列传》载战国四公子之一的孟尝君以五月五日生，其父田婴命其母"勿举"，理由是："五月子者长与户齐，将不利其父母。"也就是说，这一天出生的孩子将给父母带来厄运。

　　为何五月被视为恶月呢？这是因为五月时节白昼越来越长，天气渐热，古人认为此月阴阳不和，很危险。《礼记·月令》载五月"是月也，日长至，阴阳争，死生分"。五月是阴阳相争、死生分判的关键时期，人们要特别慎重。在这个月里，君子要斋戒，即使在室内也要遮掩身体，不得裸露；不能近女色，饮食要清淡；要节制嗜好和欲望，平心静气；百官要安静地办公，不能动用刑罚；以此稳定阴阳争斗所形成的格局。正因为这个月是凶月，所以人们要采取一些措施来遏制凶月带来的不利影响。先秦时期五月节的习俗只有沐浴、斋戒。《大戴礼记·夏小正》篇指出，在五月，"蓄兰，为沐浴也。"兰，即兰草，又名泽兰，是一种香草。在古人的眼里，兰是一种非常高洁的草，用兰汤沐浴可以洁净自己的身体，从而除去一切不祥的东西。而《太平御览》的卷三十一载《夏小正》曰："此月畜药，以蠲除毒气也。"

事实上，在先秦时期的典籍中，记载的是五月的一些禁忌，并没有明确记载五月五日作为一个节日的习俗。到了汉代，五月五日作为固定的节日，受到了人们的普遍重视。而且在汉代，人们已经把端午节与屈原联系起来，如东汉应劭的《风俗通义》佚文："五月五日，以五彩丝系臂……辟兵及鬼，命人不病瘟。又曰，亦因屈原。"把五色丝带绑在手臂上避邪，而且已经出现了用端午节来纪念屈原的说法。

（二）丰富时期

魏晋南北朝时期是端午节发展完善的重要时期，端午节的习俗在这一时期丰富起来，并逐渐固定下来，端午节的名字也正式确立。端午节之名最早出现在《风土记》："仲夏端午，端，初也，谓五月五日也。俗重五日，与夏至同。"这一时期，人们不仅延续了五月的诸多禁忌，还增加了更多的禁忌。南朝梁代宗懔的《荆楚岁时记》对此有详细的记载，曰："五月俗称恶月，多禁忌曝床荐席，及忌盖屋。""五月盖屋,令人头秃。""五月人或上屋,见影魂便去。"五月不能盖房子,不能晒床,否则就有一系列严重后果。所以这一时期,端午节习俗中很重要的一项还是禳灾驱毒避邪,如捉蛤蟆配药、踏百草、采杂药、采艾、悬艾草于门户、臂系五彩丝线、饮药酒(菖蒲酒、雄黄酒),等等。

魏晋南北朝时期,端午节的主要习俗(竞渡与食粽子)已经开始与屈原联系起来。但是,其他地区还是保留了不同的说法,如并州地区认为端午节是为纪念介子推,浙江地区认为端午节是为纪念越王勾践,江浙一带吴国故地认为端午节是为纪念伍子胥。

隋唐时期,端午节是为纪念屈原的说法普及开来。唐代的文献记载,端午节是纪念屈原的。唐代很多诗人都有咏端午的诗篇,如文秀作《端午》诗曰:"节分端午自谁言,万古传闻为屈原。堪笑楚江空渺渺,不能洗得直臣冤。"殷尧藩《端午》诗曰:"少年佳节倍多情,老去谁知感慨生。不效艾符趋习俗,但祈蒲酒话升平。"这些诗都在为屈原鸣不平,感慨一代忠臣的无奈与悲怆。

端午节的节日气氛亦开始发生变化,由原来的神秘、恐怖、不祥转变为轻松、欢乐、喜庆。在魏晋南北朝时期,端午节已经洋溢着节日喜庆气氛,端午节开始被看作是"良节""嘉辰"。端午节各种娱乐活动热闹非凡,龙舟竞渡的场面异常壮观。唐代诗人张建封在其《竞渡歌》中热情地描述当时的场面:"鼓声三下红旗开,两龙跃出浮水来;棹影斡波飞万剑,鼓声劈浪鸣千雷;鼓声渐急标将近,两龙望标目如瞬;坡上人呼霹雳惊,竿头彩挂虹霓晕;前船抢水已得标,后船失势空挥挠。"与悼念屈原

○观竞渡

的感伤情怀不同，竞渡的娱乐性功能明显增强，逐渐演变为一种娱乐竞技的体育活动。

除了竞渡之外，吃粽子的习俗也是越来越普及，而且粽子越做越精致，花样增多。据记载，唐代的粽子有九子粽、百索粽、粉团粽子等。唐代还出现了射粉团角粽的游戏，即用细小的弓箭去射放置在盘中的粉团角粽，射中者胜，射不中则要受罚。唐太宗时期，端午节遵从五日贺节的传统习俗，节日期间，唐太宗赠送长孙无忌、杨师道每人飞白扇两把，"庶动清风，以增美德"，其意其情，感动上下。

（三）确立时期

至于端午节究竟何时才算真正确定，众说纷纭。有日本学者认为宋代嘉兴地区端午节已有张贴钟馗画像、插菖蒲和艾草，屋内用苍术和白芷熏蒸，吃五黄和粽子以及饮雄黄酒等习俗，端午节作为江南庶民的重要节庆才真正确定下来。可以肯定的是，不迟于宋代，端午节作为一种传统节日已在民间确立并广为流传，其文化内涵也已稳定和固化。

清代时期，端午节的民间风俗也传入宫廷之内。清末内宫以雄黄酒驱毒虫，慈禧太后甚至亲自用小刷子蘸了雄黄酒，在皇后、妃嫔、女官等女眷们的鼻子和耳朵下分别点上两点，以防毒虫。喜爱戏剧的西太后还命人在宫中编演屈原故事的历史剧，并命宫眷们都穿上虎头鞋，场景相当有趣。清宫中的妇女们端午时还要做鞋子、槟榔荷包、烟荷包、绣花手巾等，在五月初三这一天，送给西太后及其他女伴，西太后回赠衣物、首饰等给她喜欢的内廷女眷。

都说烟花三月下扬州，可是端午前后的扬州更是热闹。清末，扬州城南运河上的龙舟竞渡，吸引了许多富商大户，后来还有"抢标竞渡"的活动。有钱人家将赏票放在掏空的鸭蛋里，这就是所谓的"标"。再将鸭蛋壳扔到运河中，鸭蛋壳在水面起起伏伏，划龙舟的水手前去"抢标"。这个"抢"的过程也是有讲究的，不能用手抓住，而是要用嘴去咬住鸭蛋壳，才算是"得标"。这个功夫，这个巧劲儿，也是很考验水手的技艺。

除此之外，普通的龙舟竞渡自汉代以来就已经很普遍了。宋代《梦粱录》载，官府在西湖举办游船式竞渡，"龙舟六只，戏二丁二湖中"，船上有"七圣""二郎神"等装饰，划船人戴"大花""卷脚帽子"，"穿红绿戏衫，像演戏一般"，进行速度比赛，终点夺标。

Chapter One
History of the Dragon Boat Festival

The Dragon Boat Festival(also called the Duanyang Festival), which falls on the fifth day of the fifth lunar month annually, is one of the traditional festivals the Chinese people value most.

Compared with other festivals, the Dragon Boat Festival owns the largest number of names, (including) more than 20, Such as Duanwu (Double–Fifth Day), Chongwu (also Double–Fifth Day), Chongwu Quarter, Duanyang, Dila (a Taoist festival), Girls' Day, Yulan (Orchid Bathing Day) and Tianzhong etc. Besides the Han people, some other Chinese ethnic groups (e.g. the Yi, the Dai, the Tujia, the Naxi, the Dong and the Bouyei) also celebrate the Dragon Boat Festival but with varied customs. To this day, everywhere around China you can see customs such as rowing dragon boats, eating zongzi (rice dumplings), drinking realgar wines and hanging calamus & wormwood. Especially in Southern China, where the local people celebrate it more and more ceremoniously.

Our readers may ask, "How did the Dragon Boat Festival come into being?" "Why did it fall on the very day (the fifth day of the fifth lunar month)?" "Why have the Chinese people held those customs like rowing dragon boats, eating

zongzi (rice dumplings), drinking medicinal (realgar) wine and pasting 'Master charms' ?" "Who is Qu Yuan?" "What totem does the dragon boat symbolize? " We could find the answers to these questions if we seek the truth along the long river of Chinese history.

1. Origins of the Dragon Boat Festival

It can be safely concluded that customs originating from the ancient China are best preserved in the Dragon Boat Festival with the most complicated origins. Concerning the origins of the Dragon Boat Festival, there exist many arguments among which three most influential are usually mentioned: The first holds that this festival was originally celebrated by the ancient Wu-Yue people (with dragons as their totem), who always held rituals to worship dragons. The second believes that it was celebrated to commemorate some people including Qu Yuan, Wu Zixu, Jie Zitui, Gou Jian (king of the ancient state of Yue), Cao E (the Filial Daughter), General Ma Yuan and Chen Lin (the magistrate of Cangwu Prefecture, the Han Dynasty). Earnestly worshiped, these historical figures or legendary personages mainly lived somewhere ranging from Jianghan Plain (in Central China) to the Yangtze River Valley (part of the Eastern China). The third is related to preventing diseases or evils and avoiding disasters——the high temperature in the fifth lunar month causes the proliferation of snakes, insects and viruses as well, so the Chinese folks have long believed that this month is a "fierce one" and preserved some customs such as dispelling the "five poisonous creatures"(Wu Du), hanging calamus & wormwood and drinking realgar (Xiong Huang) wine in the hope of blessing themselves.

Based on the research of Mr. Zhang Zhengming, a scholar, the Dragon Boat Festival proves to be the evolution of one cultural matter (with varied origins), which has resulted from the mutual restraint yet harmonious coexistence between human beings and the nature.

1.1 The Most Common Story

The Dragon Boat Festival is generally believed to commemorate Qu Yuan , a great poet , and that is why it is also called "Poets' Day". Wen Xiu, a monk in the late Tang Dynasty, once wrote a poem titled "Duan Yang": "When Duanwu came into being we don't know, for Qu Yuan's sake but we all know; The rapids of Chu River run along, yet unable to wash away the patriotic poet's wrong." This poem unbosoms the people's sympathy and admiration for this great patriotic poet, while voices the writer's hatred for the fatuous monarch and those treacherous officials. Who is Qu Yuan? Why were so many customs held on the Dragon Boat Festival highly related to this great poet? All stories could date back to the Warring States Period of the Zhou Dynasty more than 2,300 years ago.

Qu Yuan

At that time in ancient China, the "seven powerful states" (namely, the Qin, the Chu, the Qi, the Yan, the Zhao, the Han and the Wei) fought against each other, plundering and slaughtering with endless battles. A great poet of the State of Chu, Qu Yuan (a descendent of the royal family), who was very young then, was appointed as Zuo Tu (the counterpart is foreign minister nowadays) by King Chu-huai. He felt much pained when he beheld the people's sufferings caused by the wars, so he resolved to help the people and serve the state wholeheartedly. He suggested that the king appoint those capable and virtuous officials and show sympathy for the people, thus earning the king's full trust.

As the strongest among the "seven powers", the state of Qin (located in the West of China then) often launched attacks on the other six states. Qu Yuan determined to contact them in person, hoping to resist the powerful Qin with united force. In the 11th year of King Chu-huai reign period, his efforts paid off——the kings of the Chu, the Qi, the Yan, the Zhao, the Han and the Wei gathered in Ying City (the capital of the Chu) and established the six-state alliance, with King Chu-huai as the leader. The strong alliance stopped the Qin's invasive expansion, and King Chu-huai put Qu Yuan in a more important position to handle both internal and foreign affairs. His glorious feats invited other villains' envy. In the state of Chu at that time, a gang of aristocrats headed by Zilan (one son of the king) bore a grudge against Qu and before King Chu-huai they frequently slandered this loyal minister: "He is arbitrary and belittles Your Majesty!" King Chu-huai became dubious about Qu's loyalty since so many slanders flooded into his ears.

When the agents of the Qin got to know such internal discord in the court, they reported it to the king of the Qin right away. Learning this important information, King Qin-hui, the king of the Qin, who had long before planned to attack the state of Qi but feared the strength of the alliance, immediately called for Zhang Yi, the Secretary of State. Zhang Yi thought the Qi and the Chu were the strongest among the six allied powers, and the alliance would collapse for sure if the two strongest were alienated. Zhang also volunteered to tear apart the alliance by taking the chance of the discord between the allied states. The overjoyed king trusted treasures as expenditure to him. Zhang cunningly handed in his official stamp and feigned resigning from his post as planned.

When he arrived in Ying City, (the capital of the state of Chu), he directly visited Qu Yuan's residence and advocated the profits of the alliance between the Chu and the powerful Qin. Qu rebuked, "By no means will we abandon the claim of the six-state alliance." Seeing Qu's stubbornness and insistence, Zhang Yi yielded and visited Zilan's residence. He encouraged, "Qu Yuan is trusted by King Chu-huai only because of the six-state alliance and he will mean nothing to you if the alliance collapses." Zilan was delighted to hear his story and soon those envious aristocrats began to collaborate with Zhang Yi. Zilan also introduced Zhang to Zheng Xiu, the favorite concubine of King Chu-huai. At their first meeting, Zhang presented a pair of priceless white jades to the woman, whose eyes shone at the brightness of the treasure. Much pleased, she promised to help promote the alliance between the Chu and the Qin. After plotting, the three queer collaborators reached agreement: "The collapse of the six-state alliance is the very premise of the alliance between the Chu and the Qin; while King Chu-huai's distrust in Qu Yuan is the very first step to reaching the goal." Then, Zilan made a plot—— Zheng Xiu was to gossip stealthily before King Chu-huai that Qu Yuan had asked Zhang Yi for a bribe.

Zilan recommended Zhang Yi to King Chu-huai soon afterwards. To induce King Chu-huai, Zhang listed many profits of tearing apart the six-state alliance and added the last bonus: If King Chu-huai agrees, the king of the Qin will cede 300km² of land in Shangyu (located in Henan Province now) to the Chu as a gift. As a greedy monarch, King Chu-huai was much delighted to hear that he would gain a vast territory with no pains. When he went back to the imperial harem, he told Zheng Xiu about it and the concubine congratulated. However, she frowned and complained, "I'm told that Qu Yuan has asked Zhang Yi for a pair of white jades but in vain. I'm afraid he will object the alliance." The king felt dubious about it. The following day, King Chu-huai treated Zhang Yi to a banquet at which they outlined the friendship between the two states in the future. Qu Yuan doubtlessly objected such prospect harshly and disputed with Zilan and Jin Shang vehemently. While bitterly retorting Zhang, Zi and Jin, he strode forward facing the king. "It matters the life and death of our country, Your Majesty! Never believe his story! Zhang Yi is just dispatched to tear apart the alliance and make our country alienated! Never believe······" Zheng Xiu's complaints occurred to the king: "The bribe! The jades!" This greedy king interrupted angrily, "Are the white jades more valuable than the 300km² of land?" Then he had the guards drag Qu Yuan out of the imperial court.

Deeply grieved, Qu Yuan lingered outside the court and refused to leave, hoping that the king could wake up and change his mind to keep the country from suffering the tragedy. In great despair, he sighed and muttered to himself, "Alas! My beloved motherland, misfortune will befall you!"

When coming back home, Qu was still depressed. In his mind's eye, the alliance he helped to build with great efforts would collapse and his country would lose her prosperity soon. Such prospect made him deeply sigh again. When his elder sister Xu, keeping house for him, got to know why he sighed, she was aware at once that his brother was framed and then dissuaded him from uttering complaints. Qu responded firmly, "I was born here and I've grown up here! I will risk my life to save my country from any danger!"

He soon composed a long poem titled "Lisao", which voiced his deep concern about the Chu and his repressive wrath. "Lisao" means "sorrow after departure." When deserted, it is so natural for a man in despair to pray to heaven and earth to voice his bitterness. "Lisao" gained wide popularity and the court learned it soon. Zilan and his followers made this poem a bullet to attack Qu Yuan, reporting to the king that Qu compared the latter to King Jie and King Zhou (the notorious tyrants in the Xia and the Shang Dynasty respectively). Outraged, King Chu-huai removed Qu from his post. The suffocating air over the capital nearly drove the poet crazy. His sister urged him to move to a new place for a rest, and under his sister's constant persuasion, Qu Yuan finally had no choice but to leave the capital city "Ying".

Soon after the political relation between the Chu and the Qi broke off and the alliance between them collapsed, King Chu-huai sent an envoy to take over the "ceded" land of the Qin. As Zhang Yi and the envoy drew near Xianyang —— the capital of the state of Qin, Zhang feigned getting drunk and deliberately fell over from the wagon. Pleading his wounded legs, Zhang waved goodbye to the envoy and entered the city alone. The envoy, residing in the hotel, visited Zhang everyday, but the latter declined to greet him for the sake of his wound. Till three months later, only after he was informed of the collapse of the six-state alliance did Zhang greet the envoy of the Chu. When referring to the "ceded" land, Zhang Yi went back on his word, "The 'ceded' land I promised to offer is that of my own, only covering 3 Kilometers. How dare I cede the land of the Qin to other states?" Stricken dumb, the envoy had to return to the Chu empty-handed. Feeling fooled and insulted, the outraged King Chu-huai, proud of his strong well-trained army and ample supply prepared in the past few years, ordered his senior general Qugai (commanding an army of 100,000) to attack the Qin.

Facing the army of the Chu, King Qin-hui changed his former plan to attack the Qi, while deciding to attack the Chu instead with the newly-allied Qi. Unable to resist the two-way attack, the defeated army of the Chu retreated after successive failures in several battles, leaving large territory of Hanzhong to the hand of the Qin. Hearing the defeat, angered yet distressed, Qu Yuan determined to hurry back to the capital to resist the Qin. On his way back, he was appointed as the envoy and dispatched to resume the collapsed Chu-Qi alliance. Very gratified at the king's change, Qu hurried to the State of Qi. The king of Qi detested King Chu-huai's betrayal but esteemed Qu Yuan's loyalty and nobility, therefore, after several rounds of negotiation, he promised to withdraw his army. But to their surprise, the news came that the peace-negotiation was being carried out between the Chu and the Qin. For fear that his lord would be deceived again, Qu bid farewell to the king of Qi and went back to Chu in a hurry. Learning his coming back, Zilan and Jin Shang went to consult with Zheng Xiu in haste, both fearing that Qu would restore to power. At that night, Zheng Xiu tearfully complained to her lord, "Minister Qu told the folks that…it was my slanderous advice that…caused the deaths of those poor soldiers! And…and this time he just comes back to revenge for those wronged souls!" King Chu-huai flew into a rage. "How dare he? He is crazy! " The following day, King Chu-huai appointed Qu Yuan as Sanlv Minister (a nominal post in charge of the education of royal kins) and required him to go to his post right away without curtsying to the king. Zilan was ordered to declare the decree. The newly-appointed Minister uttered a deep sigh, "Alas! Your Majesty! You can't be muddled once more! The State of Chu and the people of Chu all count on you! "

In the 30th year of King Qin-hui's reign, the Qin occupied 8 cities in the north of the Chu. One day, the distressed king unexpectedly received an invitation letter from the king of the Qin, inviting him to visit Wuguan (a city in the Qin) and negotiate the eternal friendship between the two states. Swayed by his hesitation, King Chu-huai couldn't make up his mind yet: if he refuses, the Qin might sweep southward; if he accepts, he might face danger. Zilan stood out first, "Now that king of the Qin has proposed peace first, it is a golden chance to negotiate!" Jin Shang also persuaded, "If your highness accept his proposal, our country will enjoy peace for at least several years." When he returned to the imperial harem, his favorite concubine Zheng Xiu encouraged him as well. Now, King Chu-huai resolved to go and wrote back to king of the Qin.

After several days' preparation, accompanied by Jin Shang and 500 royal guards, King Chu-huai left Ying for Wuguan. Half a month later, only Jin Shang fled back single-handed. As Qu Yuan had foreseen, the moment King Chu-huai and his guards reached Wuguan, they were held in custody and escorted to Xianyang, the capital of the state of the Qin. The grievous news struck the whole country. To set the people's minds at rest, Zhengxiu set up Xiongheng (the crown prince) to reign, entitled "King Qingxiang". However, the concubine herself held the power in fact and she appointed Zilan as the highest-ranked officer in charge of the army. At the risk of his life, Qu Yuan hurried back to Ying. He strongly proposed that the successor restore the six-state alliance and force the Qin to set King Chu-huai free by virtue of the strong alliance. Zilan and his faction feared that the king, if he could come back, would condemn them for the sake of their earlier persuasion, and they also dared not offend the powerful Qin. Therefore, they not only denounced Qu's proposal, but also drove him out of the capital, forbidding him to come back forever. Their evil attempt completed, those treacherous men dined and wined for another three years until one day, the news came that King Chu-huai had passed away. The Qin decided to send back his worthless remains to the Chu. When the coffin was carried to Ying, along the road the Chu people all knelt down and cried out, feeling it a burning shame. Seeing the former king's coffin, Qu Yuan was totally brokenhearted and even cried to faint, for he had long spun his hope to revive the Chu on the king's awakening. But now, all was gone. He advised King Qingxiang to reunite other states to fight against the Qin while they all had resentment against the Qin. In spite of his heartfelt advice, this young ruler closed his ears. Qu had to wait at the gate of the palace day and night, hoping that the king could be moved. His persistence annoyed Zhengxiu, and this spiteful woman had him removed from his post, "Drive him far far away! The farther the better! Never allow him to come back!"

He returned to Lingyang and stayed there for 9 years in

the rest of his life. Having no way to go back to Ying, he felt rather restless about every message that his country was weaker and weaker. One day, he got to Xupu County and stayed there. Everyday, in the depth of his heart, a burning desire like a flaming fire urged him to chant and create poems out of sadness and bitterness. In the 21st year of King Qingxiang reign period, a shocking news knocked out the poet: The army of the Qin, headed by General Baiqi, attacked the Chu and occupied the capital, ruining the ancestral temples and tombs of the royal family. The country was to be perished. Qu made a decision: Go back to the capital to meet his destiny! Hair uncombed, face unwashed, he stumbled ahead in a daze for a few days, till he got to the Miluo River. Seeing the reflection of his white hairs in the clean water, with his mind in turmoil, the poet threw himself into the river.

Ever since his death, for fear that the fishes and dragons would eat his body, the grieved folks would throw into the rivers the prepared bamboo boxes stuffed with rice in honor of him. Legend has it that in the years of Jianwu Period (Han Dynasty), for fear that the dragons might take away those sacrifices, the folks would row the dragon boats to the middle of the river to scare away the beasts. They also tied zongzi (rice dumplings wrapped with lotus leaves) with five-colored silk ribbons and threw them into the river to scare the dragons. They made it, for it was said that the dragons feared such five-colored silk ribbons.

Tips for Tourism

The Miluo River

The Miluo River originates from the Pingjiang County (Hunan

Province) and flows into the Dongting Lake after it runs through Yueyang City (Hunan Province). Among the whitewashed cottages alongside the banks of the Miluo River, there still remain some ancient relics like Qu Yuan Temple, "Sao" Altar (a local poetry—composing club to com—memorate Qu Yuan) and the suspected graves of this great poet. Scattered within an area of 1.5 Kilometers on the Miluo Hill, there are altogether 12 suspected pyramid—shaped grave mounds in front of which there stand some gravestones engraved with epitaphs like "Grave of Sanlv Minister of The Chu State". So far, on the fifth day of the fifth lunar month, the lo—cals here will hold dragon—boat races to commemorate their great patriotic poet.

Qu Yuan Temple

Standing on the Yusi Hill on the bank of the Miluo River, Qu Yuan Temple was first built in the Han Dynasty (206 BC − 220 AD) and reno—vated during the Emperor Qianlong reign period (1736 AD − 1795 AD) in the Qing Dynasty (1636 AD − 1912 AD).

Transportation

By air: After arriving at Changsha Huanghua International Airport, the travelers could take a bus or taxi to get to Miluo City and then from there take the shuttle bus to visit Qu Yuan Temple (on the Yusi Hill 15 kilometers away).

By train and bus: After arriving at Yueyang City (Hunan Province), the travelers could take a train or nonstop bus to get to Miluo City and then from there take a shuttle bus to visit Qu Yuan Temple on the Yusi Hill 15 kilometers away.

1.2 To avoid evils——by archaeologists

Long before the Qin Shi-huang (the first emperor in an-cient China) Period, the Chinese people thought the fifth lunar month was sinister and called it "fierce month", for disasters frequently happened and men were likely to fall ill in this month. The book of Shi-ji (The Historical Records by Sima Qian, the greatest historiographer in ancient China) once recorded the following story.

Tianying (son of the king of Qi in Warring States Period) married many women and they gave birth to more than 40 children. Once, one concubine would give birth to her baby just on the fifth day of the fifth lunar month, while Tianying told her not to do so in this "fierce month". However, his concubine gave birth to a boy on the very day, naming him Tianwen (Lord Mengchang, famous for his generosity). Since his father didn't allow the birth on that "fierce"day, this child was reared secretly till one day, but his brothers exposed the secret to their father. Out of temper, Tianying sent for the mother and her son. When they came, he scolded his concubine angrily. "Why didn't you obey me?" Looking at his angry father, Tianwen, a filial son caring about his mother, knelt down right away. "Father, why didn't you want me? Just because I was born in the fifth lunar month? " Tianying answered, "The child born in the fierce month will grow as tall as the door. When he grows up and gets married, he will do harm to his parents!" Hearing such fallacy, the child retorted calmly, "Man's life is granted by heaven and no one is entitled to deprive him of it. You have no right to kill him just because he might do harm to you, do you? As far as the door, you may raise its height and all will be well. In a word, the heaven won't allow such killing!" Ever since then, the ancient Chinese would celebrate the Dragon Boat Festival on the fifth day of the fifth lunar month, aiming to fend off evils and pray for the well-being of the whole family.

Solar terms may also create relations between the Dragon Boat Festival and health maybe is weather. In many places, the

Dragon Boat Festival is called the Duanyang Festival, for Duanyang means the peak of "yang-qi"——sun heat, also Summer Solstice. The Custom of eating zongzi in midsummer and racing dragon boat on the day of Summer Solstice are respectively recorded in "Records of Customs and Festivals in the Chu Region " written by Zongtan (in the 6th century) and "Book of Jade Candle——Records of Halcyon Days" by Du Taiqing (between the 5th——6th century). According to their books, the Dragon Boat Festival derived from Summer Solstice. While Mr. Gao Bingzhong, a scholar, once speculated that, due to the unfixed Summer Solstice in lunar calendar, the folks for convenience "converted" Summer Solstice into the Duanyang Festival at a fixed date——the fifteenth day of the fifth lunar month. In the Wei, Jin and the Southern and Northern Dynasties (from the 3rd to 6th centuries), Summer Solstice and the Duanyang Festival were respectively celebrated at first, and gradually the former ("Big Duanwu") and the latter ("Small Duanwu") became integrated as one, with the latter as the winner. Therefore, among those origins, there came one concerning "fierce day", say, the heated Summer Solstice.

Generally speaking, most of the customs of the Dragon Boat Festival originally came into existence following the change of weather——especially the coming of Summer Solstice. In the Han Dynasty, this special date was regarded as a taboo, which could be traced back to the Xia, Shang and Zhou Dynasty. In the Tang Dynasty, this "fierce day" ultimately became a merry gala celebrated by the mass, with more delicate foods and ornaments.

1.3 To commemorate Cao E, the Filial Daughter

There is another story which is widely handed down in the Southern China. Long long ago (in the Eastern Han Dynasty), there was a nameless village, where lived a fisher named Cao who caught fish on the Shun River all day along. Cao had a 14-year daughter named Cao E, who was pretty and smart, and more importantly, known to all for her filial conduct.

At the end of the spring and the beginning of the summer that year, the continuous heavy rains made the Shun River rise abruptly. On the river, the turbid waves rushed down, big whirls curled up and mud plats and rocks were drowned. Fishers usually anticipated the floods, for they would bring abundant fishes and shrimps; and Fisher Cao decided to take a chance when he watched the turbid river, for he knew "fish in the troubled water". Looking at the dark clouds in the heavy sky, Cao E dissuaded her father. But he insisted that fish-catching was dangerous everyday indeed and he would be safe if taking care.

After her father left, Cao E stayed at home with great anxiety, only wishing he could come home safe and sound, but he didn't come back for din-ner till late afternoon. She ran up to the riverbank again and again, only to see the rapids on the wide river, but not his father's little boat. Much upset, Cao E walked up along the river for three miles, then she turned back and walked down for six miles, both in vain. The sun setting beyond the hill, Cao called out, "Daddy! Daddy! Where are you?"

Cao E

Hearing her cry, some good friends of her father gathered around, all wet over. They deeply sighed, "We were casting nets when a huge wave suddenly pushed your dad's boat into a big whirl and … and rushed him away!" Much stunned, Cao E cried out "Daddy!" and searched down the riverbank. Night fell and it was pitch-dark now. Those fishers accompanied the filial daughter. They consoled her and persuaded her to go back home first, saying that her father was good at swimming and he might have swum ashore. "We shall get him back tomorrow!" Unable to find her father, Cao E refused to leave and looked for him all night, her cry drowned by the roaring river. The following day, some villagers sent her food but she declined. All of them helped her. For three days Cao E searched and searched but in vain, her tears drying up. The villagers consoled and persuaded, yet she said she'd rather die if she lost her father. Without eating and sleeping, she kept seeking for seven days till blood welled up from her eyes.

On the 8th day, gazing at the river, Cao E suddenly saw a huge wave lifting a dark figure, as if her father was fighting against the wave. Overjoyed Cao E thought it was her father. "Save him! Daddy, I'm coming!" With those words, she jumped into the water!

Three days later, villagers saw a big whirl in which someone seemed to be swimming. Hopefully they hurried there, only to find two deads——Cao E and her father on her back. It so happened that Cao E managed to find her father at last and carried him ashore. Everybody said it must be the daughter's filial conduct that moved the gods. From then on, where Cao E found her father was called "Hepan Village".

Cao E's filial conduct moved not only the gods, but also the neighborhood. They held a decent funeral for the father and his daughter. And at the very place where she jumped, they also built a temple and made a statue in honor of her, referring to her respectfully as "Goddess the Filial", and renaming this small fishing village "Cao E Village", the river running along-side "Cao E River". On the very day Cao E jumped, when a grand-scaled temple fair was held annually, the officials and civilians would come here to worship "Goddess the Filial". It is said that, Cao E jumped into the river to save her father just on the fifth day of the fifth lunar month, so many people thought the Dragon Boat Festival was celebrated to commemorate her.

Tips for Tourism

Cao E Temple in Shangyu District

Cao E Temple, once called the Filial Spirit Temple or the Filial Daughter Temple, was built to commemorate Cao E the Filial Daughter and publicize her filial conduct. First built in 151 AD (in the Eastern Han Dynasty), this grand-looking temple has undergone several removals, extensions and renovations, thus finally presenting before the travelers its basic architectural style: carefully-ordered and well-proportioned.

Facing east and the Cao E River downhill, Cao E Temple, half surrounded by the Fenghuang (Phoenix) Hill, covers nearly 6,000m^2 with its gross area over 3,840m^2. The main structures are arranged along three axes: along the northern axis, there successively stand 5 three-bay structures—the Archway, the Drinking Pavilion, the Stele Corridor, the Double-juniper Pavilion and the Cao E Grave; along the middle axis, there successively stand 6 five-bay structures—the Shield Wall, the Emperor-bestowed Stele Pavilion, the Gate, the Stage, the Main Hall and the Ancestral Hall; and along the southern axis, there successively stand 7 three-bay structures: the Gate, the Stage, the Tugu (god of the land) Hall, the Shen Hall (to commemorate Shen Wenkui, a high-rank official who helped to renovate

Cao E Temple), the Stage (another), the Dongyue (god of Mount Tai) Hall and the Death King Hall. Cao E Temple has won its reputation both at home and abroad for the "Four Unique Treasures", namely, sculptures, wall paintings, couplets and calligraphy works, since many of them are well-known masterpieces.

From the fifteenth to twenty-second of the fifth lunar month every year, a grand temple fair is held in Cao E Temple, where the travelers could watch wonderful performances like Kongfu, horse-riding, acrobatics and Shao Opera (a local opera in Shaoxing, Zhejiang Province). What a bustling place! For the sake of publicizing filial piety, organizers of the present temple fair are carrying out more piety-related cultural activities, such as painting, photography and calligraphy exhibitions.

Address: Filial Daughter Road, Cao E Street

Tel: 0575-82162498

Transportation

By air: After arriving at Hangzhou International Airport or Ningbo International Airport, the travelers could take a coach to get to Shangyu City and then from there take a shuttle bus or taxi to reach Cao E Town.

By train and bus: After arriving at Shaoxingdong Railway Station (Zhejiang Province), the travelers could take a coach or taxi to reach Cao E Town.

1.4 To Commemorat Wu Zixu

Wu Zixu (in the late Spring and Autumn Period), like Qu Yuan, was also a man of the Chu, but he was born 200 years or so earlier than the latter. With his wronged father and brother killed by King Chu-ping, Wu ran to the state of Wu for shelter and helped the Wu to attack the Chu for revenge. The army of the Wu, after five attempts successively, finally defeated the Chu and occupied its capital. Since his enemy King Chu-ping was dead, to vent his anger, Wu Zixu had the king's grave dug out and his remains whipped heavily 300 times. (This is the well-known story of "Digging Grave and Whipping Remains" in ancient China, but the truth of it has long been questioned.)

Fully trusted by King Helv of the Wu, Wu Zixu went on assisting his son——Fuchai, who succeeded the throne. Craving for greatness and success, King Fuchai attempted to attack the state of Yue——the southern neighbor. The high-moraled army of the Wu had tasted no failures ever since the new king came to the power, so they quickly defeated the much weaker army of the Yue and made them surrender. King Gou Jian of the Yue sued for peace in person and Fuchai accepted. Rich in both political and military experience, Wu Zixu advised the new king to wipe out the Yue once and for all, but he refused. At the same time, a high-ranked minister named Boxi (also coming from the Chu) took huge bribes from the Yue, so he took every chance to slander the prime minister before the king. Regrettedly, King Fuchai was misled and believed his rumors. He "granted" Wu a treasured sword and ordered him to commit suicide with it. As a man of integrity and loyalty, Wu feared no death. Before he lifted the "granted" sword, it was said that he spoke to everyone present, "After my death, dig out my eyes and hang them on the East Gate! I will see the ruin of the state of Wu!" Learning Wu's last words, the outraged king had his remains wrapped in leather and thrown into the river just on the fifth day of the fifth lunar month. Many years later, the folks in Suzhou (in Jiangsu Province now) called the river passing by "Xu River" in honor of him. The story above offers another possible origin of the Dragon Boat Festival——to commemorate Wu Zixu, the famous prime minister.

Tips for Tourism

Wu Zixu and Suzhou City

In 514 BC, King Helv of the State of Wu dispatched Wu Zixu to supervise the building of Helv City. After carefully observing the condi-tions of the water, soil and climate,(namely Fengshui) Wu determined

Wu Zixu

the building site——where Suzhou City is located today. Legend has it that the chosen site was one treasured lair of the dragons, so the outraged King Dragon ordered a fierce dragon to stop the project. On the first day of construction, gust and storm befell. Seeing the evil trouble-maker, Wu Zixu daringly drew out his sword to fight against him and at last, with his excellent swordplay, Wu chopped the dragon into several parts. Later, Wu had the builders build 8 gates to connect (or disconnect) the roads in all directions and another 8 gates to connect (or disconnect) the waters in all directions. Wu also had a wide canal dug outside the Western Gate to connect the newly-build capital and the Tai Lake. Moreover, he ordered to build the Baichi (one hundred feet wide) Canal, making the grain ships directly reach the Yangtze River. From then on, this so–called treasured lair of the dragons was curbed and the City of Suzhou suffered no flood any more. After his death, it is said that his head was hung over the West—ern Gate. To commemorate Wu Zixu and his great contributions, the folks in Suzhou called the Western Gate "Xu" Gate and one river passing by "Xu" River; in the meantime, they built the King Xu Temple beside Tai Lake and respectfully called him "God of the Lake".

On the Lantern Festival, the Dragon Boat Festival and the Mid–autumn Festival every year, the locals will gather just on the spacious stretch outside the old Xu Gate, merrily watching folklore performances like Dragon–Lion Dance, Lotus Boat Swaying, Copper–coin Stick Playing, Flower–basket Carrying and Stilt Walking. At the same time, the visitors' palates are greatly stimulated by those local snacks like small glutinous–rice dump–lings with aosmanthus, sweet porridge, sweet eddoes, plum blossom cakes and beancurd jelly.

Enclosed by granite, the Wu Zixu Grave in Suzhou is one meter tall above the ground, in front of which stands one gravestone engraved with an epitaph "Grave of Prime Minister Wu of The Wu State". Nearby, there still remain some ancient relics like the grave of the two wives of Shun (a great monarch in ancient China) and a general–acknowledging memorial.

Address: 38 Nianzhu Street, Canglang District, Suzhou City, Jiangsu Province

By Air: Since there is no airport in Suzhou, the travelers could first take flights to Shanghai or Wuxi.

By train: There are three railway stations in Suzhou now which are respectively Suzhou Station (the busiest one), Suzhou Hi–Tech District Station and Suzhou Industrial Park Station.

Bus routes are available for reaching the three railway stations.

Convenient coach service: Many shifts of high–speed coaches are available for reaching Shanghai (with Suzhou North Station the busiest).

1.5 Origin related to totems——a study by Wen Yiduo

Wen Yiduo, a well-known scholar in modern China, favored that the hypothesis that the Dragon Boat Festival is related to the totem of dragon. According to him, the two most important customs of Duanwu——racing dragon boats and eating zongzi—— are dragon-related. These two festive customs allegedly originated from the Wu and the Yue, where the folks long long ago had their hairs cut short and their bodies painted with varied patterns. On a certain day (with the longest daylight hours) in the fifth lunar month, the folks of the Wu and the Yue would hold grand-scaled totem-worshiping rituals more than 4,000-5,000 years ago. Inhabiting in the south region of the Yangtze River (in Southeast China), they were frequently threatened by floods and tormented by plagues, so they took the dragon with supernatural power as their ethnic totem with piety, in the hope that the mythical beast could protect them. On the day of Duanwu, after they prepared various foods stuffed in the bamboo boxes or wrapped by leaves, they would throw them into the river to please the dragons hidden under the water, while sparing some to please themselves.

Meanwhile, urged and encouraged by the intensive drumbeats, they would hold dragon boat race to please their totem.

Some other scholars are of the opinion that the Dragon Boat Festival originated from some Chinese minority nationalities. For example, in his book *New Research of the Dragon*

The Drago Boat Festival derived from dragon totem worship

Boat Festival, Long Wenyu holds that the Dragon Boat Festival was first celebrated by the Miao people, who named the festival "Duanwu" in their own Miao language (Hmong). The Miao people think "Duanwu" was first celebrated in the habitat area of their ancestors to commemorate those diseased including Qu Yuan, who was regarded as one member of their own. Based on the research of bronze drum and patterns painted on the boat, canoe/ boat coffin custom and dragon boat race, some scholars think the Dragon Boat Festival was most likely celebrated firstly by the ancient people of Pu, fishing and living on the boats, and boat race was held by them to call back and see off the spirit of the diseased. Later (no one knows since when), bird boat was changed into dragon boat and the spirit-calling ritual was developed into boat race. Influence of the Pu's festival spread over the neighboring areas gradually and this festival evolved into a multi-ethnic custom celebrated by the Pu, the Yue, the Miao and the Chu. Finally, it turned into a comprehensive festival integrating customs of Duanwu, Shang-si (the third day of the third lunar month) and Summer Solstice.

2. Cultural Inheritance of the Dragon Boat Festival

As previously mentioned, the Dragon Boat Festival with varied origins was not formed overnight as a whole, but was developed following the historical and environmental changes, with different cultural connotations added and enriched in different times. On the whole, the story of "fierce month" first appeared in the pre-Qin Period (esp. Warring States Period). In the Han Dynasty and the Tang Dynasty, the story of Qu Yuan enriched its cultural connotation. In the Wei, Jin and the Southern and Northern Dynasties, customs of the Dragon Boat Festival were gradually amplified and entertainment-oriented.

In the Sui and Tang Dynasty, customs of the Dragon Boat Festival spread all over the ancient China, which made itself a nationwide festival entertained by people. At least in the Song Dynasty, Duanwu was at the first time celebrated by the common folks as a traditional festival on a fixed day.

2.1 From "Fierce Day and Month" to the Protype of the Festival

Early in the pre-Qin Period, the fifth lunar month was taken as the "fierce", while the fifth day of the fifth lunar month the "most fierce of the fierce", which was best illustrated by the custom of " never giving birth to a baby on the double-fifth day". It is recorded in the book of "Shi-ji-Biography of Lord Mengchang" (one of the famous "Four Lords in Warring States Period", famous for his generosity) that Lord Mengchang's mother gave birth to him on the fifth day of the fifth lunar month, but his father warned his mother not to do so beforehand because he held that "the child born in the fierce month will grow as tall as the door and do harm to his parents".

Why did the ancient Chinese believe so? In the fifth lunar month, the daylight hours would become longer and the weather much hotter, so the ancient Chinese thought such phenomenon was very dangerous as the result of the imbalance between Yin and Yang (here it means cold vs. hot). "Climate Records of A Lunar Month"——one part of The Book of Rites——also pointed out that: In the fifth lunar month, the daylight hours become longer, with Yin vs.Yang competing and life vs. death fighting. Gentlemen should cautiously fast and keep bodies shaded in the house from the burning sun. They also should taste light food and restrain their lust with a placidity of mind, refusing sensual pleasure. Officials should work in a tranquil state and never conduct criminal penalty for the sake of tranquilizing the Yin, since penalty which symbolizes Yin could spoil the balance between Yin and Yang. So far as the customs in the fifth lunar month in the pre-Qin Period, we could but find bathing and fasting. In the Han Dynasty, The Book of Rites——Calendar in the Xia Dynasty (compiled by Dai De, a famous ritual expert) recorded that people collected orchids for bathing. As a fragrant thoroughwort, virtuous in the eyes of the ancient Chinese, orchid could clean the bather's body and drive away any sinisterness. It was also recorded in "Taiping Yulan" (an encyclopedia complied in the Song Dynasty) that "in the fifth lunar month, medicines should be stored up beforehand to dispel disease".

We have noticed that in the pre-Qin Period many classic works mainly recorded those taboos concerning the customs in the fifth lunar month, but recorded no customs of celebrating the double-fifth day. While in the Han Dynasty, though the fifth lunar month was still taken as "fierce" with many a taboo, the double-fifth day was celebrated as a fixed festival and gained much attention from the folks. And just in the Han Dynasty did the folks begin to associate Duanwu with Qu Yuan, which could be found in the book "Overview of Customs"(written by Ying Shao), "······on the double-fifth day, the five-color threads are tied around the arms...to avoid the war disasters or ghosts and keep the folks from diseases. Minister Qu Yuan is said to be commemorated too on this very day······" Such an account supports the idea that at least in the late Eastern Han Dynasty, the Dragon Boat Festival was celebrated to commemorate Qu Yuan partly.

2.2 The Evolution of the Dragon Boat Festival

After the Han Dynasty, the evolution of the Dragon Boat Festival met another important phase——the Wei, Jin and the Southern and Northern Dynasties (from the 3th to 6th centuries), in which the customs got much enriched and fixed gradually, with the name "Duanwu" ultimately established. "Duanwu" as such first appeared in the book "Documents of Special Customs" (written by Zhou Chu in the Jin Dynasty): "In the midsummer, the word 'Duan Wu'(端 午), with the first character Duan—— 端 which means the beginning, involves the fifth day of the fifth lunar month." What the folks call "Chong Wu" (the double-fifth day) is another name of Summer Solstice. In this period, the folks not only preserved many of those taboos inherited from the past, but also added more. Here are some of them listed in "Records of Customs and Festivals in the Chu Region" written by Zong Tan (in the 6th century): "The fifth lunar month is commonly known as the 'fierce month', in which the folks abstain from exposing the bed and mattress to the heated sun." "They also abstain from building new house, for 'He who dares to build will become bald!' or 'He who climbs onto the roof will lose his soul at the sight of the shade of his own!'" Therefore, among all of those customs in this period, there was one of much importance——how to dispel the evils and get rid of the disease——involving catching toads for a prescription, treading on the grasses, gathering herbs, hanging calamus & wormwood on the door, tying five-color ribbons around the arms and drinking medicinal (calamus or realgar) wine, etc.

Just in this period, the story of Qu Yuan spread over and became the primary concern of the folks when celebrating this festival——they raced dragon boats and ate zongzi to commemorate the patriotic poet. However, other stories were still widely accepted by the folks in different regions: in Bingzhou (present-day Hebei and Shanxi in Northren China), the people held that they commemorated Jie Zitui (famous for his loyalty to King Jinwen); in Zhejiang region, the commemorated was Gou Jian; and in what was the ancient state of Wu in the late Spring and Autumn Period (as mentioned above), the commemorated was Wu Zixu.

In the Sui and Tang Dynasties, the Dragon Boat Festival was celebrated nationwide ultimately, with the story of Qu Yuan spread over ancient China. According to the extant documents, people then mainly celebrated this festival in honor of Qu Yuan. We still could find many Duanwu-chanting poems in the Tang Dynasty: For example, Wen Xiu wrote a poem titled "Duanwu"——" When Duanwu came into being we don't know, for Qu yuan's sake but we all know; The rapids of Chu River run along, yet unable to wash away the poet's wrong." Yin Yaofan chanted another "Duanwu"——"When I was young, Duanwu always made me high; but now I am old, it could but make me sigh. Unwilling to follow the custom to avoid evils, I am too lazy to hang the wormwoods and charms; Willing to chat about the peace of life only, I am so happy to drink calamus wine with my friends."(excerpted)

The Dragon Boat Festival was always celebrated both warmly and merrily, with jubilant festive activities held everywhere. According to the historical records, the dragon boat races looked extraordinarily spectacular in the Sui and Tang Dynasties. In his poem "Song of Boat Race", Zhang Jianfeng (a poet in the Tang Dynasty) perhaps presents us the best description of such a scene: "With three drumbeats and waving red flags, two boats leap out of the water like dragons. Like thousand swords the paddles plough the whirling waves, like hundred thunders the drumbeats split the huge waves. Drumbeats get much louder to urge the rowers as the prizes are just ahead, eyes of the dragons wink at the prizes as two boats scurry ahead. The folks burst into thunderous cheers on the slopes, and the colored brocade hung on the pole dance like rainbows. The winners take away the prizes as they reach first, much excited; while the losers have but to wave oars in the air, too disappointed." (excerpted) The narration above tells us that, different from the sentimental mood of the folks mourning Qu Yuan on this day in the Wei, Jin and the Southern and Northern Dynasties, much more fun-seeking spirit of the folks was found instead in festive activities such as the boat race, which was evolved into an entertaining sport rather than the poet-saving activity.

Apart from boat race, the custom of eating zongzi became more and more popular, with this rice-dumpling prepared more delicately and increasing in variety. It is recorded that early in the Tang Dynasty, there existed "nine-son" zongzi (a string of zongzi of different sizes), "hundred-string" zongzi, "sticky-rice balls" and the like. The game of shooting "sticky-rice balls" also appeared——the players had to shoot the ball-shaped sticky-rice dumpling with tiny arrows, with the winners enjoying the trophy. During the Taizong reign period of the Tang Dynasty, the

Shorting the osier

Dragon Boat Festival was celebrated on the double fifth day by tradition. Once during the festival, Emperor Taizong presented fans with hollow-stroked calligraphy to his two senior ministers——Zhangsun Wuji and Yang Shidao, on which two lines were written——"Gentle wind breezed and virtue was raised." All were deeply moved by the implied heartfelt expectation: Be as clean as the breeze!

2.3 Festival established

So far as the accurate beginning of the Dragon Boat Festival, opinions vary. According to some Japanese scholars, in Jiaxing district (in present-day Zhejiang Province) in the Song Dynasty (from AD 960 to 1120), the folks on this day would post up the portraits of Zhongkui (a Taoist ghost-hunter), hang calamus &wormwood, burn the Atractylodes lancea and angelica root inside the house, eat zongzi and "five huangs" (five special foods with the same initial character—— 黄 ——pronounced as "huang") and drink realgar (Xiong Huang) wine. Such customs could prove one point that the folks dwelling in Southeast China began to celebrate this important festival at least as early as in the Song Dynasty. Regardless of the varied theories, we could make it sure that no later than the Song Dynasty, the Dragon Boat Festival as a traditional festival was established and widely known among the people, with its unique cultural connotations unchanged.

The folk customs of the Dragon Boat Festival were also introduced to the imperial court during the Qing Dynasty later. On the double fifth day in the late Qing Dynasty, in order to drive away the poisonous creatures, apart from the spray of realgar wine inside the inner palace, even Empress Dowager Cixi ("the Buddha", a disputable woman who monopolized power in the late Qing Dynasty) would dip a small brush into the realgar wine first, then with the wine-dipped brush slightly touch the parts under the noses and ears of some women living in the inner palace——queen, concubines and other female officers. Keen on Peking Opera, she ordered her imperial playwrights to write operas based on the story of Qu Yuan, and had the women all wear "tiger-head" shoes that day, which was a very funny scene. The women living in the inner palace would prepare shoes, areca-nut pouches, tobacco pouches and embroidered towels and present them to Empress Dowager Cixi as well as other ladies, who would grant clothes and jewels to those she favored in return.

It is widely known that the third lunar month is the best tourism season for traveling in Yangzhou (Jiangsu Province now), since at that time the willow catkins flying in the sky make the travelers lost in the scenery. But in fact, Yangzhou was much more attractive and boisterous during the Dragon Boat Festival. On the festival, some local rich merchants would insert the "reward papers" (on which the amount of money reward was written) into the hollowed duck eggs and throw these "prizes" onto the canal, left for the rowers to "scramble". These eggshells floated on the rippled water, and the rowers could only "bite" the prizes, but not "catch" them. So, besides speed and strength, their tactful "mouth" maneuver also determined the winning or losing.

Pleasure-boat races (appeared earliest in the Han Dynasty) were also popular. For example, on the West Lake (Hangzhou, Zhejiang Province), pleasure-boat races were held by the locals on the Dragon Boat Festival. According to "Liangmenglu" (a book recording the local customs and practices of Hangzhou in the Song Dynasty, written by Wu Zimu), the local government would hold pleasure-boat races on the West Lake. "There are six dragon boats in the lake, on which the images of 'seven sages' and 'God Erh-lang' are set up. Wearing 'big red flowers', 'edge-curled hats' and 'red-green costumes', the rowers are playing rather than rowing."

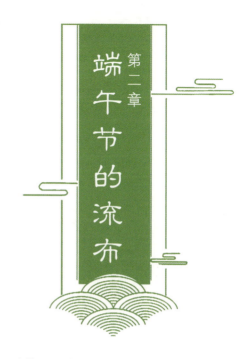

第二章 端午节的流布

端午节不仅在汉族地区，而且随着文化传播和民族融合，少数民族地区也有庆祝端午的习俗。中外文化交流也把端午节庆带到海外进一步传播。

基于前人研究中对南北端午习俗的划分，本章按照地理条件，以水域地形多寡作为一级划分的标准。对少水地区的各种活动再进行二级划分，主要包括厌胜、竞技与社会交往三种。厌胜是建立于端午避恶的文化内涵上被各地广泛采取的驱邪手段，"厌胜"意即"厌而胜之"，系用法术诅咒或祈祷以达到制胜所厌恶的人、物或魔怪的目的。这种形式非常普遍，在少水地区（其中主要在北方）较为突出，水域地区也采取类似的措施来祈求平安和健康。竞技活动是对龙舟竞渡活动的一种地域变形。社会交往的主要目的也在于相互表达避恶祛病的关心，维系社交圈子，增进邻里亲戚感情，是较为普遍的活动。

而水域地区的二级划分较为容易，主要按照龙舟的形制、使用方式和目的来进行区别，划分为竞渡、送瘟和画舫嬉游三种。

一、
北方少水地区的端午节

　　中国北方大部分地区，如华北平原、黄土高原等，水域稀少，气候干旱，这些地区过端午节的方式主要是采取清洁、避毒的各种厌胜做法，来确保家人与宅第的平安与祥和。而在南方一些少水或无水地区，由于缺乏或没有龙舟竞渡的条件，端午习俗也就基本上是围绕食角黍、悬蒲艾等。

○古人所谓的五毒

　　北方地区很早就有避"五毒"的观念和各种厌胜的物件，用以驱除毒虫和瘟疫疾病，保护小儿、妇女等家庭成员和邻里众人的健康与平安。佩戴在小儿、妇女身上的物件主要有五毒背心、五色丝、香囊；用来保护家宅平安的，主要有悬插艾草和贴各种符字。佩带五色丝的风俗，在北方地区的表现较为明显，是端午习俗中一种较为突出的表现形式，一直流传至今。另外，还有用酒或水掺和艾草、葛蒲、雄黄等中药材，用来洁身或清洁居室，以防止疾病入侵、毒虫肆虐。

北方地区的妇女常用绞罗布帛制成小虎及粽子等，把它们串在一起，或戴在头上，或系在肩头。这些物品流传到近现代，主要被称为香包、香囊等，成为端午节日期间妇女们和儿童的主要装饰佩带之

○给儿童穿的五毒衣

物。姑娘们精心缝制彩布或丝绸小袋，一般包上香草、香料或其他物品，如雄黄、艾、蒜等用以除瘟。各地民间还有男青年在此节日期间"抢"姑娘香包的习俗。在陕西，端午节前，姑娘用色布彩线，精心缝制成各种香包，形状有粽子、老虎、金鹿、蝴蝶、燕子、孔雀、金瓜、寿桃、梅花等。它们大多坠有各色丝线缨穗，内装有中药配制成的香料。过端午节时，姑娘们把香包戴在胸前，如果男青年趁其不备，将香包抢去，被抢的姑娘会认为自己的手艺受到异性的喜欢而高兴；反之，如果所佩香包始终无人来抢，就会感到扫兴。

在端午节，妇女、儿童多于鬓际、肩头等戴装饰生肖的小饰物，此外也多有诸如艾虎、健人、独头蒜、小粽子等，或五毒鞋、五毒背心等穿戴，或戴长命索、五色缕等，或带各式香包，以上种种就形成了一大文化景观。小儿和妇女，通过以上各种方式都得到了保护，男子们则主要使用水或酒来洁身健体。这种习俗在南方地区表现得较为明显。

旧时在江苏省的南京一带，人们过端午时，要用放入雄黄、小钱的清水洗眼，认为这样可免除一年的眼病。雄黄酒自从明清之后被广泛使用以来，就被认为是能保护健康的重要药品。雄黄向有杀虫驱毒的效用，在李时珍的《本草纲目》中就有记载：雄黄味辛温有毒，具有解蛇虫毒，燥湿，祛痰的功效。

此外，在少水或无水的区域，受地理条件的限制，几乎不大可能举行龙舟竞渡这样的仪式活动。有些地区，如东北、西北的居民，便继承了辽金时期"射柳祈雨"的风俗，把龙舟竞渡变成了其他方式的竞技比赛，如旱地的竞跑、械杖斗石等，其中祈雨的意义还有所保留，可以说，这也算是一种地方性的活动类型。

端午节的各种活动，在"小社区"中反映出"大社会"的面貌，其中还有一种重要的类型，亦即社区内的相互探访。这种探访因为走访者和被访者之间的关系而有区别，主要包括了三种关系之间的来往。

一是邻里之间相互赠送角黍、厌胜等物，或者邀请亲友宴饮，以便维系社区内的情感。中国南方与北方实际上都颇为盛行这种亲友关系的维系和交往。在北方，有些地方将亲友之间馈送角黍称为"解粽"。有时候，北方特有的面食如馒头，也是佳节馈赠的礼品。

二是姻亲之间的来往，主要是订婚或已婚的女儿、女婿与娘家相互来往，因此端午节也被称为"女儿节"或"探节"。有的地方是订婚而未完婚的准姻亲之间往来，有的是女儿已经出嫁或者刚刚出嫁未满一年的，要在端午节回娘家。还有的地方要接女儿和外孙回娘家，姻亲间要相互赠礼。

三是师生之间的来往。读书的孩子给先生备礼，前往拜见，先生有时也会给学生回礼，如扇子之类。社会关系来往是和个人紧密相联的一项活动，从个人拓展到周围的邻里、亲属以及重要的社会关系等。"隆师"之礼在很多地方都颇为重视，一年中重大的节日往往也是人们之间加强社会关系，维系社区往来的关键时刻。因此，这种隆师之礼并不限于端午，在年节、中秋、冬至等重要节日，看望师长都是必备的礼数。

二、
南方水域地区的端午节

在中国南方，江河纵横，湖泊遍地，水域地区较为广阔。在端午节期间，使用的过节实物以龙舟为主，根据龙舟形制、使用目的、使用方式的不同，基本上可以分为以下三种·

第一种是夺标竞胜的龙舟竞渡。这种竞赛类型的端午活动分布较广，主要是在五月五日举行竞渡的赛事，使用窄而细长的龙舟，刻有龙头龙尾，可以乘坐十几人，它以下水为目的，举行水中竞渡，先树立得胜的"标"，诸如锦旗、标彩或鸭子等。以先到、先得者为胜，参加者均以胜利为荣。

○龙舟竞赛

第二种是送瘟船的活动。这类活动的目的，在于祛疫禳灾，它主要在"大端阳"举行，基本上在五月十八日左右。一般使用木制或纸制的龙船，但其功用不是为了下水，而是由人们抬着游街，并借此收取当地百姓生活中的灾难和不祥，在游街之后即将其焚烧，认为这样就可以把灾难送走。

　　有些地方把这类习俗直接称之为"收瘟""送瘟"或"迎船"等。人们抬着龙船沿门挨户地表演，换取香火、酒食，待表演完毕，龙舟即被焚烧。如江西湖口一地，也是在五月十八日，"为纸龙舟，形如真者，皆结彩装戏，游于市中"。所过民家投以五谷盐茶，名曰"收瘟"。游毕，则送之郊外焚之。再如广东省的台山等地，使用的是打造的木龙。四月初八即开始抬着木龙游乡，以五月五日最为热闹。每到村头门口，即唱祝颂词，主人则赏给红包。回村后结束游乡，把木龙烧掉，称之为"送龙归天"。在湖北等地，多在五月十八日开始纸船祈神之会。如湖北大冶一带，使用的是纸船。他们在五月十八日"送瘟"。用纸作龙舟，长约数丈，上为三闾大夫像，人物有数十，皆衣锦绣彩绘，冠佩器用以银制，花费近百金，送之至青龙堤焚之，其盛况为他处所罕比。

　　各地对这类龙舟称谓不尽相同，但比赛性质相同，基本上都是以纸船送瘟，有的地方还会设坛打醮，活动甚至可以持续达十余天。竞渡和送瘟的活动，在有些地方两种方式都有，主要是在过大端午的地区。楚俗大多数地区均有五日为"小端阳"和十五日为"大端阳"的节期，湖北《武昌县志》对夺标的龙舟竞渡和纸船祈神送瘟之会都记述和区分得相当细致："'端阳'悬蒲艾，食角黍，泛雄黄酒，系彩辟恶。近水居民竞龙舟。舟绘黄、红、青三色，沿岸分曹，以角胜负，或晌以酒食，胜者得之，曰'夺标'。"大端阳节则是送瘟之会。"十七日，有纸舫祈神之会，小儿女系赴瘟司庙上枷。次日，庙神出游，异者盛饰，去帽答五色花，沿街拽茅船，谓之'逐疫'。"

就如同送瘟禳灾的端午一样，端午时节在家家户户的门上贴避邪的符字，并做好纸船焚烧，认为这样就可以驱除瘟疫和疾病，镇压邪祟和毒气。农业耕作圈的居民遇到大旱或水灾时都会举行这种祈禳仪式。

相比较而言，画舫嬉游的情形，其游戏和娱乐的目的则显得要更加明确和重要。画舫嬉游则是属于第三类龙舟活动。在这一类娱乐型的活动中，龙舟竞渡往往演化成为一种表演，人们更主要的是以出游消遣为乐。届时游客如织，街市买卖兴旺，娱乐、商贸活动形成为集市，规模颇为壮观。

三、少数民族地区的端午节

在民族文化相互交流的过程中，中国少数民族地区的节日体系逐渐地囊括了诸如春节、清明、端午、中秋等重大的汉文化节日。就端午节来说，黎族、土家族、京族、布依族、畲族、壮族、阿昌族、满族等每年都过端午节。

在海南黎族聚居区，五月初五那一天，有钱人家凑钱宰牛杀鸡，包粽子吃。当天清晨，妇女到河边挑水，谁家挑得早，当年的运气就最好，收成也最好，被称作"挑新水"。在湖南，当地的土家族也过端午节，但是有大端午和小端午的区别，包粽子、门边挂菖蒲叶等习俗跟汉族相同。

京族过端午节的时候要先祭祖，再全家一起吃粽子、喝雄黄酒。布依族的雄黄酒与其他族有点不一样，不只是用雄黄和白酒泡，还加上了大蒜、姜、葱等，预防痢疾以及其他流行病。有时候甚至捞出泡过雄黄酒的大蒜直接食用，预防疾病。而且，还把雄黄粉四处喷洒，防止蚊虫肆虐。包的粽子也与普通的糯米粽子不同。布依族的粽子馅也有食疗功能，例如艾菜粽可以清热解毒，草灰粽可以帮助消化等。另外，布依族人还把雄黄、菖蒲、艾叶、三角枫等放在香袋里随身携带，避邪祛病。

对于水族来说，"端午"还有另外的含义。水族人把端午称为"借端"，而"借"又是"吃"的意思，也就是新开始的含义。所以在这一天，水族人都要祭祀祖先，祈求保佑来年丰收。畲族的粽子是五月初四包好的，但是要等到五月初五这一天才全家在一起吃，而且要在中午之前吃完。据说是因为先辈的时代，白天要忙于农活，只

○白娘子喝黄酒现原形

有早晨有时间吃。而且粽子形状是圆柱形的"管粽"和横枕式的"横巴粽"，用粽叶包裹后扎上粽叶丝，通常有五节，表示"五福齐得"的含义。也有人认为，这是象征着祖先参与征战后皇上赏赐的物品，因此后人用粽子祭祖，表达了崇敬和自豪之情。粽子是要用"猴梨柴"烧灰炮制的碱水，所以味道特别可口。一些地方的畲族还有"送端午节"的习俗，父母给出嫁的女儿提早送去粽子、衣服、手帕等"送节"礼物。

广西的壮族也有五月初五过端午节的习俗，但是壮族人所包出来的粽子各式各样，有肉馅的，也有绿豆馅的，还有豆沙馅的粽子，甚至有的用藤叶、糯米磨成粉做成干糕状做馅等。南方初夏时节十分潮湿，壮族人不仅在家门口插上枫叶或艾草，还煮醋液、烧柚子皮来驱虫杀蚊，并且把雄黄酒用来喷洒在房屋的四周，以祛除病邪。有些地方的壮族人还在端午节划龙舟比赛。

阿昌族在端午节所包的粽子也很有特点，小三角粽、枕头粽、裹脚粽、草灰粽等，还要加上草果作为香料，有咸有甜，味道诱人。另外，还要专门制作祭祀祖灵的素粽，挂在家堂上，生病腹泻的时候可以吃这对素粽。除此之外，还要制作药酒，绣香包给妇女小孩佩戴，炒十多种野菜混在一起的"八宝菜"吃，预防疾病。

○粽叶

满族不仅在端午节吃粽子，而且还供奉"祖宗板子"。还有一个关于粽子的传说：

○食粽

很久以前，天帝派人下凡体察民情。在五月初五这天，天帝的使臣扮成卖油翁吆喝："一葫芦二斤，两葫芦三斤。"大家争相购买，只有一个老人没有买，还告诉卖油翁账算错了。等油卖光后，卖油翁对老人说："你是个好人，今天晚上要降瘟疫，你在自己家的房檐上插上艾草，就可以躲过瘟疫了。"老人听后，就挨家挨户告诉了乡亲，家家都插上了艾草，瘟神也就不能降下瘟疫了，人们都得救了。

满族人除了在屋檐瓦片上插艾蒿、用露水洗脸、采"百步草"、制作荷包香囊和长命缕以外，老北京的满族小姑娘还在端午这一天头戴石榴花，火红的石榴花远远望去亮丽夺目。

有些少数民族的端午节内容与汉族相似，以避邪、清洁为主，但也有一些少数民族的端午节意义则与汉族完全不同。云南的拉祜

○ 簪榴花作发饰

族在端午节时种树种竹，相传这一天是种植树木最容易成活的日子，此外还要与亲朋好友一起进食。施甸的布朗族要在五月初五这一天举行"洗牛脚"的仪式。在五月初四这一天晚上，布朗族人用红纸包裹

香烛，插在厅堂里，门前插一面红纸旗幡。第二天，寨子的头人和寨老共牵一只羊，拿着杨柳、桃枝、黄泡树枝扎成的树枝，到各家门前扫一下厅堂，给主人带来祝福。主人将一瓢冷水洒在两人的雨帽蓑衣上，表示已经洗去牛的足迹。之后，将羊牵到树下宰杀，每家每户带一些米，煮羊肉稀饭，大家共食。哈尼族五月初五的"牛纳纳"也与牛有关。"牛纳纳"的意思是让牛歇歇气，对耕牛表示谢意，让其休养生息。在五月初五这一天，寨子里的各家各户将紫色的兰草煮成紫水，染糯米饭供奉祖先，还要用紫水洗脸擦身，祛除病邪。带着公鸡和紫糯米饭上山祭祖，给牛喂肉汤糯米饭，对耕牛表示感谢。

四川省凉山州雷波及金沙江沿岸等地的彝族，在五月初五过"都阳节"。都阳节的由来还跟民族互助有关呢。据说在古代，有一次彝族寨子里病疫盛行，江边的汉族同胞把菖蒲、艾叶和雄黄送给彝族，还告诉他们，端午节的草药可以治百病。彝族人用艾蒿洗澡，用雄黄酒擦身，后来就痊愈了。从此，彝族把"端"念成"都"，也过"都阳节"了。这一天，彝族人除了挂艾叶菖蒲以外，还有摔跤、斗牛、跳舞等活动。

　　云南的纳西族过端午节时在门口插上一枝青刺枝，用野生青刺果油炸鸡蛋祭祀狮子山，男女歌手对唱歌颂狮子山。纳西族人在端午节时要在手上、脚上缠带五色丝线，也给当年出生的小马驹、小牛犊的脖子上缠上彩线，祛邪保平安。在火把节的最后一天即六月二十七时烧掉五色续命缕。

　　四川甘肃交界一带的藏族在五月初五过"采花节"，也叫"女儿节"。据说以前，当地一片荒凉，莲芝姑娘教大家种地、采花治病，

○藏族的女儿节

061

可惜莲芝姑娘在五月初五上山采花时摔死了。人们为了纪念她，在这一天举行抢水、采花的活动，祈求保佑和祝福。

在采花节这一天的清晨，人们抢着去泉水边打水洗脸洗身，据说用太阳还未照到的泉水洗浴，可以得到吉祥的祝福。青年男女们穿上盛装，到山上去采花。姑娘采花，小伙子负责砍柴搭棚等，傍晚时唱歌跳舞。第二天，姑娘们戴着鲜花背着草药回到寨子，将采回的鲜花草药赠送给村民，送上吉祥与祝愿。

蒙古族有端午打大围的习俗，也称之为"端午猎日"。相传很久以前，某一年的五月初五，蒙古族部落的成员都出去打大围了，刚好这一天有其他部落侵袭，而蒙古族部落的成员都不在，因此一场厮杀得以避免。所以五月初五打大围就成为一种习俗传承下来。还有一种说法与成吉思汗有关。据说成吉思汗是在五月初五这一天围猎受惊而死，因此这一天作为猎日以纪念成吉思汗。打大围开始的前几天，需要确定围猎的路线和范围，推举总指挥"阿宾达"。有两种方式打大围，一种是在山区，从山口把猎物往山沟里围。另一种是在平原地区从四面八方往中间围。猎人们带着猎枪或弓箭，赶着猎狗，从早到晚，满载而归。

博峪采花节

博峪采花节是甘肃省甘南藏族自治州舟曲县博峪一带藏族群众的传统节日，每年农历五月初举行，节期两天。采花节是祭祀花神的节日，在这一天，寨老带领村寨的藏族民众祭祀、唱歌、抢水等，还有盛大的集会活动。

地址：甘肃省甘南藏族自治州舟曲县博峪乡

交通：舟曲县位于甘肃省东南部，兰州至舟曲县，每天有汽车对发。

县城到博峪乡乘舟曲至武都的班次，再乘武都到文县至博峪乡的班次。

四、
港澳台地区的端午节

港澳台地区亦属于中国东南沿海，端午节的习俗与相邻的省份习俗接近，主要采用各种方式进行祛疫禳灾。在香港和台湾某些地区，至今还保留着相当完整、复杂的龙舟竞渡仪式。

每年端午节，香港多个地区都会举行龙舟竞渡，特别是仍有艇家生活的香港仔、西贡、长洲、大澳、南丫岛、屯门、沙田城门河、大埔海滨公园等。1983 年，日本学者渡边欣雄详细地考察了"香港长洲岛的龙舟祭"，并根据对长洲岛的实地观察和访谈记录，对当地的端午节礼仪进行了深入的分析。长洲岛位于香港最大的岛屿大屿山东南部的洋面上，面积约有 2.4 平方千米，算是一个小岛。据说这个岛上有人居住，已有几百年的历史了，自古就作为一个渔业小镇而繁荣。长洲岛因系香港少有的水上村落而广为人知，在船上起居生活的水上居民，云集于长洲湾内，包括那些已经开始在陆上生活的渔业从业者在内，战后最繁盛的时期，据说有一万多人。可是，现在他们的人数逐渐减少，已不足一万，在长洲岛注册的渔船的数量，大约有 500 只（1983 年）。长洲岛的龙舟祭，是以旧历的五月五日为正日，亦即在"端午节"这天举行的。节期是从旧历五月二日（初二）到旧历五月六日（初六），是以水上居民和渔民们为中心而传承举办的，它是长洲岛代表性的大节之一。

端午节的各项传统活动中，又以大澳的游泳活动最特别，为香港独有。每年农历五月初五，乡民都会划着龙舟，后面拖着载有神像的"神艇"，巡游在各水道间，并沿途焚烧宝烛。而棚屋居民又同时会朝着龙舟拜祭，祈求合家平安、驱除疾病、风调雨顺。游泳仪式过后便会举行龙舟竞渡。游泳活动已有逾百年历史，2011 年更被列为第三批国家非物质文化遗产项目。

○ 荡秋千

还有人会专门选端午节这天去游泳，叫作"游龙舟水"。在香港，人们相信这天游水有祈福、改变运程和辟走邪气的作用。因此这天各个泳池和海滩，都会挤满想要祈求好运、游龙舟水的人们。

　　台湾的端午习俗，保留有古老的悬艾、系五色丝等事象，随着时代的推移，逐渐增加了新的内容，如竞技比赛、龙舟赛事等。在《台湾府志》中记载了清代的端午习俗。其中对龙舟竞渡之戏有不同的记述，有的说竞渡只残存着一部分内容，无法做到真正争胜。有的却说它可以同福建一带夺标竞争，还有的更为详细地记载了祀神和争斗的经过。例如，《台湾府志·岁时》的记载有："五月五日，家折松艾，悬之门首，以五色丝系儿童臂上，呼为长命缕。又以兰作虎子形贴儿额上，到午时脱而投之所在。竞渡船不过杉板小艇，大海狂澜难以击楫，仅存遗意。亦渍米裹竹叶为角黍。"《台湾府志·风土》也有类似的记载，但不同的是增加了夺标的内容："端午日昔人取艾悬户，采蒲泛酒，今合艾与蒲共悬之，谓蒲似剑也。以五色长命缕系儿童臂上，以兰作虎子贴额上，至午时脱而投之所在。竞渡虽云吊屈，亦以辟邪，无贵贱，咸买舟出游中流，箫鼓歌舞，凌波游人置竿船头，挂以锦绮，捷者夺标而去。人家俱为角黍，按《风土记》取阴阳包裹未分之义也。"

　　而《重修台湾府志》中的记载则更为详细，补充了很多上述文字所没有的信息，如"五月五日清晨，燃稻梗一束向四隅熏之，用褚钱送路旁，名曰送蚊。门相间艾叶菖蒲兼插禾稗一茎，谓可避蚊。榕一枝，谓老而弥健。彼此以西瓜肉粽相馈遗。祀神用诸红色物，自初五至初七，好事者于海口浅处，用钱或布为标，杉板渔船争相夺取，胜者鸣锣为得采。土人亦号为斗龙舟"。对此，还注有小字称："三月尽、四月朔望、五月初一至初五日，各寺庙及海岸各船，鸣锣击鼓，名曰龙船戏，谓主一年旺相。"这些记载都反映了台湾端午风俗。

龙舟竞渡的习俗在台湾也是颇为昌盛的，台湾当地称之为"扒龙船"。据《民俗台湾》记载，日据时代士林的端午习俗是自五月初一起，就先到水边"迎水神"。初二则开"龙船会"，商议有关事情。初五正午，即敲响锣鼓，扛起龙舟到河岸，沿途都有居民烧香、祭拜。俗语说，"五月五，龙船鼓，满街路"。龙船到达河岸后，先到的龙船要鸣锣举桨，表示欢迎，此称为"接龙船"。赛过龙船后，还要在初十"送水神"，举行"谢江"的仪式。

○端午节门口挂菖蒲、艾草和榕树叶

1996年，台湾编辑节日丛书的序中，对端午习俗的描述是"以清领台湾为上限，对三百大庙。咸粽便是其中不可或缺的祭品。咸粽分米粽及板（粿）粽两种，纯粹用来解馋"。

台湾的闽南人一般认为在端午节要吃桃、茄子、菜豆等，认为这样能够健康长寿。俗语有云："食茄吃到会摇，吃豆吃到老老。"台式粽子因为制作方法不同，有南北两种风味。北部将米浸泡，沥干后用油炒香，并加入五香粉、胡椒粉、酱油等调味料，再将米蒸熟。有的用油将米炒到半熟，再用竹叶包裹后，填馅重蒸一次。南部则是将白糯米浸泡后加肉馅，以绿竹叶包裹，用水煮熟。所以，北方粽子有浓郁的五香胡椒味，南方的肉粽有竹叶的清香。粽子馅可以是猪肉、香菇、虾米、花生、咸蛋黄、红葱头、栗子、蚝干等，完全可以按照个人的喜好增减。

五、
其他国家的端午节

　　以节日习俗而言，端午节虽然发源地在中国，但是在长期的流传和国际交流中，它已经被中国周边的国家和民族所吸纳、所接受，并被置于他们自己的文化土壤之中，形成了周边国家民族独特的节日习俗。

　　韩国江陵端午祭的原型深受中国文化的影响。韩国也称五月初五日为"重午""重五""端阳""五月节"，韩国特有的词是称"端午"为"上日"，意为神的日子。按照传统的风俗，人们在端午这一天，要吃"艾子糕"，喝益仁汁，妇女们要用菖蒲汤洗头发或饮用菖蒲水，或者用菖蒲露化妆——"菖蒲妆"。士大夫人家的门柱上，要贴朱砂符借以避邪，君臣之间还要互赠端午扇表示祝贺。

　　韩国江陵端午祭包含了丰富的内容，祭祀、演戏、游艺是其主要的内容。其中的祭祀仪式，据说保存了颇为完整的形式和内容，是韩国江陵端午祭的核心。祭祀仪式主要与神话传说有关，祭祀的神灵是"大关岭山神"金庚信、国师城隍"梵日国师"、大关岭国师女城隍郑家女等。

　　江陵端午祭有繁琐的祭祀仪式，时间跨度大。如果从迎神的"前夜祭"算起是五个昼夜，从"山神祭"算起是 20 多天，从"谨酿神酒"算起则长达一个月。神酒的酿制拉开了江陵端午祭的序幕。在农历四月五日，用江陵旧官府"七事堂"发放的大米和柚子酿制神酒。四月十五日举行"大关岭山神祭"和"国师城隍祭"。农历五月初三傍晚时分，回到江陵国师女城隍祠（郑家女）接受"奉安祭"（即"前夜祭"）。祭祀结束之后，将大关岭山神和国师城隍牌位送往南大川露天祭场。从初四到初七，每天的早晨举行"朝奠祭"。江陵端午祭总体上分为"儒教式祭仪"和"巫俗祭仪"两种。前者是奉读汉文祝祷词，祈祷平安繁盛。后者是歌舞戏剧表演，一直到夜深。

江陵端午祭的活动丰富多彩。除指定的祭礼（谨酿神酒—送神仪式）、巫祭、假面戏、农乐竞赛外，还有众多的民俗活动。例如，汉诗创作比赛、乡土民谣竞唱大赛、全国时调竞唱大赛、拔河、摔跤、荡秋千、射箭、投壶等。庆祝活动包括烟火游戏、端午放灯等，还有国乐表演、伽椰琴并唱等夜间活动。

越南人的端午节包括赛龙舟、食粽子、祭祀屈原。大约在陈朝的时候，端午节传入越南，并逐渐成为越南人重要的传统民俗节日之一。越南老百姓过端午，既有对中国爱国诗人屈原的缅怀，又结合了刘神、阮召的动人事迹，以及早稻丰收的喜悦，庆祝刘神、阮召的功劳。

越南人民把这个节日越南化，并创造出符合越南生活的习俗。如除害虫、染手脚指甲、戴辟邪香袋、香茅草沐浴、爬树采果、午时采药、插艾叶葛蒲等习俗。除害虫是因为人们认为虫会隐避在人的腹中，五月五日会出来。除掉的方法是在五月五日一早起床漱口后吃糯米酒把它弄醉，然后吃水果把它们弄死。采草药是因为人们认为这些叶子能降温，能解除气候反常引起的热。所以在正午时分，人们到偏僻的地方采药草，把叶子晒干熬水喝，解热降暑。拷树取果的风俗，是因为民间认为每一棵树都有灵魂，如果树多年未结果，人们就拷树，逼树开花结果。在挂艾草时，越南人把艾草编成与当年对应的生肖形状，挂在门口以避邪驱魔。人们认为艾草有强大的生命力，能为生肖注入力量，有保卫人们的任务，避免人们受邪气、瘟疫病毒的侵害。越南人在端午节期间食用的粽子，是用芭蕉叶包裹的，有圆形和方形两种。他们认为，圆形的粽子代表天，方形粽子代表地，天地合一，大吉大利。咸粽用糯米加虾米、瘦猪肉、红豆，再加半只咸蛋包成；肥肉粽用糯米、肋条肉、虾米、绿豆和五香调料包成，煮熟剥壳切片而食。端午节吃粽子，被认为可以求得风调雨顺，五谷丰登。

　　朝鲜和日本的端午节习俗，也有一些中国端午节的文化元素。朝鲜的粽子，被称为"车轮饼"，人们把鲜嫩的艾叶煮后捣碎加在米粉中，再做成车轮形状，味道可口。朝鲜人会在端午节带着珍贵的艾饼和松皮饼去祭奠祖先，女孩子们则用菖蒲煮汤洗澡、洗头。在节日期间，还有摔跤、荡秋千等传统的娱乐活动。

○端午用菖蒲水洗发

日本人包粽子不用糯米，而是用磨碎的米粉，形状也与中国的不同，是锤形粽子。在阴历五月五日吃的粽子被称为"茅卷"，这是用竹叶或蒿叶包成，形状则是长圆柱的形状。日本的粽子有各种不同形状，有筒形、菱形、锥形、秤锤形等，并按照形状命名。还有按照功能命名的粽子，例如百索粽是希望男孩子吃了以后能健康成长。在日本，五月有男孩节，人们在房顶或院内用竹竿悬挂鲤鱼旗，期待孩子能有鲤鱼那种激流勇进的精神。

　　随着华人的足迹逐渐遍布世界各国，华人的节日文化也随之传播出去，尤其是春节、端午、中秋等主要节日，日益成为海外华人和其他国家重视的中国节庆。新加坡在端午节期间要举行全国范围的龙舟大赛，从下午起，龙舟就披红挂彩，船头站着装扮成"狮子"和"狗熊"的司鼓手。22 名桨手奋力拼搏，一直赛到夕阳西下。美国波士顿儿童博物馆在 1979 年 5 月举行了第一届波士顿龙舟游艺会，中华民族的舞蹈、武术和娱乐活动都有。

Chapter Two
Spread of the Dragon Boat Festival

The Dragon Boat Festival is not only widely celebrated by the Han people, but also has become an indispensible festival in many minority nationality regions with the ethnic integration. Meanwhile, its unique customs have long been circulated abroad through cultural communication between China and other nations.

Based on the past studies of the classification of the local customs in Southern and Northern China, in this chapter we propose a general standard for the classification of the local customs on the ground of the geographical conditions and distribution of waters. Then, we hope to subclassify those festive activities in the water—lacking areas into three kinds, namely, "overcoming the hated", sports and social interactions. The custom of "overcoming the hated" — to overcome someone or some devil who you hate—was widely adopted to drive away the evils, deeply rooted in the spirit of evil—avoiding. Such a custom spread over China, especially in those water—lacking areas (mainly in Northern China). While in those areas rich in water resources, apart from boat race, similar custom was adopted to pray for

peace and health. Sports activities (other than boat race) could be taken as regional variants for boat race, or some kind of cultural substitution. Social interactions in the Dragon Boat Festival, as popular as the custom of "overcoming the hated", mainly helped the folks to express mutual concerns about health-keeping, maintain their social circles and promote the feelings among the relatives and neighbors. The subclassification of the customs in those areas rich in water resources is relatively simpler—boat-racing, plague-dispelling and pleasure cruise of painted-boats, which could be classified and distinguished by the shapes of dragon boats, modes of usage and purposes of boat-racing.

1. The Dragon Boat Festival in Water-lacking Areas

In most parts of Northern China (e.g. Hua-pei Plain and Loess Plateau) with scarce waters and arid climate, the folks usually preserved the custom of "overcoming the hated" via

keeping body or house clean and avoiding poisons to maintain the peace of the family and residence. Meanwhile, in those water-lacking (even waterless) areas of Southern China, the custom of boat-racing has long been excluded due to lack of waters, so the folks there had to eat zongzi and hang calamus & wormwood.

In most parts of Northern China, the idea of "Wudu" (avoiding

Wudu

five poisonous creatures) and the tiny articles to "overcome the hated" have long existed, by means of which they hope to dispel the poisonous insects or plagues and prevent the children, women and neighbors falling ill. The tiny articles worn by the children and women mainly include "Wudu"-driving vests, five-color silk threads and perfume pouches. By hanging calamus &wormwood or posting charms, they hope to maintain the peace of the family and residence. In addition, they will clean their bodies or houses with wine or water blended with calamus or realgar in order to keep healthy.

The women in Northern China used to make some handicrafts like tiger cubs, bottle gourds and dried fruits with gauze, wearing them (tied in a string) on the head or on the shoulder. Mostly called perfume pouches or satchels, such articles are still popular now and the children and women will wear them on the Dragon Boat Festival. To avoid plagues, girls in the past would stuff into their elaborately-sown color-ribboned or silk pouches vanilla, spices or other odorous materials——realgar, wormwood and garlic etc. There was one funny custom—— "pouch-snatching": some young men would "snatch" the perfume pouch (es) from the girls. In Shanxi (its present capital is Xi'an), long before the festival, the girls would elaborately sew various perfume pouches with colored threads in the shape of zongzi, tiger, golden deer, butterfly, swallow, peacock, gourd, birthday peach and plum or the like. Colored silk-tassels drooping, these pouches were often stuffed with medicinal spices. On the Dragon Boat Festival, seeing the girls wearing perfume pouches on their chests, some young men would "snatch" the pouch(es) from them "off their guard". In fact, the "robbed" girls would feel delighted since their crafts were favored by the opposite gender; while, if no one came close, they might feel daunted for their "ignored" poor skills.

On the Dragon Boat Festival, the children and women often wore some petty ornaments in the shape of Chinese zodiac animals on their shoulders or beside their temples. They also wore some other ornaments——wormwood-weaved tigers, Jianren (purl-embroidered ornament in the likeness of a kid riding a tiger), one-clove garlic and even small zongzi. Meanwhile, they would prepare "Wudu"-driving shoes and vests, or wear longevity cords, five-color silk cords and various perfume pouches as well. Subsequently, a grand cultural landscape has been formed due to the variety of those lovely and meaningful ornaments, by which the children and women were protected. As far as the male adults, they would wash their bodies with water or wine to keep healthy, which could be seen more often in Southern China.

In Nanjing (present-day capital of Jiangsu Province) and its surrounding areas, the people there in the past would put realgar and copper coins into clean water and wash their eyes with it, for they believed such water could drive the eye disease away in the whole year. As far as realgar (Xiong Huang) wine, regarded as a very important medicine protecting the whole family, it has been widely consumed ever since the Ming Dynasty (1368—1644 AD) and the Qing Dynasty (1644—1912AD). It was recorded in "Bencaogangmu" ("The Compendium of Materia Medica", the greatest medical book in ancient China compiled by Li Shizhen) as follows: Xionghuang (realgar, a mineral containing sulphur and arsenic) is characterized by its pungent smell and warmth-stimulating effect. This mineral medicine is slightly poisonous while it could effectively detoxify those bitten by poisonous snakes and insects with its unique dampness-and-phlegm-eliminating effect.

However, in those water-lacking or waterless areas, festive rituals such as dragon boat races or the like could be hardly held due to the limited geographical condition. Therefore, some people in Northeast China and Northwest China preserved the custom of "shooting willow twigs to pray for rain" inherited from the Liao and Jin Period. Boat race was also converted into other forms of races——games of running on the dry land, stick-fighting and stone-hurling, with the purpose of rain-praying maintained. Such activities, as it were, were only held locally.

Among all of those festive activities, which could reflect the panorama of the whole society via a small community (like a drop of water), there is another important custom unmentioned yet——mutual visits in the same community. Due to the different relationships between the visitor and the visited, such visits could be classified into three categories as follows:

1.1 Neighbors and relatives

To strengthen the emotional bond, the neighbors would present zongzi and articles of "overcome the hated" to each other, and one would invite his relatives and friends to a banquet. Whether in the north or in the south, the Chinese all favored such customs to maintain their relationships. In the north, when people presented horn-like zongzi to their relatives and friends, they would call it "unwrap the zongzi". In addition, some unique wheaten foods popular in the north, for example, "Mantou" (steamed bun), could also become favorite presents.

1.2 Among the in-laws

The Dragon Boat Festival was also called "Girls' Day" or "Parents-Visiting Day". On this happy day, the interaction between the in-laws (to-be) was active——the fiancé with his family would visit his fiancée's home and the married daughter with(out) her husband would reunite with her parents. In some places, the in-laws-to-be would visit each other, and the married daughter (or who had just got married less than one year) also returned to her parents' home. In some other places, the married daughters and grandchildren would be picked up by her natal family, with gifts presented between the in-laws.

1.3 The students and the tutors

The students would go to visit their tutors with prepared presents, and the latter would give gifts in return, for example, a fan or the like. Social interaction, closely related to "avoiding five poisonous creatures"——an individual activity more or less, was regarded as one important festive activity, which in a larger range involved the relations between an individual and his neighbors, relatives and other social members. Some important festivals in a year were always the critical occasions on which the people could strengthen their social relations and promote the kinship. Since the rite of "tutor-honoring" was much valued, apart from the Dragon Boat Festival, other important festivals such as the Chinese New Year, the Mid-Autumn Festival and the Winter Solstice were also critical days on which the students should pay a visit to their tutors.

2. The Dragon Boat Festival in Southern Waters

In Southern China, intersected by numerous rivers and countless lakes, many places rich in water resources are flat and open stretches. On the Dragon Boat Festival, people there used to celebrate it by racing the dragon boat——the most conspicuous tangible tool. Dragon boat race, in the light of the shapes of boats, modes of usage and purposes of boat-racing, could be classified and distinguished as the following three kinds.

Dragon boat Race

2.1 Dragon boat race for winning the prizes

Held mainly on the double-fifth day, such a kind of race took place annually all over Southern China. The dragon boat for prize-winning competition, narrow and slender, could hold 10 or more rowers (depending on the length, up to even 80), with a head carved like an open-mouthed dragon and the stern a scaly tail. The boat race, held on the rivers or lakes of course, had a simple rule——"reaching or grabbing first": the boat first reaching the prize-pole or finish line would win, or the rowers first grabbing the silk flag, prize-lottery or ducks would defeat others. Such a rule encouraged the competitors to row all out to win the race.

2.2 Sending away the "plague-boat"

To drive away plagues and avoid disasters, such a special activity was mostly held on the day of "Big Duanyang" (Summer Solstice), around the 18th day of the fifth lunar month. Carrying a dragon boat made of wood or paper, people would parade through the streets in the hope to "collect" the misfortune and unluckiness of the locals. After the parade, they would burn the boat, believing that the misfortune and unluckiness had been sent away.

In some places, such a custom was also called "collecting plagues", "sending away plagues" or "greeting the plague-boat". People would carry such dragon boats and parade through the streets, stopping to perform before every door and gain incense or some food and drink in return. The boat would be burnt right after the parade. For example, on the 18th day of the fifth lunar month, the folks in Hukou County (in present-day Jiangxi Province) would make a lifelike paper-made dragon, get it festoon-adorned and parade through the streets, where the residents would throw "five cereals" or salt or tea leaves upon the paper dragon. They called it "collecting plagues". After that, the dragon was sent to the outskirts and burnt right away. While the folks in Taishan district (in present-day Guangdong Province) preferred to make a wood-made dragon. Starting on the eighth day of the fourth lunar month, they would carry that dragon for a parade, with the whole village most cheerful on the double-fifth day. When passing by every house, the performers would sing out prayers or praises and gain a "red packet" (money left in a red envelop as bonus/prize) from the host. The boat would also be burnt right after the parade, which was called "sending the dragon back to the heaven". On the eighteenth day of the fifth lunar month, the people in some places in Hubei Province would hold temple fairs to pray for rain by carrying paper-made dragons. The people in Daye (in Hubei Province) would "send away plagues" via parade and burning (of) dragon. On this 10-meter paper dragon would stand the portrait of Sanlv Minister (Qu Yuan) and dozens of other figures, all wearing colored brocade with painted patterns and silver crowns or waist-ornaments. This costly paper dragon would be carried to Green-Dragon Dam and burnt there, a spectacular scene rarely seen in anywhere else.

Though people in different places named such dragon boat differently, they all hoped to "send away plagues" by carrying and burning the paper dragons. In some places, the locals would even set altars and ask Taoists to tell fortunes, which could last more than 10 days. The customs of boat-racing and "sending away plagues" were preserved simultaneously in some places (mainly in the places where "Big Duanwu" was celebrated). "Small Duanyang" (lasting 5 days) and "Big Duanyang" (lasting 15 days) were both celebrated in many districts of the ancient Chu. Found in Xianning District (Hubei Province), the book of "Local Chronicle of Wuchang" (Volume X, the carving copy in Qianlong reign period of the Qing Dynasty) respectively elaborates on the custom of dragon boat race and "sending away plagues" via burning the paper dragon: On the day of "Small Duanyang", to fend off the evils, it is conventional to eat zongzi, hang calamus & wormwood, drink realgar wine and tie colored cords. The riverside folks will hold dragon boat race——lines of spectators standing along the riverbanks, the boats painted yellow, red and green dash ahead to win the game. The winner who grabs the red flag first may enjoy the prize——food and drink. On the day of "Big Duanyang", however, it is a custom to send away plagues. On the 17th day, at the temple fair to pray for rain, boys and girls will present incense to the Gods of Plagues (in charge of the plagues). On the next day, the Gods of Plagues are carried out for a parade, standing beside are those strange make-up figures decorated with gorgeous clothes and five-colored flowers. The locals will drag the straw boat along the streets, which is called "driving away the plagues".

Apart from "sending away plagues", every household would post talismans or charms upon the door and burn the prepared paper boats to avoid evils, drive away diseases and overwhelm devils. When stricken by droughts or floods, the farmers would hold such activities to pray for blessing.

2.3 Pleasure cruise of painted-boats

Relatively speaking, pleasure cruise of painted-boats was held as a game to entertain the spectators for the most part. In such an activity, the boat race was evolved into some kind of grand show for the pleasure-seeking people, who strolled and shopped on the bustling streets, making the busy fair a grand view.

3. The Dragon Boat Festival in Minority Nationality Regions

During the cultural interactions among different nationalities, some important festivals of the Han nationality, e.g., the Spring Festival, Qing Ming (Tomb-Sweeping) Day, the Dragon Boat Festival and the Mid-Autumn Festival, have gradually become one part of the holiday system of other Chinese minority communities. So far as the Dragon Boat Festival, the Li, the Tu, the Tujia, the Jing, the Dong, the Bouyei, the She, the Zhuang, the A-Chang and the Manchu all celebrate this festival. The Li people living

Hanging wormwood during
the Dragon Boat Festival

in Hainan Island also celebrated the Double Fifth Day. On the fifth day of the fifth lunar month, some well-off families would club together to have an ox butchered and share the beef, enjoying chicken, duck and zongzi respectively. Early in the morning one woman of each family would be asked to fetch water from the river running alongside, which was called "fetch fresh water". It was said the family who fetched water the earliest would have the luckiest year and the best harvest. Besides, the Tu people living in Hunan also celebrated Duanwu —— but "Small Duanwu" and "Big Duanwu" respectively. They had some customs similar to those of the Han people —— eating zongzi and hanging calamus and wormwood on each side of the door.

On the Dragon Boat Festival, each family of the Jing people (inhabit mainly in Guangxi Zhuang Autonomous Region now) would worship their ancestors in the morning first and at noon, the family would gather to eat zongzi, drink realgar wine, smear a little of it on the kid's forehead and hang wormwood on the door. Just on this day, in order to prevent diarrhea and other illnesses, the Bouyei people would drink realgar wine blended with garlic, ginger and green onion, or eat realgar wine-soaked garlic. In addition, sometimes they would spray realgar powder at the corners to fend off the crazy attacks of bugs and mosquitoes. Of course, all families would prepare zongzi stuffed with various fillings as the staple food that day, including goat-ear-shaped "wormwood-leaf" zongzi to clear heat or detoxify and "Caohui" zongzi (dyed dark by straw ash) to help digestion with a longer storage period. They would wear perfume pouches stuffed with realgar, calamus, wormwood and trident maple upon the chests, hoping to avoid evils and prevent diseases.

For the Shui People, Duanwu meant something a little different: They called it "jieduan" ("Duan-borrowing") and "jie" also meant "eating". Therefore, Duanwu symbolized the beginning of a new day on which the Shui people would worship their ancestors and pray for a harvest.

The She people (mainly living in Southeast China now) would prepare zongzi on the fourth day of the fifth lunar month but could only eat them the next day (must eat them up before noon). Why? It is said that their ancestors could only have leisure time to enjoy zongzi in the morning since they were too busy farming in the daytime, But their zongzi was (is) unique for its special soda water and shapes: on the one hand, the soda water-soaked ash (of burnt "monkey-pear" firewood) made its texture flexible and the glutinous dumplings tasty; on the other hand, apart from the common "quadrangled" zongzi, they also made pillow-shaped "Hengba" zongzi and column-shaped "Pipe" zongzi. Their zongzi (usu. five knobs), after being wrapped by the reed leaves and tied by the reed ropes, would symbolize "five lucks". They also held it that Zongzi symbolized the award granted by the emperors after their ancestors won the war. By sacrificing zongzi, they expressed both their worship and pride. The custom of "seeing off Duanwu" is still preserved: Before the daughter's wedding day, her parents will see the festival off early on the first day of the fifth lunar month, leaving zongzi, clothes, handkerchiefs and fans as gifts in the in-laws' house.

The Zhuang people would worship their ancestors also by sacrificing zongzi on the Dragon Boat Festival. Their zongzi is/ was also featured by its various fillings: beans, meat fillings and soda water-soaked rice etc. In some places where Zhuang people lived, the glutinous rice ground with vine leaves & water would be filtered and the boiled dumplings with such mixed dry paste would look pitch-dark. On the festival, every household would hang maple leaves (or wormwood) on the door, boil vinegar and burn grapefruit peel indoors, hoping that the steam and scent could drive away the mosquitoes and fresh the air. Realgar wine would also be drunk and sprayed in the corners. The Zhuang living near the riverside (in the cities or suburbs) would hold boat race.

Zongzi

The A-Chang people would eat zongzi and celebrate the Dragon Boat Festival as well. They would prepare "triangle-shaped", "pillow-shaped", "ball-shaped", "foot-binding" and "straw-ashed" zongzi stuffed with amomum and fresh/preserved pork, much tasty. So far as the sacrifice offered in their family ancestral temple, they would make "plain" rice zongzi——with no fillings as mentioned above. They all believed that when one family member had diarrhea, he would get recovered should he eat the pair of "charred" plain zongzi taken down from the ancestral temple. Meanwhile, the herb wine and embroidered perfume pouches (for both women and children to wear) would be prepared. To prevent diseases, they would also pick wild vegetables and fry 10-20 kinds together to make "eight-treasure" dish.

The Manchu people would make glutinous millet zongzi and put them as sacrifices into a unique wooden-case in honor of their ancestors. Here is a story popular among the Manchu people about their special zongzi:

Legend has it that long long ago Emperor of heaven sent an immortal to investigate the living of the mortals (human beings). On the fifth day of the fifth lunar month, the envoy, dressed up as an old cooking-oil peddler, yelled out for promotion: "Two catties of oil in one gourd and three catties in two!" (In fact, there should be four catties in two gourds but the envoyed immortal deliberately charged less.) Many villagers snapped up to cash in on him, but an old man refused and warned the "confused peddler" that he charged less. His "business" over, the envoy said to the old man, "You are kind-hearted! A plague will fall tonight and you can be freed if you hang wormwood on the door of your house." Hearing that, this kind-hearted man hurried to tell every neighbor from door to door about the horrible news. Hanging wormwood on the doors, all of the villagers were saved, for the God of Plagues couldn't spread plagues over the clever immortals.

The Manchu people enjoyed their customs like "hanging wormwood" over the roofs, going to outskirts to "tread on the dews" and picking herbs and wearing five-color longevity cords and perfume pouches. In the past, the little girls of the Manchu living in Beijing would wear "fiery" pomegranate flowers on the double-fifth day, a beautiful landscape in the old capital.

In this section, we have mainly dwelt on the festive activities of the minority nationalities that have become similar to those of the Han people. For example, some minority communities would also hold similar rituals with the same connotations such as avoiding evils and cleaning. But in fact, connotations of the festival celebrated by the minority nationalities may differ.

The Lahu people (in Yunnan Province)would plant trees and bamboos on the day of Duanwu, which was taken as the best sowing time for the corn seeds to sprout and the seedlings to survive. Additionally, they would invite their relatives and friends to a big dinner.

The Blang people in Shidian district (Yunnan Province) would hold the ritual of "washing cattle feet" and eat zongzi as well. On the eve of Duanwu, every household would wash the feet of their cattle and offer scented candles wrapped with red papers in the parlor. On the day of Duanwu, a bundle of willow twigs, peach twigs and "Huangpao" (obcordatus) twigs bound together in one hand, the tribal chief and patriarch of the village would lead a goat together to visit every household. Having hung a red-paper banner on the door, the two reverend villagers would sweep the doorway with those two bundles, a blessing for the family. While the house owner, as prepared beforehand, would pour water onto their rainhats and bamboo cloaks, which referred to "washing away" the footmarks of the cattle. At noon, the goat was led to one big tree and butchered there, while the representatives of every family would congregate with some rice to cook mutton-porridge, praying peace for the stockaded village.

The Hani people (mainly inhabiting in Yunnan Province) had one festival of their own——"Niu-Nana"——the transliteration of Hani language, meaning "the cattle stops laboring for a while". On the double-fifth day, to show respect to the laborious cattle toiling a whole spring, the Hani villagers would let the cattle get relaxed to replenish energy. They would worship their ancestors and gods by offering glutinous rice dyed purple by boiled water blended with orchid. In the early morning, they would wash their faces and bodies with the "purple" water. When worshiping, they would offer sacrifice (usu. a rooster and a bowl of "purple" glutinous rice) to their ancestors first and then feed the cattle with glutinous rice mixed with chicken and broth, with a prayer in their mouths: "Oh! The busy spring is over and you may graze on the slope now!"

On the double-fifth day, the Yi people living in Leibo County (Liangsahn Yi Autonomous Prefecture, Sichuan Province) would celebrate "the Duyang Festival". Legend has it that it was once very hot there and the Yi people were scared by the plague haunting their stockaded village. Hearing their misfortune, the Han people living along the riverbank down the hills sent the calamus, wormwood and realgar they prepared for the Dragon Boat Festival to those Yi villagers, asking the latter to clean the ulcers with the herbs and wash their bodies with realgar wine. It turned out that the Yi got recovered soon. From then on, the Yi people also celebrated the Dragon Boat Festival. Duanwu had another name——"Duanyang" and the Yi pronounced "Duan" as "Du", so their offspring called the Duanyang Festival "the Duyang Festival". On the festival, every household would hang calamus and wormwood on the door and wrestle, dance, ride horses and play games of bullfight and goatfight, a merry moment once a year.

The Naxi people in Yunnan would celebrate the Dragon Boat Festival on the double-fifth day. At noon, they would drink cups of green bur oil and hang a thorned twig of green bur on the door to prevent disaster and subdue demons. With the bur-oil fried eggs as the special sacrifice, they would worship the Mount Lion, where Naxi youths would sing antiphonal songs at their best to worship their holy mountain. All the Naxi people would bind five-colored cords around their wrists and the children would tie colored threads around their feet additionally. It was also common to yarn colored threads around the necks of the newly-born ponies or calves, a custom to avoid poisonous snakes or insects and pray for their healthy growth. "Longevity cords" weaved with five-colored cotton threads would be burnt on the last day of Torch Festival——the 27th of the sixth lunar month.

The Zang people (Tibetan nationality) would celebrate the "Flower-picking Day" (Girls' Day) on the double-fifth day, a traditional festival lasting two days popular in Boyu district, located at the shared border of Sichuan Province and Gansu Province. Long long ago, it is said that on the barren land of Boyu, it was a girl named Lianzhi who taught the locals how to farm and how to cure illness with the picked flowers. Before long, however, Lianzhi fell dead when she picked flowers in the hill on the double-fifth day. In honor of her, the locals began to celebrate "Flower-picking Day", on which the Zang people would hold festive activities like "scrambling for spring", "picking flowers" and "praying for blessing".

At the dawn, for the sake of washing and drinking, the locals would "scramble" for the spring. They held that if they could wash their bodies with the spring before the sunrise, they could be blessed; and if they could drink such water, the illnesses could be prevented. Then, in their holiday dress, they would pick flowers in the hills. When girls picked flowers, the boys would gather firewood, set up pots and put up sheds. Starting at twilight, the happy songs and dances would last until midnight. When returning the next day, the girls would carry back baskets full of fresh flowers and herbs, flowers and garlands on their heads. Those lovely flower-pickers would offer fresh flowers and herbs to the villagers left at home as their blessing.

The Moggol people would play "Dawei" (grand-scaled hunting activity by prey-enclosing) on the double-fifth day, and that was why "Dawei" was also called "Duanwu Hunting". Long long ago, legend has it that one Mongolian tribe was raided by an alien tribe. Fortunately, a retaliative slaughter was avoided since most of the tribal members had gone out for hunting. It so happened that the raid took place just on the double-fifth day, so, from then on, it became a fixed date on which the "Dawei" hunting was practiced. There exists another story: Genghis Khan (the founder and emperor of the Mongol Empire) was shocked to death when hunting wild ass on the double-fifth day, so it was taken as the hunting day for the Mongols to shoot the beasts and commemorate his greatness. Several days before the "Dawei" hunting, the tribal members would gather to arrange the route and range of hunting, electing a chief ——"Abinda", who was usually a man of virtue and integrity with excellent hunting skills. There were usually two hunting ways: one was "Entrance Hunting"—— generally took place in the mountainous area, where the hunters would chase the preys into a valley from the entrance of the mountain; and the other was "Enclosure Hunting" —— usually took place on the plains, where the hunters could slowly encircle the preys and chase them from all directions. When the hunting began, with rifles (or bows) on their backs and packs of hounds barking and running ahead, the excited hunters went on chasing till it was dark and till they would finish their fruitful hunting then.

The Flower-picking Festival in Boyu

Falling on the fifth day of the fifth lunar month, the Flower-picking Festival (lasting for two days) is traditionally celebrated by the Zang people (Tibetan) inhabiting in Boyu Township, which is located in Zhouqu County, Gannan Zang Autonomous Region in Gansu Province. The Flower-picking Festival is held to worship the Goddess of Flower, so the reverend old will lead the villagers to finish the sacrifice activity first and then they will join in a big fair and other festive activities like "scrambling for the spring" and "antiphonal singing".

Address: Boyu Township, Zhouqu County, Gannan Zang Autonomous Region, Gansu Province

By coach: Zhouqu County is located in the southeast of Gansu Province. Every day from Lanzhou (the capital of Gansu Province) to Zhouqu County, there are two shifts to go and another two to return.

From Zhouqu County the travelers could take coaches to reach Boyu Township via Wudu District and Wenxian County.

4. Customs & Rituals of the Dragon Boat Festival in Hong Kong, Macao and Taiwan Regions

The Chinese people living in Hong Kong, Macao and Taiwan regions, located in the southeast coast of China, would also celebrate the Dragon Boat Festival with customs similar to those of the neighboring provinces. To prevent plagues and avoid disasters, the people there would hold various festive activities, among which dragon boat race was (is still) most common, esp. in those places rich in water resources. Some complicated festive rituals are still preserved intact to this day in some places of Hong Kong and Taiwan.

On the Dragon Boat Festival every year, dragon boat races will be held in many places in Hong Kong, in particular, where there still live boatmen —— Aberdeen, Sai Kung, Cheung Chau Isle, Tai O, Lamma Island, Tuen Mun, Shing Mun River and Tai Po Waterfront Park. In 1983, via a thorough investigation in the dragon-boat sacrificial ritual held in Cheung Chau Island of Hong Kong, and based on his field observation and interview records, Mr. Watanabe (渡辺欣雄 , a Japanese scholar famous for his research of Chinese culture and customs) made an exhaustive analysis of the local customs of the Dragon Boat Festival. Located on the open sea southeast of Lantau Island (the largest of Hong Kong), Cheung Chau Island is in fact an islet of 2.4 square kms, which has been populated for hundreds of years. As a prosperous fishing town for ages, Cheung Chau Island was famous for its "waterside village", with its afloat villagers mainly living in the Cheung Chau Bay. In its golden period after the World War Ⅱ , the number of the fishers (including those living ashore) was up to 10,000 or so. However, the number of the fishers was falling every year (less than 10,000 in 1983) and the number of registered fishing boats was only 500 or so (1983). The dragon-boat sacrificial ritual held in Cheung Chau Island usually started on the fifth day of the fifth lunar month (on the very day of Duanwu), while the holiday would last from the second to the sixth that month. The dragon-boat sacrificial ritual observed by Mr. Watanabe was just inherited and held by the afloat residents and fishers, who have long upheld the traditional economy of Cheung Chau Island. This ritual has long been one symbol of the significant festivals held on this islet.

Among those traditional festivities on the Dragon Boat

Festival, the dragon boat parade (race) in Tai O is very special , exclusive in Hong Kong. Every year on the fifth day of the fifth lunar month, the locals there will row dragon boats, behind which are the "sacred boats" carrying some statuettes of gods. The boats parade in the waterways, and along the way the joss candles are burnt. The nearby residents will also worship in the direction of the dragon boat, praying for their family peace and hoping for driving away the diseases. After the ritual ceremony of parade, the dragon boat race will be held. The custom of such a parade has been held more than 100 years and in 2011 it was listed as one of the third batch of national intangible cultural heritages.

Some locals will choose to swim on this very day in particular, for they want to share the water with the dragon. In Hong Kong, many people believe swimming that day could bring them luck and help to change their fates and avoid evils. Therefore, they will flood into every swimming pool and onto the beaches, praying for good luck and sharing the water with the dragon.

So far as the customs of the Dragon Boat Festival in Taiwan region, we may find that besides those age-old customs like "hanging-wormwood" and "tying five-color silk threads", some new customs like "competitive races" and "dragon boat race" have been absorbed with time going on. Customs of the Dragon Boat Festival in Taiwan region in the Qing Dynasty were once recorded in the book "Local Chronicle of Taiwan Prefecture". Some different accounts of dragon boat race were given: one believed that custom of boat race was partly preserved, with the competitiveness lost; while the other held that like the dragon boat race in Fujian Province, the race in Taiwan also encouraged the racers to win the prize; even another record covered the sacrificial rituals and tough races. Here is an account of Duanwu in the "Local Chronicle of Taiwan Prefecture——Festivals": "On the double-fifth day, every household will hang the picked wormwood on the door and tie five-color silk threads around the kids' arms, calling them 'longevity Cords'. Additionally, they will weave cub tiger with orchid to paste them on the kids' foreheads, while only at noon could these straw articles be taken off and thrown away from where the kids stay. The racing boat is but a deals dinghy, unable to plough the waves of the sea, so only the will to thrive for victory remains. The locals also wrap the glutinous rice to make zongzi." The similar account also appeared in the "Local Chronicle of Taiwan Prefecture——Customs Ⅱ ", but the description of "prize-winning" was added: "In the past, the locals would pick wormwood for hanging and calamus for inspiring wining; but now, they will hang wormwood and calamus together for the latter looks like a sword, able to fend off evils. They will tie five-color 'longevity cords' around the kids' arms, and weave cub tiger with orchid to paste them on the kids' foreheads, while only at noon could these straw articles be taken off and thrown away where the kids stay. The boat race is held to commemorate Qu Yuan and fend off evils as well. Rich or poor, all will buy dragon boats and row the boats towards the mid-stream for pleasure, singing and dancing accompanied by flutes and drums. A good swimmer will erect a pole on the bow of a boat, upon which he hangs a brocade banner——a symbol of victory. The rower who snatches the banner first will win the prize. Every household will make zongzi, which means the close contact of 'yin and yang', no way of taking apart."

More details were added in the revised version of "Local Chronicle of Taiwan Prefecture". For example: "On the morning of the double-fifth day, the locals will burn a bundle of rice straw and fumigate every corner of the house, or leave the saved coins by the roadside to send away 'wen'——mosquito (In ancient China, the minimum denomination of coin was 'wen'——a homophone for mosquito). They will also hang wormwood, calamus and a stem of barn grass upon the door to repel mosquitoes, and hang a banyan twig, which means 'the older yet the stronger'. They will present each other watermelon and pork zongzi, and worship the gods with sacrifices in red. From the fifth day to the seventh day, in the shallows of the bay, somebody will erect a pole upon which coins or a piece of cloths are hung. The rowers row dinghies or fishers to snatch the prize and the winners will bang gongs excitedly. The locals call it dragon-boat fight." Under the descriptions, we can read some notes: "At the end of the third lunar month or the beginning of the fourth lunar month, or from the first day to the fifth day of the fifth lunar month, on the boats owned by the temples or those living along the seashore, gongs and drums are banged. This custom is called 'Dragon Boat Show', which could bring the owners a prosperous year!" The customs described above could be taken as a comprehensive record of all customs of the Dragon Boat Festival in Taiwan region in the Qing Dynasty.

In fact, the custom of dragon boat race was popular in Taiwan region, which was called "Ba (Row) Dragon boat". During the Japanese Colonial Period, according to the book "Customs of Taiwan" (Volume I), the locals in Shi-Lin community (a famous night fair in Taipei) preserved customs as follows: "On the first day of the fifth lunar month, they will go to the riverside to greet the 'God of Water'. On the second day, they gather to discuss the agenda of boat race. At noon on the double-fifth day, banging the gongs and drums, they carry the dragon boat to the riverbank, with the locals burning incenses and praying for blessing on their knees all the way. As the saying goes, 'The drums are banged on the dragon boats on the double-fifth day,

Long strand

when all the locals crowd along the narrow streets all the way.' When the boats arrive at the riverbank, the rowers who get there earlier will lift the oars high for greeting, a custom called 'greeting dragon boat'. After the race, they will hold 'River-appreciating Ritual' to 'send off God of Water' on the tenth day."

In 1996, the Dragon Boat Festival was listed as an object of study when a series of festivals was compiled in Taiwan. So far as the customs of Duanwu in Taiwan Province, the chief-editor refers to the rule of compiling in the preface: Study of the customs of Duanwu will be traced back to the Qing Dynasty. For those 300 temples, soda water-soaked zongzi is an indispensible sacrifice, while salty zongzi is divided into meat dumpling and rice dumpling, quenching the hunger only.

The Minnan people living in Taiwan usually eat peaches, eggplants and green beans on the Dragon Boat Festival, believing they could live longer and healthier by doing so. There is a saying goes, "Eggplant and green bean every day, happy and healthy till hair is grey." Owing to different makings, Taiwan-styled zongzi could be divided into that of North flavor and South flavor. In the north of Taiwan, after soaking and draining the rice, the locals will fry it with five-spice powder, pepper powder and soy sauce before steaming it. Some locals will fry the rice till it is half-cooked, then wrap the filling-stuffed rice with bamboo leaves and steam it again. While in the south of Taiwan, soaked glutinous rice is wrapped with fresh bamboo leaves before these meat-filling-stuffed dumplings are boiled. As a result, the zongzi steamed in the north has a strong flavor of five-spice powder, while the zongzi in the south smells faint scent of bamboo leaves. The fillings of zongzi could be pork, mushroom, tiny shrimp, peanut, salt egg yoke, red onion, chestnut and dried oyster, but of course, you may add or reduce as you like.

5. Customs of the Dragon Boat Festival in Other Countries

Customs of the Dragon Boat Festival undoubtedly originated from ancient China, however, due to their long-term spreading and the international interchanges between China and other nations, many of this festival have been accepted and absorbed by the neighboring countries and nations, who have developed their unique customs nourished by their own cultural soils.

As far as the prototype of "Gangnung Danoje Festival" (강 릉 단 오 제), it was undoubtedly influenced by the Chinese culture. Several explanations for the Dragon Boat Festival have been recorded in many Korean classics, tallying well with those of the Chinese people. For example, the Korean would call the double-fifth day "Chongwu", "Double Fifth", "Duanyang" and "Fifth Lunar Month Day". In Korean, "Duanwu" referred to "high day"——"day of god" in another word. Following the customs, the locals would eat wormwood seed cakes and drink adlay juice. The Korean women would wash hair with boiled montanum (calamus) water or drink it, and put on makeup with montanum dew——"calamus makeup". Scholar officials would post cinnabar talismans on the doors to fend off evils, while the Korean king and his ministers would present "Duanwu fans" mutually to celebrate the festival.

However, "Gangnung Danoje Festival" has been famous for its abundant festive customs, with sacrificial rites, mask dramas and games as the core. Derived from the legends, these rites are held to worship some gods or goddesses like "God of Taegwallyong Ridge" or "town/village/street gods", as well as other 12 tutelary deities——like General Kim Yu-Sin 김 유 신 (who helped to unify the Korean peninsula first), Holy Monk Boemil (a reverend Korean monk who learnt Buddhism in China, the Tang Dynasty) and "Goddess of Taegwallyong Ridge"——representing sufferings from natural disasters.

Once popular everywhere, many customs of Danoje have disappeared with the development of the society, yet they are preserved intact in Kangnung region with its cumbersome sacrificial rites. Considering the "Eve Rite" to greet the gods, the ritual will last five days and nights; the ritual may continue almost 20 days if you finish the process from "Worshiping Gods of Mounts" to "Sending Back Gods"; and the whole course will keep as long as one month ever since "brewing wine for the gods". Starting on the fifth day of the fourth lunar month, for worshiping gods and drinking at the sacrificial ritual, the locals will brew the "nectar" with the rice and pomelos provided by the government in the old office hall (옛 관청이었던 사당). On the fifteenth day, rites to worship "God of Mount Taegwallyong" and Holy Monk Boemil are held. The rites over, guided by a piece of sawn "holy wood/trunk" hung with green and red satins, the locals will parade in a line to bring down the gods. At the dusk of the third day of the fifth lunar month, when they go back to "Temple of Town Goddess" in Gangnung, they will hold the rite of "Placing Tablets of Gods"——the "Eve Rite". After the rite, tablets of "God of Mount Taegwallyong" and "Holy Monk Boemil" are carried to the open Guksayeo Altar by the Namdaecheon Stream (남대천) in Gangnung City. Then, from the fourth day to the seventh day, "Morning Memorial" will be held every day. The rites of "Gangnung Danoje Sacrificial Ritual" consists of "Confucian Scholar-Hosted Rite" and "Wizard-Hosted Rite". The former is finished by reading out Chinese prayers, concerning eliminating misfortunes and welcoming lucks, praying for health and peace, curing diseases, harvesting fishes and crops and raising numerous live stocks. "Confucian Scholar-Hosted Rite" over, comes the "Wizard-Hosted Rite", followed by singing and dancing and mask drams, till mid-night.

Festive activities of "Gangnung Danoje Festival" are rich and colorful. Apart from the designated sacrificial rite ("brewing nectar" and "sending back gods"), wizard-hosted rite, mask dramas, Nongok (farmers' song) race, children Nongok race and 학 산 오 도 쓰 songs...(most of which were designated as the "Intangible Cultural Properties"), there still exist some folk activities: Chinese poem writing competition, folk songs competition, national Korean verse competition, tug-of-war, wrestling, swinging, archery and pot-cast. As for celebrations, we can find fireworks, lantern-flying/floating, traditional Korean music performance and kayagum performance.

In the eye of the Vietnamese, Chinese Dragon Boat Festival means dragon boat race, eating zongzi and commemorating Qu Yuan. the Dragon Boat Festival was first introduced into Vietnam in Nhà Trần period (one dynasty in ancient Vietnam, 1225—1400 AD) and became one of the important festivals of the locals. The Vietnamese celebrated this festival to pay homage to Qu Yuan's lofty patriotic loyalty on the one hand, and on the other, integrating the joy of harvest and the poetic stories of Liu Shen and Ruan Shao (transliterations of Vietnamese), they commemorated their contribution.

In order to get the newly-introduced festival integrated with their living conditions, the local people in Vietnam "localized" the Customs of the Dragon Boat Festival and created some other customs like killing pests, dying nails, wearing evil-avoiding pouches, bathing with lemon grass, picking fruits on the tree, picking herbs at noon and hanging wormwood and calamus. Here are some unique customs believed by the locals. For example, they held that the pests doing harm to them usually hid in their stomachs and would come out only on the double-fifth day. How to kill these nasty pests? After getting up and rinsing their mouths with water that morning, they would drink glutinous rice wine to get the pests "drunk" and eat fruits to "kill" them. Holding the view that the herbs could cool their bodies from the abnormally hot weather, they would pick herbs in some remote places at noon and drink the boiled water fortified with sun-dried herbs. We may find another custom of "torturing trees"——since the locals believed that every tree had a soul, they would "torture" the trees by beating to force them to bear fruits if they had failed to do so for many years. When hanging wormwood, they would weave the grass into the shape of the Chinese zodiac animal matching that lunar year to fend off evils. Why? They thought that the strong vitality of wormwood could infuse power into the zodiac animal to protect them from evils and plagues. During the festival, the Vietnamese would wrap round-shaped or square-shaped zongzi with banana leaves. They would make salty zongzi with glutinous rice, small shrimps, lean pork, red beans and half a salted egg; or wrap diamond-shaped soda water-soaked zongzi with glutinous rice flour, coconut shreds, small shrimps and mung, served with a sugar dressing. As far as the fat pork zongzi, they would prepare rib pork, small shrimps, mung and five-spice seasonings and slice the cooked zongzi for eating. In their belief, the round-shaped zongzi could symbolize the heaven while the square-shaped zongzi the earth, so the "Unity of heaven and earth" would bring good luck to them. They would be blessed with a smooth and harvest year if they could eat zongzi on the Dragon Boat Festival.

Some cultural elements of the Dragon Boat Festival could be also found in those customs kept by Korean and Japanese

In Korea, zongzi was called "wheel cake"——after boiling the fresh wormwood, they would put the mashed leaves into the glutinous rice flour to make "wheel-shaped" cakes, much tasty. The Korean would worship their ancestors and recall their family members with precious wormwood cakes and crisp cakes. The girls would wash bodies or hair with boiled calamus water. In addition, they would take part in some traditional festive activities like wrestling and swinging.

The Japanese would wrap "hammer-headed" zongzi (different from Chinese zongzi in shape) with ground rice flour instead of glutinous rice. On the fifth day of the fifth lunar month, they would eat column-shaped "straw-roll" zongzi wrapped with indocalamus leaves or water bamboo leaves. Zongzi in Japan could be named according to its various shapes —— the tube, the diamond, the cone and the hammer. It is also named according to its functions. For example, they make hundred-rope zongzi in the hope that their children could grow healthily. The Japanese now celebrate Boys' Day, on which they would hang "carp banners" on the top of roofs and upon the bamboo poles, hoping that their boys could "swim upstream" (to be successful) like the brave carps.

With their footprints all over the world, the overseas Chinese have spread Chinese festive cultures all over the world too. Some traditional Chinese festivals (like the Spring Festival, the Dragon Boat Festival and the Mid-Autumn Festival in particular) have become more valued by both the overseas Chinese and other nations. In Singapore, a nationwide dragon boat race will be held during the Dragon Boat Festival. In the afternoon, on the bows of the colorfully decorated dragon boats will stand drummers dressed up as "lions" or "bears", and the 22 rowers in the same boat will dash ahead until sunset. In the May of 1979, the first Boston Dragon Boat Festival was held by Boston Children's Museum, in which Chinese songs, dances, martial arts and entertainments were all presented.

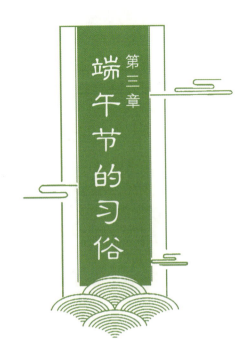

第三章

端午节的习俗

　　端午节习俗是与端午有关的禁忌、娱乐、饮食、节日服饰、仪式仪礼、家庭活动、亲友往来等民俗事项的总称。在长期的历史积淀中，端午节已经形成了形式多样的端午习俗。本章将介绍这些丰富多彩的端午活动和习俗。

一、
端午活动

　　中国的端午节习俗，如龙舟竞渡、采药，踏、斗百草以及女儿归宁等仪式行为，大都是表演性的。通过龙舟竞渡仪式，不单传达了民众希冀获得龙神护佑，禳灾避祸、五谷丰登的愿望，还抒发和宣泄了主体的情感，表达了自己对生活的喜悦，对未来的美好期盼；踏、斗百草也主要是为了娱乐、游玩，舒展身心；亲朋互赏端阳，互赠礼物，女儿归宁，也并不在乎礼物的轻重，关键是增强了亲友之间的友好关系，烘托欢快、喜悦的节日心境。

（一）兴龙舟竞渡，吉祥喜庆

　　龙舟竞渡是端午节中最具特色的节俗活动，范围几乎遍及大江南北。关于龙舟竞渡的起源，苏州一带传说是为了纪念春秋后期吴国功臣伍子胥；浙江地区则由越王勾践卧薪尝胆，为复国而操练水师演化而来；福建沿海传说是纪念妈祖；云南白族传说是纪念杀蟒英雄段赤城；傣族传说纪念为除恶魔而献身的七个傣族姑娘；贵州清水江流域的苗族传说是为纪念一位杀死恶龙的英雄久保。而影响最为深远和广泛的要算荆楚地区纪念屈原的说法了。有学者认为它最早是一种送灾巫术仪式，发源地在江南水乡；也有学者认为龙舟竞渡起源于古越族的图腾祭祀等。

○龙舟竞渡

　　人们面对各种自然灾害无能为力，于是采用龙舟竞渡的方式，企求得到龙神保佑，以期祛凶消灾、风调雨顺、五谷丰登。随着历史的发展，人们增加了各式各样的历史和传说人物，用龙舟竞渡的方式来纪念先贤。这是人们对"龙"神的信仰，相信它能避邪，通过这种形式来表达对正义的弘扬，对邪恶势力的抗争，反映了抑恶扬善的民族情怀。而各种传说最终凝聚在"纪念屈原"这样一个集中国传统伦理道德和价值观于一身的著名历史人物上，体现了中华民族爱国、爱家的精神气概和强烈的民族认同感，表达了人们对民族繁荣昌盛的祝愿，彰显了民族的美学文化。

　　中国民间的龙舟种类也很多，主要有游玩龙舟、祭祀龙舟和竞渡龙舟三大类。

游玩龙舟除了供帝王游乐的大型豪华龙舟外，民间也有不少，如江浙一带的"文龙舟"。再有南方各地节日里在旱地玩耍的"旱龙船""彩龙船"等，或以龙船象形，举行化装赛跑活动，或陪衬、点缀玩龙舞狮。在江苏镇江还有一种特技龙舟，在龙舟上，一些杂技表演如倒立、小孩悬于船尾等，把龙舟娱乐表演结合起来，体现了南方城市生活的一种面貌。

○游玩龙舟

○精心制作的龙头

　　祭祀龙舟主要流行在湘、鄂、赣边区，是一种由巫师用肩扛着串游乡间的祭祀器具，长约2米，宽、高约为0.4米，这一活动俗称"敬干龙船"。还有一种是由众多乡民抬着登高地、游街市，俗称"迎鬼船"。

　　竞渡龙舟是专用于水上竞渡的龙舟，船身是特制的，用于争抢竞渡，龙头龙尾都有华丽的装饰。近代以来，凡用于竞渡的船，无论有无龙饰，都统称"龙舟"，包括那些临时用来竞渡的渡船、划子（一种小渔船）或运输船。而这一水上竞赛活动也就统称为"划龙船"或"龙舟竞渡"。竞渡龙舟可分为"专业龙舟"和"业余龙舟"两大类。"专业龙舟"只作竞渡，不作他用；"业余龙舟"则是以生产、生活用船临时改装而成，用后又恢复为生产生活的功用。

各种龙舟的构造大致相同，由船体（包括桨梢或橹）、龙头、龙尾、各种装饰物和锣鼓组成。龙头大多用整木雕成。无论专业龙舟还是业余龙舟，龙头都是竞渡前才装上船头的。龙头造型千姿百态，根据各地风俗而定。广州西江水系的鸡公龙头和东江水系的大头狗龙头，别具特色。龙头多染成红色，称"红龙"。也有涂为黑色或灰色的，称"黑龙"或"灰龙"。龙尾大多用整木雕成，装饰鳞甲。船上装饰最繁杂的以顺德的鸡公头龙舟为代表。其中有一个神楼，一个大鼓和一个铜锣。龙舟上有龙头、龙尾旗、帅旗和罗伞等装饰。

龙舟的大小按人数区分：3人、5人、10人的为小龙舟，长约1丈半到2丈；20到50人左右的为中龙舟，长5丈到7丈；60到100人以上的为大龙舟，长9丈到10多丈；还有200多人的特大龙舟。小龙舟只有桡手和舵手，中龙舟配鼓手和锣手各1人，大龙舟配鼓手和锣手各2人。珠江三角洲的龙舟比较大，容纳60多人以上的算较普通的，容纳100多人的龙舟也很多。

龙舟竞渡主要在节日期间。在楚越民族居住的广大江南地区，龙舟竞渡的习俗很盛行。有文献记载的龙舟竞渡在汉末时期。南宋时，广东已有民间的大型龙舟竞渡；明清时，广东官方和民间的端午节赛龙舟活动更普遍。明代杨嗣昌的《武陵竞渡略》详细记载了明朝沅湘一带的竞渡习俗。

明朝沅湘习俗中，竞渡是为了禳灾避害，划龙舟前要举行种种祭祀，请巫师来作法以祈求顺意。龙舟竞渡结束后，当地人还会争相从龙舟中舀水回家，和药草煮，然后用煮开的水来洗澡，目的在于避恶驱邪。竞渡为禳灾是最为原始的形态，它在许多地区以"旱龙船"的形式表现出来。江西等地有旱龙舟之俗，龙舟有竹制和木制，在当地是以禳灾为目的。

清代人厉愓斋曾详细记述了当时扬州的龙舟竞渡情况，从五月初一至五月初五，都有龙舟竞渡。各种各样的龙舟都要争奇斗巧。龙舟上还有种种表演，主要以杂技为主，不仅以竞渡的快慢、胜败来吸引人，而且也以杂技表演来丰富龙舟的奇与巧。

广州地区流行的龙船景，也叫"趁景"，每年农历五月初一至五月二十，人们在指定水域邀集各乡龙船前来"应景"。因轮流在各乡举行，不设竞渡的名次，只展示表演技巧，所以称作"趁景"。有些乡村很看重"龙船景"，像过盛大节日似的热闹，家家户户包粽子、蒸糕，招呼着观景，涌到岸边观看龙船表演，抢吃龙船饭。龙船景这项习俗甚至可以追溯到宋代。外村嫁来的妇女，看到娘家来的龙船"应景"，就要和丈夫、小孩带鞭炮、饼食，划小艇去表示欢迎。

从龙舟竞渡可以看出，竞渡除了早期的禳灾除邪、速度较量而外，更多的还是节日里以娱乐和表演的方式获得观众参与，把平日里在戏台上观看的表演搬到龙舟上，不仅提高了表演的难度，而且更具节日情趣和观赏性。

当代龙舟赛事既与端午节有关，又有一定的独立性。按照国际龙舟联合会的规定，在单数年举办世界龙舟锦标赛，在双数年举办世界龙舟俱乐部锦标赛。而世界龙舟俱乐部锦标赛只限代表龙舟俱乐部的赛队参加，赛队必须以俱乐部名义参赛，不享有国家队地位。比赛必须至少有六支国际龙舟联合会正式会员或基本会员的俱乐部赛队参加，方有资格将比赛级别定为锦标赛。

目前国际性或全国性的比赛都为标准龙舟赛，而我国民间作为传统风俗项目的多为传统龙舟赛。传统龙舟赛与标准龙舟赛的竞赛规则有很多不同。传统龙舟赛中顺德和东莞分列赛是在湍急的河流中比赛，龙船上有一名队员摇旗呐喊，为队员鼓气，同时有一名队员在船头表演，体现当地的民俗文化。另外，标准龙舟赛的参赛龙舟有"龙头"和"龙尾",而传统龙舟大赛在展示时将会"全副武装",把自己最好的一面全面展示,但在比赛时一般都会摘下装饰"轻装上阵",只让两名龙舟队员担当。而且,传统龙舟赛作为端午节俗的重要活动,往往要举行一些与端午节俗相关的仪式。如2006年湖南汨罗江国际龙舟节在赛前举行祭祀屈原的仪式与表演,为龙舟赛涂抹了浓郁的民族文化与民俗风情的底色,使得龙舟、龙舟赛都被赋予了深厚的文化韵味。

居住在贵州黔东南的苗族同胞在端午节时有一个盛大的龙舟竞渡比赛,当地叫作独木龙舟节。据说这个节日是为了报仇、杀龙(烧龙)而举行的。农历五月二十四至二十七,黔东南州施洞的苗族同胞驾着雕有精美雕刻的龙头船,在清水江的不同江段举行比赛。每年农历五月二十四日,从施秉县的平寨开始,经台江塘龙、榕山到施洞结束,历时四天。一般来说是二十四日在平寨,二十五日在塘龙,二十六日在老屯、旧州两个地方分龙,二十七日在芳寨。活动除赛龙船外,还有斗牛、赛马、踩鼓、跳芦笙、游方等。节日内容丰富,民族风情浓郁,毗邻的凯里、黄平、镇遍、三穗、剑河的各族人民都赶来赴会观光,约三四万人,是县境内任何一个节日也比不上的。

独木龙舟由三根粗大、笔直的杉树挖成槽形的独木舟并排捆扎而成。中间一只长约七丈,称母船;两侧各有一只独木舟,长五丈,称子船。龙头选用七尺多长的一根水柳树雕刻龙的形象,龙头两边还有一对水牛角,分别书写"风调雨顺"和"国泰民安"。龙舟上的人员包括鼓头、锣手、撑篙、理事、艄公、桡手等,鼓头是主角,以鼓点的节奏指挥整个龙舟的竞渡。比赛开始后,桡手们齐声呐喊,奋力划桨,江面浪花飞溅。此时,观众们也踮起脚尖,扯起喉咙呐喊助威。

旅游小贴士

苗疆古镇——施洞

施洞的苗名叫掌响，即赶集的地方，位于贵州台江县北部，坐落在苗岭山脉余麓，地处长江流域清水江畔。距离县城 38 千米，距离凯里市 48 千米，与黄平、镇远、施秉、剑河四县毗邻，辖 21 个行政村居，96 个村民小组，苗族人口比例为 98%，是典型的苗族聚集区，是台江县重要的古集镇。

素有"歌舞海洋""银饰之都"和"艺术之乡"称誉的施洞，1994 年贵州省文化厅将其命名为"刺绣银饰剪纸艺术之乡"。施洞苗族姊妹节和独木龙舟节举世闻名，苗族飞歌蜚声艺坛。此外，建于清代的苏公馆、两湖会馆也值得一游。

施洞镇依山傍水，气候宜人，清水江穿境而过，镇内古树葱郁，田园风光秀丽，群山雄伟壮观。施洞有工艺精湛、精美绝伦的苗族银饰和手工艺品，有蕴含苗族特色文化的手工刺绣，还有鲜嫩健胃的酸汤鱼，味美价廉的施洞肉鹅等。

交通：

去施洞建议先到凯里。贵阳到凯里有多趟列车，约 3 个小时的车程。

台江县城台拱镇到施洞有穿梭往返的中巴，途经老屯、偏寨等乡寨。

气候与游季：

端午节

施洞镇属于亚热带湿润气候，冬暖夏凉，夏天最高温度29℃，冬天最低温度1℃，终年无结冰和积雪，3月到5月平均气温在22℃左右。最佳的旅游时间每年的5~10月。

作为端午节民俗活动之一的龙舟竞渡活动，包含着民众祈求丰收的动机。在竞渡活动中，人们企图通过"龙舟"与"龙神"之间建立某种积极的丰收增产的期望关系，向龙神示好，以期实现农作物丰收的农耕祈愿。"端午……各乡俱操舟竞渡，祈年赛歌。""龙兮龙兮绘出太平象，酬神合谱丰年篇。"反映了人们对农业生活的良好愿望，寄托着人们对农耕生活的祝愿和祈求。"送圣后奉太子于画舫中礼拜，祈禳收灾降福，举国若狂。"人们期望通过激烈的龙舟竞赛，将瘟神送走，以求未来的生活幸福平安。

（二）抚尘踏斗草，娱乐祈福

斗草游戏是一项有益和有趣的活动，历史源远流长。据学者考证，最早有文献记载的斗草游戏见于南朝宗懔的《荆楚岁时记》："五月五日，四民并踏百草，又有斗百草之戏。"唐宋社会生活繁荣时代，这种风气最为盛行，到了清代仍然存在，并一直延续至今。

斗百草又称斗草，是江南地区端午节传统游戏。早在《中吴纪闻》中就有记载吴王与西施斗草的逸闻，唐代文人刘禹锡的诗句中有"若共吴王斗百草，不如应是欠西施"。白居易《观儿戏》有诗句"弄尘或斗草，尽日乐嬉嬉"。南宋淳熙十三年，隐居苏州石湖的范成大，在《春日田园杂兴》中吟咏了天真无邪的儿童斗草的情景，"青枝满地花狼藉，知是儿孙斗草来"。明田汝成在《熙朝乐事》中也说，杭州"春日，妇女喜为斗草之戏"，后面还引用了《绮罗香》词，生动形象地展现了杭城妇女斗草嬉戏的画面。在斗草活动中，赢者可以获得玉制小耳饰等物质奖励，参加此竞赛的众多女性可以休闲放松、娱乐身心。清袁景澜的《吴郡岁华纪丽》中也有"端午结庐蓄乐，斗百草，缠五丝"的记载。

所谓斗草一般有两种斗法，文斗和武斗。文斗分两种：一是把各自的盆景放在一起，争妍斗艳，比一比，看谁的花草最为珍奇、优美；另一种则是把花草集中放在一起，一人报出自己的草名，他人各以手中之草对答，如果对不上就算输，答对就算赢。如"月月红"应对"星星翠"，"鸡冠花"应对"狗尾草"。《红楼梦》第六十二回形象地描述了斗草的情况：

○（明）斗百草

一时吃毕，大家吃茶闲话，又随便玩笑，外面小螺和香菱、芳官、蕊官、藕官、豆官等四五个人，满园玩了一回，大家采了些花草来兜着，坐在花草堆里斗草。这一个说："我有观音柳。"那一个说："我有罗汉松。"那一个又说："我有君子竹。"这一个又说："我有美人蕉。"这个又说："我有星星翠。"那个又说："我有月月红。"这个又说："我有《牡丹亭》上的牡丹花。"那个又说："我有《琵琶记》里的枇杷果。"豆官便说："我有姐妹花。"众人没了，香菱便说："我有夫妻蕙。"豆官说："从没听见有个'夫妻蕙'！"香菱道："一个剪儿一个花儿叫作'兰'，一个剪儿几个花儿叫作'蕙'。上下结花的为'兄弟蕙'，并头结花的为'夫妻蕙'。我这枝并头的，怎么不是'夫妻蕙'？"豆官没的说了，便起身笑道："依你说，要是这两枝一大一小，就是'老子儿子蕙'了？若是两枝背面开的，就是'仇人蕙'了？你汉子去了大半年，你想他了，便拉扯着蕙上也有了夫妻了，好不害臊！"香菱听了，红了脸，忙要起身拧她，笑骂道："我把你这个烂了嘴的小蹄子！满口里放屁胡说。"

　　武斗主要是斗草的韧性。由相斗之双方各持一草在手，然后使两草成十字相交状，两人用力一拉，以草不断者为胜，草断者为负。这一斗法，无锡人叫"打官司草"。所用的草，多为车前子、牛筋草等，所以车前子的别名在吴语中叫"打官司草"。这种斗法虽然在典

○斗草图局部

籍中缺乏详细记载，但从上引的"青枝满地花狼藉，知是儿孙斗草来"等诗句来看，可以判断所描写的正是这种斗法。

武斗多在儿童当中流行。今故宫博物院珍藏的清代宫廷画家金廷标作的《群婴斗草图》，对这种斗法有极细致而生动的描绘。画中共有十个男孩，其中有弯腰找草的，有伸手拔草的，有捧了一兜草匆匆赶来相斗的，有两人正在用力拉扯的，也有酣斗暂休，几个孩子围着满地狼藉的残枝，正在拿草欲续斗的。全图描绘了"找草、拔草、运草、斗草等全过程，同时也真实地展现了儿童们节日斗草的欢快气氛"。

斗草游戏不仅在妇女、儿童中盛行，这种在花间草边充满野趣的游戏也逐渐被文人们接受，成为文人雅士们酒筵上的"雅玩"了，演变成了一种酒令，即"斗草令"。这种"斗草令"的方法为："合席各以门类如天文时令颜色数目珍宝之类，以花草字为经，出两字对，令合席对之。加入天文门出月桂，或对凤兰，或对天花之类。又次至颜色门，出青萍，或对绛树之类。评定甲乙，总宜平仄调叶（xié），裁对新颖。"

踏百草也是江南地区端午节传统习俗，是一项愉悦身心的活动。踏百草是端午野外踏青、郊游的活动，"是日，织染佣工多酿游吴山"。在北方，踏百草又称"踏青""耍青""游百病"等。

端午季节，正是草绿花红、禾苗青翠之时，人们在端午这天去野外游玩，"跑山""登高"。据说这天登山玩水可消百病，所以一到此时，人们便倾城出动，满山人头攒动，遍地欢声笑语，充满娱乐游玩的轻松和自由。北京地区，端午日"挈酒游高粱或天坛……"五日游为"耍青"，十日游为"送青"。东北铁岭山一带五日"男女纷纷登龙首山，游览竟日"。锦州府"少长出郭游，具饮高歌"，亦有携酒游观音洞者，曰"耍青"。

○端午时节登高踏百草

　　此外，端午节踏百草活动在少数民族地区也很盛行。端午节这天，白族支系那马人的未婚青年男女都要穿上最好的衣服，带上酒、肉、饭、粑粑等好吃的东西往大山里去。上山后，姑娘、小伙子一块吃东西、唱调子，谈情说爱，痛快地玩上一天。端午节对男女青年来说，就是狂欢节、恋爱节。五月初五，正值小麦已经收割进仓，大麦下种完毕，宁蒗县托甸乡的普米族借此节日休息联欢一天。青年男女穿上节日盛装，前往深山"绕岩洞"，在岩洞的石坑上点酥油灯，大人小孩都要喝几口泡有菖蒲、雄黄的药酒。药酒有时还泡入熊胆、麝香等贵重药品，一般是泡菖蒲、樟目子、雪通、雪草之类中草药。这一天，还要特地做小麦粑粑，蘸着蜂蜜吃，然后到瀑布下洗澡、歌舞。在端午节中午，温泉乡的普米族全家出动转山念经，插一炷香，叩三个头，虔诚地祈祷神灵保佑风调雨顺，粮食获得大丰收。在端午这天，凡能外出走动的羌族人都尽可能到山上踏青染露，强身健骨。

　　端午节因为有了踏百草、斗百草等具有娱乐、游戏色彩的活动，且为群众喜闻乐见，被广大民众接纳，延续至今，不断散发出持久的魅力。

（三）亲朋赏端阳，美满和谐

端午节对于中国人而言也是走亲探友、家庭团聚的日子。人们往往带着一些节日礼品，走亲串友，互致节日祝福。上海地区"亲戚以角黍、枇杷相饷"；苏州地区也多"以角黍、艾花、香珠、画扇并组织杂物相馈"；杭州一带"亲戚竞以角黍、彩缯相馈"，彩缯多用菖蒲、通草，皮金雕刻仙佛、禽鸟、百虫、猛兽之形，作钗头、符胜，备极工巧。端午节除送一些节令时物外，各家这天还备有宴会，"人家各有宴会，庆赏端阳"。工人通常还有机会放假半天，"百工亦各辍所业，群入酒肆共饮，名曰'白赏节'"。在这难得清闲，难得相聚的节日里，人们邀上三五好友，或在家里，或在酒肆，谈笑风生，倾吐工作和生活的愉悦和不快，不仅放松了心情，而且传达了朋友、亲戚之间的关爱，增进了友情和亲情。

中国端午节，亲友之间除了馈赠粽子、香囊以外，还以扇子为节礼。端午节之际正值盛夏到来之时，扇子具有招风纳凉、驱赶虫蚊、掸拂灰尘等功用。端午送扇，其本意可能是端午日的避瘟祈福。早期的扇子大多以蒲叶制成，由于菖蒲具有禳毒的功效，所以也把这种扇子称为"避瘟扇"。据明陆容《菽园杂记》卷一载："奉天门常朝御座后内官持一小扇，金黄绢以裹之。尝闻一老将军云：'非扇也，其名卓影辟邪，永乐年间

○避瘟菖蒲扇

外国所进。但闻其名，不知为何物也。'"扇子称"卓影辟邪"，这也与端午节辟邪的宗旨一致。端午日，人们互赠扇子，同时还传达着一种美好的祝愿，希望亲朋好友平平安安。

在端午这一天，也有医家赠送消病除疾的药物给常往来的顾客。"药肆馈遗苍术、白芷、大黄、雄黄等品与常所往来之家。以礼盒为囊，带之云疗疾。"医家所送这些苍术、白芷、大黄、雄黄之类药品，大都有防病、消毒、杀菌之功用，满足了民众祛病除疾的心理，顾客很愿意接受这些所赠之物。同时，被认为能够除灾避祸的僧道之人，在端午节之日或前后，制作各种符篆送经常往来之家。"道家以天师符，僧家以黄纸符馈檀越，谓之'送符'。女僧则以彩绒作花，谓之'送老虎花'"。受符的人必到寺庙或者道观烧香，并酬以钱文，谓之"符金"。自魏晋南北朝以来，江南地区俗信很强，佛寺、道观很多。人们相信各路神灵能够庇佑他们逃避灾祸，度过各种灾难。

端午节的节俗活动中还有一项是姻亲交往。它最突出地表现了端午节的社交功能，许多地区称端午节为"女儿节"。在节庆前后，订婚的男方要给未来的岳丈家送礼物；如果是女儿回娘家，则要带去酒和肉等礼物，同时娘家也要给女儿、女婿一些礼物。端午节时，上海一带嫁女之家，以角黍、绒符、蒲扇、手巾馈婿家，甚有制纱罗衣裙等馈之者，谓之"送夏衣"，间有不备衣而折钱者。嘉兴地区"新妇"经第一个"端节"，节前数日母家必备角黍、巾扇、彩绣、艾虎馈遗，谓之"致端午"；南京"端午、中秋之次日，吾乡均谓之拗节，方言也。吾乡女子之出嫁者，率于拗节归宁"。女儿归宁的习俗不仅在江南一带盛行，而且也传播到少数民族地区。重庆市石柱县的土家人，在端午节这天，一定要接已出嫁的女儿一家回来过节。跟随妻子过节来的女婿，必须送糖、烟、酒、面条和猪肉"五色礼"给岳父母。岳父母准备好粽子、麻花等款待女儿一家。女儿、女婿回家时，父

115

母要送他们每人一把花雨伞,俗称"鸳鸯伞",象征夫妻感情天长地久,经受人生风雨而白头到老,风雨同舟、忠贞不渝。过去土家山寨贫穷,送的是"油布伞"或送"草帽"。现在,山寨人富裕了,送的是各式各样的新潮雨伞。端午"送花伞"已然成为土家婚俗中约定俗成的风俗。

福建省福州人的端午习俗,还凸显了婆媳的伦理关系。节日期间,媳妇要给公婆赠送节日礼物,这些礼物大多与日常生活有关,如寿衣、鞋袜、团粽、扇子。端阳节里,各家朱门半掩,厅堂里妯娌婆媳团团围坐,包粽之时,也是婆媳、小姑拉家常的时间。如果平时关系比较紧张,媳妇喊一声:"娘(或妹妹),包粽粽吧!"这时对方不管再忙也会答应。这一喊一应非常协调,原有的矛盾也就化解了。有时媳妇还说:"娘,今年您老能吃几捆?"婆婆说:"前几年能吃一捆,去年吃一盖,今年只能吃半盖了。"说得大家哈哈大笑。在欢声笑语中,密切了婆媳关系,充分显示了人们的生活情趣和智慧。

二、
端午饮食文化

在江南的端午节习俗中，作为节日民俗符号的饮食文化，传承着数千年的历史文化积淀，蕴含着江南民众驱邪纳吉、祈保平安、企求康泰的美好意愿。

（一）吃粽子

吃粽子是端午节的重要习俗。粽子，又称"角黍"。早在晋代粽子就已作为夏至节的节令食品出现了。南朝时期，端午节的节俗意义增加了与屈原有关的内容，许多传说都把粽子的产生、演变与拯救、祭祀屈原很密切地联系在一起。随着屈原在端午节中核心地位的确立，包粽子、吃粽子也成了端午节最有代表性的节日习俗。

据考证，粽子最初用来祭神和祭祖。粽子成角

○端阳佳节吃粽子

形，源于周代先民盛行用牛或牛角来祭祀天地社神和谷神的习俗。粽子还用以祭祖，"以芦箬裹米熟之"，俗名"粽子"，即古之角黍也，用以祀灶祀先。粽子最迟出现在魏晋时期，"粽"字最初写作"糉"，其右偏旁的本义是"敛足"，即裹脚，合米旁表示一种把米包裹起来的食物。至唐宋时，粽子已成为市肆小吃，品味多样，粽馅各异。南方大多用花生、红枣、咸肉做馅，而北方多用枣、栗子及果脯，其中花生、枣及栗子的象征意义与"婚俗"中祈求生育（花生）、早立子（枣、栗子）同。南朝吴均《续齐谐记》载，缠粽子所用的线是"五色丝"，祝愿孩子能健康地长大。

○ 苏州健粽

随着社会的发展，粽子文化也越来越丰富多彩，社交、娱乐功能也愈加明显。人们用粽子相互表达深厚的友情和亲情，衷心地传达美好祝愿。苏州地区有一种名曰"健粽"的特色粽子。"以束粽之草系手足而祝之，名曰健粽，云令人壮健也。"以健粽馈亲朋，祝愿亲戚朋友身体康健。

生活在云南元阳乌河湾河坝的傣族，农历五月初五过"粽包节"，这是傣族人非常重要的节日。相传，以前有一对傣族青年，从小青梅竹马，相互爱慕，情深意浓，希望能生活在一起。但是，他们的父母都不同意他们的婚姻，坚决反对这门亲事。无奈之下，两人都患上了相思，最后为爱殉情。人们为了颂扬这两位青年追求爱情婚姻自由的精神，每年五月初五，都要举行"粽包节"来纪念他们。傣族粽包工艺精巧，味道清香。节日期间，傣族未婚青年男女身着盛装，在村边树下围成一圈唱情歌。然后，小伙子把粽包投给自己所看中的姑娘，若姑娘也有意，就拾起粽包，双双到附近僻静处谈情说爱，至日落西天时才离去。傣族粽包节，为青年男女提供自由选择对象的机会，祝愿人们都能过上幸福美满的生活。

（二）喝雄黄酒

雄黄酒是端午节必备的饮品，在中国几乎各个地区和民族都有饮雄黄酒的习俗。《松江府志》载：端午节期间，"浮菖蒲，雄黄酒"。《苏州风俗》记载，苏州端午节"日中饮雄黄酒，佐以石首鱼，并洒雄黄酒于屋隅，以驱虫豸"。《清嘉录》还介绍了制作雄黄酒的方法以及用途，"研雄黄末、屑蒲根，和酒以饮，谓之'雄黄酒'。又以余酒染小儿额及手足心，随洒墙壁间，以祛毒虫"。仲夏疾病流行、毒虫活跃，将雄黄酒喷洒在房屋壁角阴暗处，以避毒蛇蜈蚣等物，驱散瘟疫毒气。有水井的人家，以雄黄一块，裹以丝绵，投入井中，亦驱水中之毒。南京一带，端午节有用雄黄"破火眼"的习俗。"唯宁省各家，皆以清水一盂，入雄黄少许，鹅眼钱二枚（鹅眼钱，小钱别名，言其小如鹅眼也），阖家大小，均以此水涤眼，谓之破火眼，一年可免眼疾。""取蚕豆和雄黄炒之，曰雄黄豆。"

为什么人们认为雄黄具有杀毒、辟邪的功效？雄黄是一种矿物质，又名鸡冠石。据载，最早使用雄黄的是道家，雄黄是道家炼丹中常用的药材。葛洪在《抱朴子》里就提到用雄黄泡酒，《道藏》有"神仙酒炼雄黄方"，用雄黄做主药，酒为辅料，认为此酒可以心开目明，使人威武，入水可以辟蛟龙，入山可以辟虎狼，入军可以辟五兵。道家对雄黄的价值大肆推崇，后来在民间便形成了喝雄黄酒的风俗。民间亦有"喝了雄黄酒，百病都远走"的谚语。

端午节，中国各地还饮菖蒲酒，或者将蒲根切细、晒干，拌上少许雄黄，浸白酒，制成菖蒲雄黄酒。苏州一带，端午节"饮雄黄、菖蒲酒"；无锡一带"屑蒲根、雄黄和酒饮之"。崇祯版的《嘉兴县志》还谈了雄黄、菖蒲的作用："雄黄，太阳之精，能避诸邪，解诸毒，菖蒲亦能□鬼气，杀诸虫，午日泛菖蒲于雄黄酒中，各以余酒染额、胸、手、足心，以辟邪毒，洒之墙壁门窗诸处，以辟蛇虫。"菖蒲酒具有性温味辛的特点，对肺胃均有益，可延年益寿。药书有云："五月五日，饮菖蒲雄黄酒，可除百病而禁百虫。"《本草纲目》记载："菖蒲酒，治三十六风，一十二痹，通血脉，治骨瘘，久服耳目聪明"。唐殷尧藩有诗云："少年佳话倍多情，老去谁知感慨生。不效艾符趋习俗，但祈菖蒲话升平。"宋朝诗人梅尧臣在端午节时，没有菖蒲浸酒，宁可不饮。傍晚得菖蒲，还专门写诗咏引，"薄暮得菖蒲，犹胜竟日无。我焉能免俗，三揖向尊壶"。明朝时，菖蒲酒受到皇室的欢迎，被列为皇家宫廷时令御酒。明代太监刘若愚写的《酌中志》中说：宫廷"初五日午时，饮朱砂、雄黄、菖蒲酒，吃粽子"。

三、
端午服饰文化

无论是为了避邪禳灾，还是祈求平安，端午节这段时间的服饰装扮也与往常不同。从虎头帽，到五色缕、百岁索，以及香包香囊，制作繁琐的服饰背后是人们浓浓的情谊和美好的祝愿。

（一）儿童虎头帽

儿童在端午节这天要佩戴一些虎形饰物。长辈往往给孩子穿上老虎鞋，戴上老虎帽。上海地区"闺中制绣囊成虎头形，系小儿胸前，以示服猛，谓之'老虎头'"。南京一带小儿着老虎被，以"五色绢布，饰为天师骑虎形，系小儿背后，曰'老虎被'"。苏州地区"小儿衣以黄衫（曰'雄黄衫'），服以肚兜（曰'老虎肚兜'），佩以钱文（编钱为虎头形，谓之'老虎头'）。"浙江地区，民众往往以黄布制成老虎头形，系在小儿襟带间，亦有穿虎衣的，较大者往往画虎脸。

○豆娘健人

江南一带乃至全国，端午节这天还有给儿童画额的习俗。典型的方法是用雄黄酒在小儿额头画"王"字，一借雄黄以驱毒，二借猛虎以镇邪。因"王"字似虎的额纹，虎为兽中之王，所以代虎。

○端午画额

　　端午节为什么要用虎形为佩饰？虎，威猛强悍，自古以来受到民众的崇拜和敬畏。相传张天师征服天下恶魔，是从江西龙虎山骑着老虎去的。据考证，虎是先民的图腾，"虎被看作是强有力的象征，也是凶猛的象征。这里的人敬仰它的神威和机灵，膜拜它，祈求获得勇气，消除灾难"。东汉应劭的《风俗通义》云："虎者阳物，百兽之长，能执搏挫锐，噬食鬼魅。"历代民众以虎为灵物，始终强化着它的英武形象和伸张正义的守护神地位，赋予它以避邪镇恶、保佑安康的作用。俗话说虎可使"五毒化灰尘，妖邪归地府"。因此，端午节，妇女和儿童往往佩戴一些虎形佩饰，意借老虎的威猛，赶走百毒的侵袭，辟邪、去灾、防病，确保生命安全，求得生活平安。

（二）索饰求安康

端午节期间，中国各地用彩色或五色的线、缕、索作为象征驱邪辟凶的节物。《清嘉录》还介绍了端午索的制作及佩戴方法："结五色丝为索，系小儿之臂，男左、女右，谓之'长寿线'。"另外，苏州一带还有由端午索饰发展出来的端午佩饰。如用彩线结网，包裹不分瓣的大蒜头，做成的"独囊网蒜"和以五彩丝线缠绕在铜钱上，或者做成虎头的形状的"袅虥铜钱"。

以前，端午索形制和种类特别丰富。从材料的色彩着眼，称朱索、五色丝、五彩缕、五色缕、五彩缯等；从辟兵的角度着眼，称辟兵缯；从延寿的角度来看，称寿索、长命缕、续命缕、续命丝、延年缕、长寿线、百索、百岁索等。

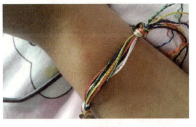

○五彩绳

从形制上分大体有以下几种：一是简单地以五色丝线合股成绳；二是五彩绳上缀饰金锡饰物；三是五彩绳折成方胜或结为人像等；四是以五彩丝线绣绘日月星辰鸟兽等物。

中国古代还在端午节前后形成了端午索饰的观赏、游艺以及买卖集市。美轮美奂的端午索堪称中国丝索手工艺制品的一大瑰宝，记录着民众对美好生活的向往和希冀。

端午节期间，长辈们会在孩子的手腕、脖子或脚腕拴上五彩丝索，或系于小儿手臂，或挂于床帐、摇篮等小孩用品上。端午索一直要到端午节过后才可以剪掉。端午期间，佩戴用五色丝线或彩线编制的各种索饰，其用意在于辟邪延寿。古人认为，青、黄、白、赤、黑五色，即代表金、木、水、火、土五行，而五行之间相辅相成，循环往复，周而复始，生生不息，五色便具有了辟邪延寿的效应和功用。"五月五日，以五彩丝系臂名曰辟兵，令人不病瘟"；"系以五色长命缕，俗传以为服猛"；"以红绿线系小儿臂（男左女右，以验日后肥瘠）"。佩戴端午索饰的目的是为了孩子能够健康成长，辟邪镇恶、保佑安康。

端午索饰除了驱邪辟祟以外，还是一种装饰品，作为表情达意的节日礼物馈赠亲朋。唐代端午节有皇帝赐大臣百索之仪。辽朝时，皇帝在端午节朝贺时身上佩戴"寿缕"，并将"寿缕"赐予诸位大臣，以示皇帝对臣下的关心和祝福。不仅如此，端午索饰还被用作情物，吴曼云《长命缕》诗曰："编成杂组费功深，络索轻于缠臂金。笑语玉郎还忆否，年时五彩结同心。"妇女送给丈夫的五色端午索一般有两种形制，一是"长命缕"，希望丈夫能够延年益寿；一是"辟兵缯"，寄托着妇女们希望丈夫能够躲避兵灾，不染瘟疫。而五色丝则象征东西南北中五个方位，借此隐喻丈夫能够五方大吉、处处平安。

（三）毒饰辟邪祟

端午节期间，中国各地民众制作各种端午毒饰，希冀用以毒攻毒的办法来驱邪消灾。长辈要给孩子们穿上精心织成的花裹肚和五毒绣肚兜，上面绣有花、鸟、鱼、虫等可以制毒防毒的动植物图像，色彩鲜艳，有的地方还专门为小孩制作五毒衣，在衣服上绣上老虎、蝎、蜥蜴、蜘蛛、蜈蚣等五毒，有时壁虎、蟾蜍、蛇也被列入五毒之中。妇女也常在端午节插戴五毒之形的头饰。浙江杭州地区，午日在扇子上画五毒之形，谓之"五毒扇"供小儿用之。

把端午索饰和端午毒饰结合在一体的端午佩饰，表达的意义与其大体相似。浙江地区，"是以红绿线制成圆形盘老虎、蝎、蜥蜴、蜘蛛、蜈蚣等在其上，系于小儿之臂，称'五毒索儿'"，为以毒制毒之意。端午节这天，清代的妇女头上佩戴一种称为"健人"的头饰。此种头饰一般用金银丝或铜丝金箔做成，形状为小人骑虎，也有另加钟铃、缨及蒜、粽子插于妇女发髻或用以馈送亲友。浙江嘉兴一带还有一种"健人虎"或者叫"健人老虎"的头饰。此头饰一般为虎形，或以艾为人形跨之，或制缯作人形跨之，供妇女插戴或互赠亲朋。

　　驱邪降福钱最能体现两者功能的完美结合。据徐家华先生介绍，他所收藏的两种端午驱邪降福钱，一种可能是明代后期的端午佩饰物，这是一种黄铜色圆形的"驱邪降福钱"，钱的中心为挖空的圆。币的正面有蝙蝠图案和楷书繁体"驱邪降福"字样，币的反面有蛇、壁虎、蜘蛛、蟾蜍和老虎图案和"钟馗驱五毒"字样。

○ 驱邪降福花钱

　　还有一种可能是民国时期的驱邪降福钱，这是一种紫铜挂璧式的花钱，钱币的正面是钟馗一只手高举宝剑，另一只手拿着黄旗，币文简写"驱邪降福"字样，币的反面是张天师手拿宝剑和符，币文简写"诸神回避"字样。这些驱邪降福钱综合了端午索饰和端午毒饰的功能和方法，并把民间鬼神的信仰习俗、道家降魔捉鬼的宗教信仰寓含于一体，集中体现出民间社会驱邪避灾的生活理念。

（四）香包传吉祥

　　每到端午时节，闺阁女子、媳妇、妯娌们就要早做准备，缝制香囊。香囊多以棉布、丝绸为材，工艺讲究，需裁剪、刺绣、挖补、粘贴缠绕。姑娘们各展身手，争奇斗巧，一旦完成，到时候拿出来交流品评，互相馈遗。"兰闺彩伴，各赌神针，炫异争奇，互相投赠，新制日增。"

　　香囊形状多呈长方形、正方形，也有三角形、菱形、鸡心形、棱角形、斗形、月牙形、扇面形等。上面绣有十二生肖、狮子、双鱼、蟠桃、花草、虫鸟、瑞兽、蔬菜、瓜果等吉祥图案及罗汉钱等，里面放雄黄、朱砂，或者苍术、香草等中草药，用五色丝线弦扣成索，做成各种不同形状，结成一串，形形色色，款式极为精美，小巧玲珑，十分可爱，所以称"香包"，或称"雄黄荷包"。带在身上，不仅可以装饰点缀节日气氛，而且还有清香，可以驱瘟散毒。

　　端午节之日，无论男女老少，往往都佩戴香包图个平安，故而香包的种类特别丰富。有的是以单一的物体或形态为主题，有的绣上汉字，如福、禄、寿、禧等，还有的是多个吉祥图案组合而成，祈求吉祥与平安。

○佩戴香囊

四、
端午家居装饰文化

五月仲夏，恶气最盛，挡灾、挡邪不能漏了家居环境。家家户户门上挂艾草菖蒲，贴桃符和钟馗像。宝剑出鞘一般的菖蒲赶走恶鬼邪祟，钟馗更是镇邪去祟，禳灾报平安。

（一）艾草辟邪，服食延年

端午节时，时至夏至，正值菖蒲、艾草药性最佳的时候，人们往往采集菖蒲、艾草挂在门口，以避邪祟。

端午节时，江南人家通常将艾草、菖蒲用红纸绑成一束，或者将艾蒿、菖蒲扎成人形，悬挂在门前，用以祛鬼禳邪、保持健康。

○艾叶　　　　　　　　○菖蒲

上海地区，人们在端午前后"系艾叶、菖蒲于门，悬大蒜、彩符"。苏州太仓的人们在端午节时也家家户户"门悬艾蓬、菖蒲、蒜头"；浙江杭州"门户挂蒲剑、艾虎，并插桃枝"，《清嘉录》亦云"截蒲为剑，割蓬作鞭，副以桃梗、蒜头，悬于床户，皆以却鬼"。

为什么要在端午节时悬挂艾草、菖蒲和大蒜呢？民间深信，菖蒲叶形似宝剑，蓬形似钢鞭，而艾叶、大蒜头散发出一种奇特的气味，这些都可用来逐妖驱鬼。沪语中有一句俗语是"鬼摸大蒜头"，意思是糊里糊涂昏了头做了不该做的事。菖蒲是一种水生草本植物。《道德经》有《菖蒲传》一卷，谓菖蒲为"水草之精英，神仙之灵药"，并详细介绍了菖蒲采摘、炮制和服食的方法。《神农本草经》将菖蒲列为药中上品："菖蒲，味辛温，主风寒湿痹，咳逆上气，开心孔，补五脏，通九窍，明耳目，出声音。久服轻身，不忘不迷，延年。"《本草纲目》补充菖蒲的主治病症："四肢湿痹，不得屈伸，小儿温疟，身积热不解，可作浴汤。治耳鸣头风泪下，鬼气，杀诸虫恶疮疥瘙。除风下气，多忘，除烦闷，止心腹痛，霍乱转筋，及耳痛者，作末炒，乘热裹罨，甚验。"可见，菖蒲在实际生活中与健康有着极大的关系。大诗人李白也曾作《嵩山采菖蒲者》诗，云："我来采菖蒲，服食可

○市民捧着购买的艾叶和菖蒲

延年。"古代普通民众认为疾病皆因鬼邪作祟所致，所以恶月恶日里挂上药用价值极高的菖蒲，以辟邪祟，保平安，求健康。

虽然有极高的药用价值，但在中国文化中，菖蒲又被历代术士、文人赋予了正义、公平和勇敢的内涵。菖蒲又名尧韭，叶片呈直长的形状，像一把利刃宝剑，象征正义、斩除妖孽的宝剑。古籍《典术》记载："尧时天降精于庭为韭，感百阴之气为菖蒲，故曰尧韭。"屈原在《楚辞》中多次提及和歌颂菖蒲，例如《少司命》中所写的"夫人自有兮美子，荪何以兮愁苦？""荪"就是石菖蒲。宋代诗人苏轼对菖蒲更是赞赏有加，说它"渍以清水，置盆中，可数十年不枯，虽不甚茂，而节叶坚瘦，根须连络，苍然于几案间"，并且能够"忍寒苦，安淡泊，与清泉白石为伍"。端午节的"蒲剑"象征正直高洁、绝不屈服的高贵人格。在古代日本，因"菖蒲"与"尚武"同音，端午节时，男孩子们玩打菖蒲，佩菖蒲刀，击菖蒲剑，喝菖蒲酒，洗菖蒲澡等。菖蒲被赋予了对男孩子茁壮成长、勇猛刚强、出人头地、飞黄腾达的美好祝愿。

（二）天师镇宅，钟馗捉鬼

端午节之日，各地区特别是江南人家，家家堂中通常悬挂天师像或者粘贴天师符，而且要挂整整一个月之久。《清嘉录》"天师符"一项说"朔日，人家以道院所贻天师符，贴厅事以镇恶，肃拜烧香。至六月朔，始焚而送之"。杭州人家则以"菖蒲、通草雕刻天师驭虎像于盘中，围以五色蒲丝，剪皮金为百虫之像铺其上，或以蒲榴、艾叶或以彩绒杂金线缠结经筒、符袋，互相馈遗"。门挂天师像的风俗在这首词里有形象的描述："挂天师，撑着眼，直下觑，骑个生狞大艾虎。闲神浪鬼，辟懔他方远方，大胆底，更敢来，上门下户。"

可以看到一个骑着艾虎凝神直视的张天师，还有把守门户、吓跑了鬼的雄姿。

不仅是天师像，只要刻有"天师"二字的符，也被称为"天师符"。吴曼云《江乡节物词》小序说："杭俗，道家于端午送符，必署天师二字，以见其神。"1929 年的调查所记录的广州午时符有两种图，一是天师像，一是太极八卦图。所配的文字是一样的，中间是"敕令五月五日午时书破官非口舌鼠蚁蛇虫一切尽消除"，两侧写有"艾旗迎百福"和"蒲剑斩千邪"。

张天师镇邪，钟馗斩五鬼。明末清初，江南人家过端午节开始挂钟馗像，"堂中挂钟馗画图一月，以祛邪魅"。李福《钟馗图》诗云："面目狰狞胆气粗，柳红蒲碧座悬图。仗君扫荡幺麽枝，负使人间鬼画符。"卢毓嵩专门有诗描画："榴花吐焰菖蒲碧，画图一副生虚白。绿袍乌帽吉莫靴，知是终南山里客。眼如点漆发如虬。唇如腥红髯如戟。看彻人间索索徒，不食烟霞食鬼魄。何年留影在人间，处处端阳驱病疫。呜呼！世上魍魉不胜计，灵光一睹难逃匿。仗君百千亿万身，却鬼直教褫鬼魄。"传说故事里的五个小鬼逐渐演变成五只小蝙蝠——"五福临门"的意思更吉祥喜庆。

各户人家端阳节张贴、悬挂钟馗像，钟馗斩五毒，作执剑起舞状，画上盖有"灵宝神判"大印或加以"敕令"

○悬挂钟馗像

的五雷符。小幅者贴于门户，大轴画悬于中堂。有的人家还在端阳正午用朱砂点钟馗的眼睛和剑上的七星，认为这样就有辟邪的神力。在日本的民间信仰中，钟馗也占有一席之地。刊行于 1838 年的《东都岁时记》是记录江户时代岁时风俗的书籍，书中有一幅描绘江户（即现在的东京）端午节市街风景的插图，图中钟馗旗高于屋脊，迎风招展。

（三）张贴符图，桃木驱邪

以符图驱邪避毒也是中国民间端午节的传统习俗。端午辟邪的符早在汉代就已经形成了。《后汉书·礼仪志》云："五月五日，朱索五色印为门户之饰，以止恶气。"清代，江南地区小户人家亦有粘五色桃印彩符用以辟邪者，"小户五色桃印彩符，每描画姜尚父及财神、聚宝盆之类"。

人们以桃木刻门神之像，源于古人对"桃"的崇拜。据《孟子》等书记载，后羿的仆人逢蒙曾用桃木大棒砸死了本领高强的羿。因为羿生前曾造福于人间，后世将其奉为宗布神，专门管理和统辖天下的魑魅魍魉。桃木棒既然能砸死万鬼首领羿，那么桃木定能镇服各类鬼怪。因此，古人将桃木崇拜为除灾、制鬼、驱怪的灵物，称其为"仙木"。《典术》云："桃者，五木之精也，故压伏邪气者也。"

端午节除了桃符以外，有的道教宫观用朱砂笔在黄表纸上画符，谓之"天师符"，馈送或出售常所往来之家。一些"梵寺亦多以红黄白纸，墨画神符，分贴比户，则非天师符矣。"供信佛的人家张贴。仕宦之家还有用朱砂笔写"五月五日天中节,赤口白舌尽消灭"之句，张贴于门户，这也是一种辟邪驱鬼的符箓。

端午节这天，江南人民还在门窗上贴纸剪的"五毒"图像。五毒是民间所指的五种毒虫，即蝎子、蜈蚣、壁虎、蟾蜍和蛇。对于这五种毒物，各地说法不一。"尼庵剪五色彩线，状蟾蜍、蜥蜴、蜘蛛、蛇、玄之形，分贴檀越，贴门楣寝室，以厌虫毒，谓之'五毒符'"，或者图绘或纸剪五毒图挂在门首。人们把"五毒"图像贴在墙上，取以毒攻毒之义，有的人家还用针刺在五毒符或五毒图上，表示钉住了五毒，辟邪驱祟，以免祸害人间。

○五毒符　　　　　　　　　○五种毒物

延伸知识

中国保护和传承端午节庆文化的举措

　　自 2008 年起，端午节被列为中国国家法定节假日。2006 年 5 月，中国国务院将其列入首批国家级非物质文化遗产名录。2009 年 9 月，联合国教科文组织正式审议并批准中国端午节列入世界非物质文化遗产，成为中国首个入选世界非遗的节日。

在当今非遗保护的大背景中，不少地方采用端午节展演方式传承和保护。不仅有申报联合国非遗代表作的四个申报地区每年举行端午节展演活动，其他地方也积极举办端午节展演活动，从龙舟竞渡到庙会集市，吸引老百姓的目光。

端午节的传承离不开传承人的努力。无论是湖北秭归县县级木雕技艺非遗传承人，还是四川自贡剪纸传承人、莱芜民间文化传承人等，他们付出时间和精力，只为将瞬间的美凝固在艺术之中。

近些年，非遗项目逐渐走进课堂，走向年轻人，让小学生们能近距离接触、感受非遗项目的魅力。在端午节的展演活动中，不少父母带着孩子前来观看，让下一代对传统文化有更多自豪感，同时也为文化的传承与延续提供一些可能。

Chapter Three
Customs of the Dragon Boat Festival

The Customs of the Dragon Boat Festival include all the folk customs like taboos, entertainments, festive costumes, ceremonies & rites, family gatherings and mutual visits among close friends and relatives. As the result of the historical accretion, The Dragon Boat Festival has witnessed a great variety of customs which may be different from each other in different places. In this chapter, we try to give an overview of these colorful customs of the Dragon Boat Festival.

1. Entertainments of the Dragon Boat Festival

The customs of the Dragon Boat Festival like dragon boat race, herb-picking, grass-treading (spring outing), matching herbs (grass-fighting) and daughter's reunion with her parents were usually performative rites. Dragon boat race not only conveyed the common people's desire to be protected by the dragon lord, avoid disasters and have a harvest, but also expressed or led off their emotions and demonstrated their love for a happy life and hoped for a good future. Grass-treading or matching herbs (grass-fighting) was in fact an entertainment or a game to help people get relaxed. When the in-laws presented each other gifts on the day of daughter's returning home, what really counted was not the gift, but the promoted relationships among the relatives and friends on this happy festival.

1.1 The Dragon Boat Race to Pray for Luck & Happiness

Among all customs of the Dragon Boat Festival, dragon boat race has long been the most symbolic festive rite (entertainment) almost spread all over China.

So far as the origins of dragon boat race, we may find many as follows: The locals in Suzhou (Jiangsu Province, Southeast China) hold that the festival was celebrated to commemorate Wu Zixu (in the late Spring and Autumn Period), the meritorious minister of the state of Wu; while the people living in Zhejiang Province think it originated from the story of Gou Jian, the king of Ancient Yue, who endured hardships to revive his country by training the navy secretly. People in the coastal area of Fujian Province believe that the race derived from the story of Goddess Matsu. The Bai people living in Yunnan Province celebrate this festival to commemorate Duan Chicheng, the python-beheading hero; while the Dai people would tell you

Dragon Boat Race

the story of seven Dai girls who dedicated their lives to slaying the demon. In the valley of Qingshui River running through Guizhou Province, the Miao people will worship Jiubao, their own hero slaying the fierce dragon. Of course, the most profound and popular story is concerned with the patriotic poet of the state of Chu——Qu Yuan. But different from the legends of some historical figures, some scholars regard dragon boat race on the Dragon Boat Festival as a wizard-hosted ritual to send away disasters in the earliest time, which originated in the south of the Yangtz River; and some others, after textual research, infer that this race came from the totem-worship ritual held by the ancient Yue people.

Feeling so helpless before the natural disasters, the ancient Chinese had to turn to the dragon lord for guarding by means of dragon boat race, hoping to avoid disasters and have a smooth and harvest year. With time going on, people began to associate Duanwu boat race with various historical or legendary figures and hold dragon boat race to commemorate their ancestors or sages. Via such race, they believed that their piety to the dragon lord could fend off the evils and protect the souls of their ancestors or sages. Meanwhile, they also hoped to show their strength to carry forward justice and fight against demons, a strong national feeling to suppress the bad and support the good. Finally, among all the legends, the story of Qu Yuan became the most prominent: They commemorated this well-known poet in history, who nobly integrated Chinese traditional ethics and values, which embodied the Chinese nation's love for both their country & home and their strong sense of national identity. Moreover, such custom also expressed the Chinese people's wish for the thriving of the nation and demonstrated their unique aesthetic value.

Among the various dragon boats, here we want to mainly discuss the following three, namely, painted-dragon boats for pleasure cruise, dragon boats for sacrificial rituals and dragon boats for prize-winning.

1.1.1 Apart from those luxurious painted-dragon boats provided for the emperors, there were still some other boats for pleasure cruise owned by the folks. In East China, there were "civil" boats (only for pleasure cruise). In the south of China, on the Dragon Boat Festival, the locals would carry and play "dryland" dragon boats or "painted" dragon boats, or organize "make-up" race (running while lifting dragon-or-elephant-shaped boats), or play the game of dragon dance or lion dance. In Zhenjiang district (Jiangsu Province), there were some unique dragon boats——"stunt-show" boats, on which some stunts (like headstand and standing of kid on the stern) were shown. The integration of dragon boat and show demonstrated one mental aspect of the cities in South China.

1.1.2 Dragon boats for sacrificial rituals were mainly welcome in the Hunan-Hubei-Jiangxi border area. 2 meters long and 0.4 meter wide and tall respectively, such a boat was one sacrifice utensil carried by the wizards on their backs when they cruised from village to village on the Dragon Boat Festival, and this custom was called "worship the dryland dragon boat" by the locals. There was another "sacrifice" boat carried by the locals who paraded uphill and across the streets, a custom called "greet the ghosts".

1.1.3 Dragon boats for prize-winning referred to those canoes only to be used in the boat race, with their bows decorated like the heads of open-mouthed dragons and the sterns the scaly tails. However, in modern times, all the racing boats for prize-winning (whether decorated with dragon images or not) have been called dragon boats, including those ferries, dinghies or small cargo ships for temporary usage. Such water sports is called "dragon boat rowing" or "dragon boat race for prize-winning", which can be classified as "professional" and "amateur" race. The "professional" dragon boat is used only for the race, while the "amateur" boat refers to the "modified boat" (used for working and living usually) whose function will be restored after the race.

The structures of dragon boats are almost the same: the hull (including oar tips and oars), the dragon head, the dragon hail, all kinds of decorations and the gong and drum. Usually carved out of a piece of whole wood, the dragon head could be installed only before the race, whether for the "professional" boat or the "amateur" boat. The dragon heads have a variety of shapes according to varied customs: The dragon heads of the boats used in the Xijiang river basin (Guangxi) are rooster-head-shaped, while the dragon heads of the boats in the Dongjiang river basin are cricket-head-shaped, both distinctive.

Dragon Boat Race

The dragon heads are usually painted red and are therefore called "red dragons". Some others may be painted black or white, so they are called "black dragons" or "white dragons". The "scaly" tail is also carved by a piece of whole wood. The rooster-headed dragon boat in Shunde (Guangdong Province) perhaps owns the most complex decorations: There is a wood-made "divine" pavilion set in the middle of the boat, together with a big drum and a gong beside. Some other decorations are dragon head, tail flag, command flag and brocade umbrella.

Depending on the number of rowers, the dragon boat can be classified as small-sized, medium-sized and large-sized. The small-sized boat can hold 3 or 5 or 10 rowers, ranging from 4.5-6 meters in length; the medium-sized boat can hold 20-50 rowers, about 15-20 meters long; and the large-sized boat with 60-100 rowers will be up to 27-30 meters long. You can even see an extra-large-sized boat which is powered by more than 200 rowers. There are only rowers and a steersman in a small-sized boat, while a drummer and a gong player are added in a medium-sized boat and two drummers and two gong players can be held in a large-sized boat. The rivers in the Zhujiang River Delta are usually wide enough, so the well-off locals can afford large-sized boats, which usually hold 60 rowers, or even more than 100.

Dragon boat race for prize-winning used to be held on the festivals (esp. the Dragon Boat Festival). In the regions south of the Yangtze River where the Chu and the Yue people once lived, customs of dragon boat race for prize-winning were very popular. Such race was at least recorded in the late Han Dynasty. In the Southern Song Dynasty (1127-1279 AD), large-scaled dragon boat races held by the folk appeared in Guangdong, and in the Ming and Qing Dynasties, both the official and folk boat races became more popular in Guangdong on the Dragon Boat Festival. Among the thousands of extant local chronicles around China, about 300 have recorded the dragon boat races. The earliest record appeared black and white in the book "An Account of Dragon Boat Races in Wuling Region" written by Yang Sichang (1588—1641 AD), who elaborated on the customs of boat race in the regions by the Yuan River and Xiang River (in present-day Hunan Province) in the Ming Dynasty.

In the Ming Dynasty, dragon boat races were held in the "Yuan-Xiang" regions to avoid disasters and fend off poisonous insects, so a variety of sacrificial rituals were required before the races started, and wizards were invited to hold rites to pray for good luck. The race over, the locals would scramble to fetch water from the boat and take it back home. After boiling the water blended with herbs, they would have a bath with such "magic" water to avoid or drive away the evils. Boat race, the protype of the sacrificial ritual to avoid disasters, was soon developed into "dryland dragon boat race" in many regions. In

Jiangxi region (to the east of Hunan), the bamboo-or-wood-made dragon boats would be worshiped when the boat race was held on the dryland. Such festive activity was also held for the purpose of avoiding disasters, much similar to that of "Yuan-Xiang" regions in the Ming Dynasty.

The Dragon boat races for prize-winning held in Yangzhou

Dragon Boat Race

(Jiangsu Province) in the Qing Dynasty were recorded in detail by Li Tizhai as follows: Boat races were held every day in Yangzhou from the first to the fifth in the fifth lunar month, extremely joyous and boisterous on the very day of Duanwu. Various dragon boats would compete with each other by dashing ahead or performing wonderful "talent shows" to attract the spectators. And on the boats, many acrobatic performances would be demonstrated. As a result, the boats changed into movable "stages" and attracted the spectators with "shows" other than racing or winning, which tremendously enriched

141

the boat races and enhanced their charms.

In some other regions (e.g. Shunde, Guangdong Province), dragon boats would gather for fun in a certain water area, a custom called "occasional" gathering. Every year from the first day to the twentieth day of the fifth lunar month, the invited locals would row the dragon boats to some designated place, where the boat race with no prize-winning was held and the folks only showed their rowing skills for fun. Such "occasional" gathering would be held in turn in every village, a different scene every day. Some villages thought a lot about the "gathering" and took it as a grand party. When seeing the boats from their "old" home, the married women, together with their husbands and children, would row small boats to greet those fellow villagers, with firecrackers and cakes as presents.

Apart from the functions of avoiding disasters and fending off evils as well as racing speed in the early time, what the people later valued more might be the joyful performances to attract the spectators. Operas or acrobatic shows, presented on the boats instead of stages, would of course make the performances more difficult, more interesting and more ornamental.

In the modern time, on the one hand the dragon boat race is of course related to the Dragon Boat Festival, but on the other it owns its uniqueness. According to the rules set by the International Dragon Boat Federation (IDBF), the World Championships will be held in the odd-numbered year and the World Club Championships in the even-numbered year. Only the club teams could attend the boat race, in the name of the "club", not the "nation"; and only when at least six club teams (owning the full or basic membership of IDBF) attend the race, can it be qualified to be listed as World Club Championships.

Nowadays, the international or national dragon boat races

are all standardized, while those races held by the folks are usually conventional. Their competition rules are different from each other. For example, the conventional boat races held in Shunde and Dongguan (Guangdong Province) take place on the rapid rivers. In the conventional boat race, on the boat there will stand one rower who cheers his team members by waving flags and shouting slogans, while on the bow another fellow will present the local folk performing art. However, such "stunts" are excluded in the standardized races. Additionally, a dragon head and a scaly tail are placed on the boat used for the standardized race; while in the conventional boat race, the boat will be "armed to the teeth" to show its best image to the spectators, but before the race, such decorations will be taken down and two rowers will stand there instead of the dragon head and tail. More importantly, some rites related to customs of the Dragon Boat Festival are to be held during the conventional boat race, since it is one vital festive activity of this festival. In 2006, the rites and performances to commemorate Qu Yuan were presented in the Miluo River International Dragon Boat Race, which made the race impressive by its unique national culture and folk customs, endowing special and profound cultural flavors to both the boat and the race.

In Southeast Guizhou Province, the Miao people living there will hold a grand dragon boat race on the Dragon Boat Festival. Locally it is called "the Dragon Canoe Festival". It is believed that this festival was held to take revenge against the vicious dragon by killing and burning him. From 24th to 27th of the fifth lunar month, the Miao people in Shidong Town, rowing their "dragon-head" boats which are elaborately carved, will race fiercely along different sections of the Qingshui River. On 24th of the fifth lunar month, setting off from the Ping

Village of Shibing County, the racing boats will pass by Tanglong Town and Rongshan Town (all in Taijiang County) and finally get to Shidong where the race is over. Usually, the race will take place in Ping Village on 24, in Tanglong on 25, in Laotun and Jiuzhou on 26 and in Fangzhai on 27. Apart from the boat race, there are other festivities like bull-fighting, horse-racing, drum-stamping, reed-pipe dancing and gathering party (like blind dating for the young). The colorful festivities featured by their unique folk customs will attract nearly 30,000—40,000 neighboring locals (from Kaili, Huangping, Zhenyuan and Sanhui) of different ethnic groups to come, since no one wants to miss the most boisterous festival of the year.

Why is it called "the Dragon Canoe Festival"? The villagers first dig a thick-and-straight fir trunk hollow in the shape of a groove, and then bind three such big "canoes" together to make a dragon boat. The canoe in the middle is about 21m long, which is called the "mother boat"; and the other two beside it are about 15m long, the "son boats". The bow of the boat is made of a 2-mteter water willow carved in the shape of dragon. Inset into both sides of the "head", there are a pair of long buffalo horns, on each of which it reads "May favorable weather and bountiful harvest come! " and "May our country prosperous and our life peaceful!" The boat team consists of the drummer, the gong player, the poler, the helmsman and the rowers, with the drummer as the core member who controls the racing pace by his drum-beating. When the race begins, with full strength the rowers row their oars, their own cheering cry heard far away and the water under splashing away. At the same time, with their necks stretching, the excited spectators cheered and cheered.

Tips for Tourism

Shidong——an Old Town Inhabited by the Miao Nationality

Shidong Town has its original name "zhang xiang" in Miao language, which means where a fair is held. Located in the north of Taijiang County, Guizhou Province, this town is nestled at the foot of the Miaoling Mountains, with a clean river (Qingshui River running through Changjiang River Basin) passing by 38km away from Taijiang County and 48km away from Kaili City, Shidong Town, with four neighboring counties——Huangping, Zhenyuan, Shibing and Jianhe, administering 21 villages and 96 villager groups. As one important old market town in Taijiang County, it is a typical Miao community, since 98% of the inhabitants here are the Miao people.

Known as the "Sea of Singing and Dancing", "Capital of Silver Ornaments" and "Home of Art", in 1994 Shidong Town was granted the title of "Home of Embroidery, Silver Ornaments and Paper-cutting" by the Provincial Department of Culture. It is also famous for its "Sisters' Day" (similar to Lover's Day) and "the Dragon Canoe Festival", with the happy Miao songs (Hxak Yeet) flying over its valleys. In addition, the Su Mansion and the Lianghu (Hubei and Hunan Province respectively) Guild Hall built in the Qing Dynasty are really worth visiting as well.

With green mountains embracing and a clean river flowing by, Shidong Town is sheltered by those lush old trees. Apart from the agreeable climate, the idyllic scenery and spectacular mountains will make the travelers unable to tear their eyes away from them. When they come here, what greet them are exquisite silver ornaments/handicrafts and hand embroideries characteristic of unique Miao culture. Of course, their mouths will water at the fresh and tender "sour soup fish" and the inexpensive tasty goose meat.

The travelers are advised to go to Kaili City first. From Guiyang (the capital of Guizhou Province) they could get to Kaili City by train and this 3-hour trip just costs about ¥24. The fair for the sleeper coach from Gui-

145

yang to Kaili is ¥ 55 and the charge for renting a car is ¥200 per day.

The shuttle coach from Guiyang will leave for Kaili (8:30 a.m. – 13: 00 p.m.) every 30 minutes and the fair is ¥18.

From Taigong Town (Taijiang County) to Shidong Town there are shuttle mini—buses which will pass by some old villages like Laotun and Pianzhai.

Influenced by the humid subtropical climate, it is cool in summer and warm in winter, with the highest temperature at 29 °C in summer and lowest temperature at 1 °C in winter. Therefore, it is free from ice and snow all the year round. The average temperature from March to May is about 22 °C and the best time for touring starts in May and ends in October.

The locals' motivation to pray for a harvest was deeply contained in the dragon boat race——a folk festivity of the Dragon Boat Festival. By means of spectacular dragon boat race, the locals hoped that the positive relationship between the dragon boat and the dragon lord would contribute to harvest. And via manipulating such a competitive race to please the dragon lord, they also hoped to fulfill their wishes——favorable weather and bountiful harvest. "On the Dragon Boat Festival…Dragon boat races are held everywhere, and the villagers sing and dance, praying for a good harvest." "The lord of dragon brings us a halcyon day, and before the gods for a harvest we pray." Their sensitivity to the change of water and soil, as well as their attachment to the much-cared harvest, could clearly reflect the farmers' wishes for the idyllic life and praying for the farming life. "After seeing off the 'sages', they will hang the portrait of Qu Yuan in the painted pleasure-boat and worship this great poet, praying for good luck and avoiding disasters, all wild with joy. " Via the competitive races, the locals hoped to send away "God of Plague" and embrace a happy life with no diseases or disasters.

146

1.2 Sand-Play and Herb-Match for Fun and Luck

"Grass-fight" is a rewarding and interesting folk activity of long standing, which was earliest recorded in the book "Records of Customs and Festivals in the Chu Region" written by Zongtan (in the 6th century, the Southern Dynasties): "On the double-fifth day, all the folks will tread the grass and play the game of 'grass-fight'". Such customs were at their peak during the booming times of the Tang Dynasty, and still existed in the Qing Dynasty, even preserved nowadays.

Herb-match, also called "herb-fight" or "grass-treading", has long been one traditional game of the Dragon Boat Festival in the regions south of the Yangtze River. The anecdote of "herb-match" between King Fuchai (of the state of Wu in the late Spring and Autumn Period) and Xishi (one of the "Four Beauties" in the history of ancient China) was once recorded in the first column of the book "Anecdotes of Suzhou City". In his poem "Watch Kids Playing", Bai Juyi (a great poet in the Tang Dynasty) described one amusing scene on the day of Duanwu: "Playing sand or herb-match all the day, they 'hee hee' till the end of the day." In the 13th year of Chunxi reign period of the Southern Song Dynasty, living in seclusion in Suzhou, Fan Chengda (a famous poet then) chanted the herb-match of the naive children in his poem "Song of Idyllic Garden": "Seeing the picked twigs and flowers scattered on the lawn, I know the kids must have played the game of herb-match". In his book "Anecdotes in the Halcyon Days", Tian Rucheng (in the Ming Dynasty) said that "in the springtime, women in Hangzhou are fond of playing the game of herb-match." He also quoted another Ci-verse to depict the scene of women grass-fighting vividly. In the game of "herb-match", the winner would gain prizes like jade earring. More importantly, the women participants could get relaxed and amused. We may also find the description of herb-match in the book "Records of Customs of Suzhou" (written by Yuan Jinglan in the Qing Dynasty): "The locals build cottages and store up medicinal herbs on the double-fifth day, and play the game of herb-match or tie five-color silk cords as well."

The game of herb-match could be classified into "verbal fight" and "grass-fight".

"Verbal fight" could also be subdivided into two ways: The first is to place two pots of plants side by side, judging whose flowers are more graceful or much rarer. The second is to place the flowers or herbs together, and one girl (woman) will speak out the name of one plant with her rival answering another (like couplet-composing). If the rival could find an appropriate answer, she will win; if not, she will lose. For example, monthly-crimson is the appropriate counterpart of starry-green, while cockscomb corresponds to dogtail flower.

In the masterpiece "A Dream of Red Mansions", the scene of herb-match is wonderfully presented as follows:

Xiaoluo, Xiangling, Fangguan, Ruiguan, Ouguan and Dougaun had been romping all over the Garden and picking flowers and herbs. Now they sat down on the grass holding these on their laps to play the game "matching herbs".

One said, "I've bodhisattva-willow."

This was capped by "I've a arhat-pine."

Another said, "I've a gentleman-bamboo."

Yet another answered, "I've a lovely-lady plantain."

"I've a starry-crimson."

"I've a the peony of Peony Pavilion."

"I've the loquat of the Romance of the Lute."

Then Dougaun said, "I've a sister-flower," and nobody

could match that until Xiangling said,

"I've a husband-and-wife orchid."

"I've never heard of such an orchid," Dougaun protested.

"A stem bearing one flower is the lan orchid, and a stem bearing several flowers is the hui orchid," Xiangling told them, "When there are flowers above and below that's brothers-orchid; when two flowers bloom side by side that's a husband-and-wife orchid. This one of mine is like that, with two flowers side by side. How can you deny it? "

Unable to refute her, Douguan rose to her feet and teased, "In that case, if one flower is large, the other small, it should be a father-and-son orchid. Two flowers confronting each other should be an enemy orchid. Your husband's been away for nearly a year and you're longing for him, so you dream up a husband-and-wife orchid. Shame on you!"

Blushing, Xingling got ready to spring up to pinch her.

"You foul-mouthed bitch!" She swore, laughing. "What drivel you talk!"

What a merry festival!

"Grass-fight" mainly tests the toughness of the stalk. Holding one piece of grass in one hand and making it intersected with another grass of the rival, the players will tug the grass backward (just like a tug-war). He whose grass is broken is the loser. In Wuxi (Jiangsu), the locals used to call the game "grass-lawsuit", and would use plantain seed (which they called "lawsuit" grass) and goose grass for the "fight". Such a game might not have been clearly recorded in those classic works, but judging from the pomes as mentioned above (e.g. "Seeing the picked twigs and flowers scattered on the lawn, I know the kids must have played the game of herb-match."), we may conclude that such a "grass-fight" was just what Fan the poet described.

"Grass-fight" was usually welcome among the children. The wash painting "Grass-Fight of Kids", a masterpiece of the court painter Jin Tingbiao (which is collected in the Palace Museum) presents us a vivid scene of such a game with delicate touches. There are ten boys in the picture: some are stooping to find grass, some are picking and some fetching a handful for the fight; two boys are "fighting" with some at recess, and some boys are sitting around the deserted stalks, preparing for another fight. This masterpiece in panorama presents the course of "grass-fight"——finding, picking, fetching and fighting, and meanwhile vividly records the merry "fight" among the children on Duanwu.

Grass-Fight of Kids

Not only popular among the women and children, such a rustic-charmed game was also accepted by the literati and became one "elegant" play at the banquet, evolving into a drinking game——"grass-fight wager". The basic rule is as follows: A two-character phrase is put forward——the first character may be concerned with astronomy, season, color, number or treasure with the second character the name of flower or grass, and the participants are required to figure out another antithetical phrase to match the former. For example, if the phrase "laurel" (in Chinese, "monthly" laurel) is questioned, the matching phrase could be Neoinetia falcata or variolosa (sky flower in Chinese, say, monthly vs. sky); green duckweed may find its counterpart crimson tree (green vs. crimson). If the pair of antithetical phrases could match each other in rhyme with novelty, the game player wins.

Grass-treading was also a delightful traditional festivity of the Dragon Boat Festival in the regions south of the Yangtze River. They would go for an outing and tread the grass. On this very day, the dyeing workers would go outing in Mount Wushan and club for a dinner there. While in Northern China, grass-treading was also called "spring outing", "grass-playing" or "illness-preventing by outing".

During the the Dragon Boat Festival, when the plants were green and the riceshoots were fresh, the folks would go for an outing, "running uphill" or "ascending", for they held that all diseases could be eliminated by "climbing" or "swimming" those days. On the Dragon Boat Festival, the whole city would go out and crowd the hills, much relaxed and excited with their cheers and laughter heard everywhere. In Beijing, "Holding wine pots, they will play in Gaoliang or Temple of Heaven... Double-fifth-day play is called 'grass-playing', while the tenth-day 'sending off grass'." In Tieling, northeast of China, on the double-fifth day, "all the locals will climb Mount Dragon Head, playing for one day." While in Jinzhou (Liaoning Province now), "the whole city will go outing, singing and drinking; and some locals will visit the Guanyin (Avalokitesvara) Cave with wine, which is called 'grass-playing'."

It is worth mentioning that the activity of "grass-treading" was also popular in some minority communities. For example, on the Dragon Boat Festival, dressed in their best clothes, the youths of Nama people (one tribal branch of the Bai)——mostly single yet some married occasionally——would climb the mountain together with wine, meat, rice and glutinous paste. Reaching their destination, guys and girls would share the food and drink, singing and courting merrily for the whole day. Therefore, in the eyes of some Nama people, the Dragon Boat Festival was just either a carnival or a lover's day for the youths. On the double-fifth day, the Pumi people living in Tuodian Town of Ninglang County (Yunnan Province) would get together for relaxation, since the wheat had just been harvested and barley seeded. In their holiday dress, the youths would go to the depth of the mountain and walk around the grotto in circles——a religious ceremony. After lighting the butter lamps placed into the stone pits in the grotto, all the pilgrims would drink a few sips of calamus-and-realgar wine. (Generally the wine was fortified with calamus, camphor seeds, xuetong-sargentgloryvine stem and edelweiss, while precious medicines like bear galls or musk might be added sometimes.) They also ate the honey-dipped wheat paste, and then had a shower under the waterfall, dancing together. On this very day, the Pumi people living in Hot Spring Town would gather for a picnic on the hillside. All the family members would walk around the hill, chanting scriptures all the way. Then, inserting one incense stick and kowtowing three times, they piously prayed the gods' blessings for favorable weather and a harvest year. All the Qiang people (if able to walk) would tread on the grass with their feet wetted by the morning dews, for they believed that the dews on the Dragon Boat Festival could make them strong and stout.

Just because of the funny and playable festive activities such as grass-treading and grass-fighting favored by the common people, the Dragon Boat Festival could be accepted by the folks and is still ablaze with charisma today.

1.3 Duanwu-Enjoying——A Harmonious Get-together

For the Chinese people, the Dragon Boat Festival was also an important occasion on which they would visit their relatives or friends with some gifts and lots of good wishes, and the family members could reunite. In Shanghai, "the relatives would present each other zongzi and loquats"; in Suzhou, "zongzi, flowers of wormwood, scented beads, painted fans or other articles were presented"; while in Hangzhou, "relatives would send each other zongzi and colored silk fabrics". With fine craft, such fabrics were always cut into the image(s) of calamus, ricepaper pith, gold-carved immortals or Buddha, birds, insects or beasts, used as hairpins or talismans. Besides the seasonal gifts, all families would prepare big dinners. "They would enjoy the Dragon Boat Festival together via big dinners."(Even the workers might enjoy a half-day holiday) "All trades were closed and the craftsmen would crowd into the taverns, a holiday called 'Baishang'——all the trades could enjoy a day off." On such a rarely leisured festival, several friends were invited to one's home or the tavern, where they would drink and chat cheerfully, sharing (un)happiness of their work or life. By doing so, they could not only forget their pressure or trouble and get much relaxed right away, but also convey to each other their concerns, with their kinship much enhanced.

From the quoted references mentioned above, apart from zongzi and perfume pouches, we may find that the Chinese people would present fans to each other sometimes on the Dragon Boat Festival. As midsummer is coming during the Dragon Boat Festival, owing to its function of cooling, dusting and mosquito-repelling, a gifted fan could meet the practical need of people. According to some scholars' textual research, the folks presented fans on the Dragon Boat Festival with the intention of praying for plague-avoiding. The fans were made of calamus leaves (which could prevent poisonous insects) in the early time, so such calamus fans were also called "plague-avoiding fans". We may find another story about the fans in "Beans Garden Miscellany——Volume I" (Lu Rong, the Ming Dynasty): "In the Fengtian Palace, behind the throne stands a court eunuch holding a fan wrapped by golden silk. Once an old general told me, 'It is not a fan but evil-fending shadow, which was imported from abroad in Yongle Reign Period. I have heard of it but never seen its true face.'" The "evil-fending" fan is accordant with the Dragon Boat Festival in the light of its purpose——to fend off evils. On the Dragon Boat Festival, the presentation of fans among the people also conveys their good wishes——the fierce month and day could be "fanned away" and they could pass the hot summer safe and sound.

Considering the mental need of those regular patients, some doctors would present them some medicines to prevent diseases on or around the Dragon Boat Festival. "The drug-stores would present those regular patients some medicines like atractylodes lancea, angelica root, rhubarb and realgar, which were packed inside the gift box for illness-curing." The medicines mentioned above, which usually could prevent diseases and sterilize viruses, were favored by those patients as they all hoped to avoid diseases. Meanwhile, on or before-after the Dragon Boat Festival, by exploiting the people's apprehension, those monks or Taoists (thought to be able to prevent disasters) would prepare all kinds of seal-character talismans and present them to those regular donors. "Taoists will present Master charms and monks straw-papered charms, which is called 'charm-presenting'. And the nuns would present colored woolen flowers——'presenting tiger flowers' " Those who accepted the charms should visit the temples or Taoist temples and burn joss incense there, offering rewards——the "charm rewards". Since the Wei, Jin and the Southern and Northern Dynasties, for the sake of numerous Buddha-worshiping or Taoist-worshiping religious activities, the pious locals (also with strong beliefs in customs) have built lots of temples or Taoist temples in the regions south of the Yangtze River. They firmly believed that these deities could protect them from any misfortune and help them survive any disaster.

Among the festive activities of the Dragon Boat Festival, there once was one custom—— the interaction between the in-laws (to-be), which highlighted the festival's function of social interaction——in many regions, Duanwu was also called "Girls' Day". Such a custom was much colorful. On this very day, the fiancé would present his future father-in-law gifts; if the married daughter returned to visit her parents' home, she would take wine and meat as gifts and of course, while her natal family would prepare some gifts for the son-in-law. On the Dragon Boat Festival, "the natal family in Shanghai would prepare zongzi, woolen talisman, calamus fan and handkerchief for the son-in-law. They even made leno clothes——'present-

155

ing summer wear' or sent gift money instead occasionally." In Jiaxing district, "several days before the first the Dragon Boat Festival after their daughter got married, the natal family would prepare some gifts like zongzi, cloth fan, colored embroidery and wormwood-weaved tiger, which was called 'sending Duanwu'. (The gifts depended on each family's budget, either rare or cheap was acceptable)" While in Nanjing, "we call the day after Duanwu and Mid-Autumn 'AO holiday' (Nanjing dialect) and all the married daughters will reunite with their parents that day." Not only popular in the regions south of Yangtze River, such a custom was almost accepted nationwide, whose influence even reached some minority communities. On the Dragon Boat Festival, the Tujia people living in Shizhu Tujia Autonomous County (Chongqing Municipality) in the past would take their married daughters home. The sons-in-law (visiting together with their wives) should present their parents-in-law "five-colored" gifts——candies, tobaccos, wine, noodles and pork. While in return, the natal families would entertain them with zongzi and fried dough twists. When the daughter and her husband returned home, the parents would also present them painted umbrellas respectively——"mandarin duck umbrellas", which symbolized the everlasting love between the young couple——weathering storms under the umbrellas, they could be loyal to each other till the end of life. Poor as they were in the past, the Tujia could only buy "oilcloth" umbrellas or straw hats. Now, the much richer locals can present a variety of new-styled umbrellas, keeping up with the pace of the era; and "painted umbrella-presenting" on the Dragon Boat Festival has become an established custom of Tujia marriage customs.

The customs of the Dragon Boat Festival preserved by the locals living in Fuzhou (Fujian Province) highlighted the ethnic relations between the mothers-in-law and daughters-in-law. During the festival, the daughters-in-law would present their mothers-in-law some gifts——shrouds, stockings, ball-shaped zongzi and fans, highly related to their daily life. On the Dragon Boat Festival, with the red gates half-closed, the mothers-in-law and the daughters-in-law (sometimes sisters-in-law as well) would sit in a circle, wrapping zongzi and chatting merrily. If the relationship among the women in this family was somewhat strained, when the daughter-in-law asked "Mum/Sister, come and wrap zongzi, ok?" the latter would answer "Ok", whether she was busy or not. In the agreeable course of "ask" and "answer", the tension would naturally melt away. Sometimes the daughter-in-law would ask, "Mum, how many bundles will you eat?" The mother-in-law might answer, "I could eat up a bundle several years ago, one zongzi last year and only half this year." Everybody would burst into laughter, since there was a funny saying "an old granny will eat less zongzi by half each year". Just in their merry laughter, the relationship between the mother-in-law and the daughter-in-law got much closer, with the living conditions and wits of the locals fully embodied. In a sense, the significance of the Dragon Boat Festival was altered and combined with filiality, which repeatedly stressed the filial piety and obligations to the mothers-in-law. Such "altered" custom could play a vital part in establishing a harmonious relationship between the mothers-in-law and the daughters-in-law, which has long been the most difficult in a traditional Chinese family, fully embodying the living conditions and wits of the locals.

2. Cooking Cultures of the Dragon Boat Festival

Among the Duanwu customs preserved in the regions south of the Yangtze River, the cooking (diet) culture of Duanwu not only bears the cultural accumulation of millenniums here with their brilliant colors and elegant styles, but also contains the locals' good wishes for evil-fending, peace-praying and heath-pleading.

2.1 Zongzi-eating

Eating zongzi is of course one essential custom of the Dragon Boat Festival. Zongzi, also called "Jiaoshu"——"horn-shaped" paste in ancient time, appeared in the Jin Dynasty (265-420 AD) as a seasonal food on the summer solstice. In the Southern and Northern Dynasties (420-589 AD), as Qu Yuan became one vital cultural symbol of the Dragon Boat Festival, people began to consider zongzi-eating a rite closely related to the origin, evolution and rescuing of zongzi and worshiping Qu Yuan——Sanlv Minister. The later generations, though presented zongzi to their relatives and friends, still worshiped the ancestors and gods with it. When Qu Yuan as a cultural symbol became the core concern of the Dragon Boat Festival, wrapping and eating zongzi at last became the most representative festive customs of the Dragon Boat Festival.

Based on the textual research, zongzi was originally offered as sacrifice to worship the gods and ancestors. The triangled or quadrangled zongzi might originate from the ancient in the Zhou Dynasty (11th century BC-771 BC), who used ox or ox horn to worship the God of heaven and earth and the God of cereal. Apart from worshiping the gods, zongzi was also offered to worship the ancestors——"Wrap the glutinous rice with reed leafs and boil them. The cooked food owns a common name——zongzi (called "jiaoshu"——"horn-shaped" paste in ancient time), which is used to worship the Kitchen God or the ancestors." Zongzi appeared in the Wei and Jin Dynasties (220-420 AD). In Chinese, the character 粽 (zong) was firstly written as 糉 , with its right part (radical) meaning "foot-binding". Combined with the left part (radical) " 米 " (rice), the character 糉 could refer to some rice-wrapped food. In the Tang and Song Dynasties, with various flavors and fillings, zongzi became one very common snack sold everywhere. Generally, peanuts, red dates and bacons were usually filled in zongzi in Southern China, while dates, chestnuts and dried fruits were often added in Northern China. Among the fillings, peanut, date and chestnut in Chinese could symbolize "giving birth", as peanut——" 花生 " is homonym to "have children" and date with chestnut（枣栗子）is homonym to 早立子——"have children early", which tallies with one wedding custom in ancient China——wishing the couple to have children as soon as possible after marriage. According to Wu Jun's "Collection of Mythical Stories——Sequel" (in the Southern Dynasties), the quadrangle-shaped zongzi was bound by "five-colored" threads, wishing for the healthy growth of the children.

With the development of the society, zongzi-culture has become more colorful due to the wide spread of zongzi, whose social and entertainment function has also become more obvious. It is recorded in many local chronicles that the presentation of zongzi among the relatives and friends has gained popularity, through which deep friendship and kinship as well as best whishes are expressed. For example, in Suzhou (Jiangsu Province), there is one unique zongzi——"jian-zong" (fit-keeping zongzi)——"whose end is tied by weed-leaf thread to make the eaters strong." People present such a "strong zongzi" in the hope that their relatives and friends become healthy and sturdy. When the locals present zongzi with peanut, date or chestnut filling (symbolizing having children), they hope that their relatives and friends have families merrily vibrant with life and children.

The Dai people, living within the Wuhe Bay of Yuanyang County (Yunnan Province), will celebrate "Zongzi Day" on the double-fifth day, which is an important courting time for the youths. Legend has it that once there were a couple of childhood lovers who loved each other deeply, hoping to live together for ever. However, their parents were all strongly against their marriage, and the love-sick couple ultimately chose to die for love. In honor of their bravery in seeking free love, the Dai people later celebrated "Zongzi Day" with finely-crafted and faintly-scented zongzi on the double-fifth day. During the festival, in their holiday dress, the unmarried singles will sit in a circle under trees in the village, singing love songs. When a fellow falls in love with one girl, he will "cast" a zongzi at her; and if willing, the girl will pick up the love token and follow him to some quiet place to continue their "love story" till sunset. "Zongzi Day" celebrated by the Dai people could offer a golden chance for the youth to choose his (her) lover freely, blessing all of the lovers to live a happy life with their beloved.

2.2 Realgar wine-drinking

Realgar wine would be a must for the Dragon Boat Festival, for it was a custom of every ethnic group nearly all over China to drink such wine on this very day. According to the Local Chronicle of Songjiang (in Shanghai) Prefecture, "during the Dragon Boat Festival, calamus or realgar wine is drunk." It is recorded in "Customs of Suzhou" that on Duanwu, "people will drink realgar wine together with drumfish and spray the wine in the corners of the house to dispel poisonous insects." Realgar wine was also drunk in Hangzhou. The making and use of such wine was once recorded in "Qing Jia Lu" (a book recording the customs and tour sights in Suzhou): "Drink the wine blended with ground realgar powder and chopped calamus-root, which is called realgar wine. Then, smear a little of such wine on the kids' foreheads and spray the wine into the corners to dispel poisonous insects. " In midsummer, the diseases would prevail and poisonous insects would proliferate, so it was a custom to spray the "antivirus" realgar wine into the dark corners of the house to dispel vipers and centipedes and fend off plagues and toxic air. In the house owning a well, a lump of realgar wrapped with silk floss would be thrown into the well to detoxify the water. In Nanjing, there was a custom to clean the eyes (clear away heat) with realgar-blended water. "The locals in Nanjing City will put a little realgar and two 'goose-eye' coins (coins as small as goose eyes) into a basin of clean water, and all the family will wash their eyes with such water in order to avoid eye diseases in a year." "Fry broad beans with realgar and call them 'realgar beans'."

Why would the people believe in the "magic power" of realgar to kill viruses and fend off evils? Realgar is a mineral with another name cockscomb stone. It is recorded that realgar, often used as a mineral medicine in Taoist alchemy, was firstly used by Taoists. In his great Taoist classic "Baopuzi", Gehong (a great Taoist scholar living in the Jin Dynasty with Baopuzi as his literary name) referred to the making of realgar wine. And in another classic "Collected Taoist Scriptures", he put forward a prescription——"realgar-soaked immortal wine": make realgar soaked in the wine. He believed that after drinking such wine, with eyes brightened, the mighty drinker could slaughter the flood dragon in the water, drive away the fierce tiger in the mountain and protect himself from being wounded by arms. The Taoists praised the realgar for its efficacy, which made it a folk custom to drink realgar wine. There was a saying that "all diseases will part with you if you drink realgar wine".

Meanwhile, people all over China would drink calamus wine or even calamus-realgar wine as well: chop the calamus roots into tiny pieces, dry them in the sun and then soak them. In Suzhou, "the locals will drink realgar or calamus wine on the Dragon Boat Festival. While in Wuxi, "people drink the wine blended with chopped calamus roots and realgar." Such customs were not only recorded in "Local Chronicle of Jiaxing County" (during the Chongzhen reign period of the Ming Dynasty), the efficacy of realgar and calamus was also discussed: "Realgar, the essence of the sun, could fend off evils and detoxicate. Calamus could also fend off ghosts and kill all poisonous insects. At noon, soak the calamus in the realgar wine, smear the medicinal wine on the foreheads, chests, hands and soles to fend off evils, and spray some wine onto the walls and windows to dispel the snakes and insects. " The calamus wine owns pungent smell and warmth-stimulating effect, which is beneficial to both lung and stomach, helping to prolong life. One book of drug pointed out: drink the calamus-realgar wine, and all diseases will be cured and all poisonous insects kept away. "Compendium of Materia Medica" also recorded that "able to cure 36 wind syndromes and 12 numbness, calamus wine could also promote blood circulation and cure bone fistula, making hearing accurate and vision clear." As a famous alcohol traditionally, calamus wine has also aroused the interest of some men of letters. For example, Yin Yaofan (a poet in the Tang Dynasty) once wrote: "When I was young, Duanwu always made me high; but now I am old, it could but make me sigh. Unwilling to follow the custom to avoid evils, I am too lazy to hang the wormwoods and talismans; Willing to chat about the peace of life only, I am so happy to drink calamus wine with my friends." Mei Yaochen (a poet in the Song Dynasty) would like to drink nothing but calamus wine on the Dragon Boat Festival. When getting the wine at last in late afternoon once, the poet even wrote a poem to express his excitement: "Calamus wine I get at last in late afternoon, much excited since I got none till noon. Impossibly resisting the custom of drinking such wine, thankfully I bow thrice to the jug of wine." In the Ming Dynasty, calamus wine was even favored by the imperial household and was listed as the seasonal royal wine, which was recorded in "Records of the Imperial Harem" (a book of short-sketched historical records, written by Liu Ruoyu, a high-ranked eunuch in the Ming Dynasty): "Around noon on the double-fifth day, wine blended with cinnabar, realgar or calamus is drunk and zongzi is eaten."

3. Dressing Cultures of the Dragon Boat Festival

Whether to avoid evils or pray for peace, the dressing culture on Duanwu is presented always different from other days. Hidden behind the tiger-head caps, five-colored cords, longevity ropes, perfume pouches and even those fastidiously-made costumes, we could sense the deep feelings and best wishes.

3.1 Tiger-head caps

Children would wear some tiger-shaped ornaments——e.g. tiger-shaped shoes or tiger-head caps given by the elder. In Shanghai, "in the boudoir the tiger-head-shaped pouch is embroidered and hung upon the chest of the kid, which is called 'tiger head' to awe the fierce animals." In Nanjing, when sleeping, the children would be covered with "tiger quilt"——"five-colored silk cloth embroidered with the figure of a Taoist master riding a tiger, usually tied around the back of a kid." In Suzhou, "kids will wear yellow ('Xiong Huang') jerseys, 'tiger bellybands' and 'tiger-head–shaped' coin ornaments." And in

Zhejiang, the locals would tie the tiger-head-shaped pendants made of yellow cloths around the kids' waists, or prepare tiger-painted clothes and draw a tiger on the elder kids' faces. In the regions south of the Yangtze River (even all over China), painting on the kid's forehead was also a popular custom: the most common was to write a character 王 (king) with realgar wine to drive away viruses and awe the evils by "borrowing " the tiger's fierceness. (In Chinese, 王 looks like the wrinkles on the tiger's forehead and the tiger is just the king——" 王 "of the beasts.)

Why tiger-shaped ornaments were worn on the Dragon Boat Festival? With honest looking and steady steps, the mighty and valiant tiger has long been admired and awed by the Chinese people. Legend has it that riding a tiger, Taoist Master Zhang left Mount Dragon & Tiger to conquer the devils. Based on the texture research, the tiger was the totem of the ancient. "The tiger was taken as the symbol of power and fierceness as well. Adoring his prowess, cunningness and shrewdness, the people here worshiped him to pray for courage to ward off calamities." Ying Shao (in the East Han Dynasty) also pointed out in his book "Overview of Customs" : "As the king of the beasts, the strong tiger can settle the disputes and swallow the demons." Holding that the tiger is endowed with spirit, the folks have ever since fortified his valiant image and his role as a justice-upholding guardian to awe the evils and maintain the peace. As the saying goes that "tigers could change the poisonous insects into dust and drive the genies back to the hell", so the women and children would wear some tiger-shaped ornaments on the Dragon Boat Festival to drive away the poisonous insects via "borrowing " the tiger's fierceness, with the evils driven, disasters avoided, illness prevented and healthy life maintained.

3.2 Cord ornaments for health-pleading

During the Dragon Boat Festival, nearly all over China, the folks have long worn colored or five-colored threads/cords as symbolic festive ornaments to drive away evils. The making and wearing of such cord ornaments was once recorded in "Qing Jia Lu——Longevity Cords" (a book recording the customs and tour sights in Suzhou): "Weave five-colored cords with silk and tie them around the left arms of the boys and the right of the girls, which are called 'longevity cords'. "Meanwhile, there was one festive ornament deriving from cord ornament: Weave colored threads into a net and wrap a single garlic with it, then bind this "garlic net" with a copper coin by five-colored threads, or make a tiger-head-shaped "woolen coin".

Historically, the types and shapes of Duanwu cord ornaments are especially rich:

So far as the colors of the materials, there was red cord, five-colored thread, five-colored cord and five-colored silk or the like. In the terms of war-avoiding, there was war-avoiding cord. From the angle of life-prolonging, there was longevity cord, life-prolonging thread, life-prolonging cord, longevity thread and centenarian cord etc..

Evil-avoiding five-colored bracelets

And according to its shapes, there were several as follows: five-colored cord simply weaved by five-colored silk threads; five-colored cord decorated by AuSn-gilded ornament; "fangsheng" (one ornamental pattern folded by five-colored cords) and human-figure-shaped cord; five-color-thread embroidered ornaments in the shape of

165

sun, moon, star, bird or beast.

Around the festival in ancient China, there were even some festive activities like cord ornament watching, playing and marketing. Able to be classified as the treasure of the cord handcrafts in ancient China, these multi-colored fabulous Duanwu cords carried the folks' hope for a better life.

During the festival, the elder would tie five-colored cords around the kids' waists, necks, ankles or arms, or hang them on some children articles like bed curtains and cradles. These cords could only be cut off after the Dragon Boat Festival. During the festival, the children wore five-colored threads or various cord ornaments weaved by colored threads in order to fend off evils and prolong life. In the eyes of the ancient, the five colors——green, yellow, white, red and black just respectively stood for the five fundamental elements——metal, wood, water, fire and earth, which could supplement each other in a circle of life, thus causing the five colors able to fend off evils and prolong life."On the double-fifth day, the custom of tying five-color threads around the kids' arms is called 'war-avoiding' to prevent diseases and plagues." "Tie five-colored longevity cords to overwhelm the beasts." "Tie red or green threads around the left arms of the boys and the right of the girls, testing their growth in the future." Therefore, we could say that the children wore these cord ornaments for the sake of healthy growth, evil-avoiding & fierceness-overwhelming, peace-protecting and life-prolonging.

Apart from the functions mentioned above, as a festive ornament, the Duanwu cord could also be presented among the relatives and friends for feeling-conveying. In the Tang Dynasty (618-907 AD), it was a royal etiquette for the emperor to grant his ministers Duanwu centenarian cords. In the Liao Dynasty

(907-1125 AD, a state established by Qidan-Khitan minority in Northern China), the emperor would wear longevity cords for the "royal celebration ceremony" on Duanwu and grant the longevity cords to his ministers, conveying his concerns and blessings. Moreover, such cords were also regarded as love tokens. Wu Manyun once wrote a poem "longevity cords": "Weaved with efforts in a complex way, the longevity cords are tied today; smiling gently I ask my dear husband, whether he remembers the love knot I once weaved." Generally, wives would present their husbands two kinds of Duanwu cords with different types and shapes: one was longevity cord for "prolonging" their life; the other was war-avoiding cord to prevent war disasters and plagues. And the five-colored threads would symbolize the five directions——East, West, South, North and Center, implying that their husbands would be safe and sound when going out in all directions.

five-colored threads

3.3 Poison-driving ornaments to avoid evils

During the Dragon Boat Festival, the folks all over China would prepare varied "poison-driving" ornaments in the hope that via "Set a thief to catch a thief", evils could be avoided and disasters prevented. The elder would clothe the kids with elaborately- weaved flower-patterned bellybands and "Wudu" (five poisonous creatures) bellybands with bright colors, on which patterns of flowers, birds, fishes, and insects were embroidered to drive away those poisonous creatures. In some places, for the children "Wudu" clothes were specially prepared, on which tiger, scorpion, lizard, spider and centipede (sometimes including gecko, toad and snake) were embroidered. Women would also wear "Wudu"-shaped headwear. In Hangzhou, Zhejiang Province, "Wudu" creatures were also drawn on the sector——"Wudu" fans for the kids. There was a Duanwu ornament combining cord ornament and "poison-driving" ornament, expressing the similar meaning. In Zhejiang, "weave red and green threads into a round disc on which figures of the tiger, the scorpion, the lizard, the spider and the centipede are tied, and tie such 'Wudu' cord around the kid's arm to 'Set a thief to catch a thief'. "On the Dragon Boat Festival in the Qing Dynasty, women used to wear one kind of headwear——Jianren (purl/copper foil-embroidered ornament in the likeness of a kid riding a tiger), and sometimes wore Jianren plus petty bell, tassel, garlic or zongzi——inserted into the hair bun or presented among the relatives or friends. In Jiaxing, Zhejiang, there was once "Jianren tiger"——tiger-shaped cocoon headwear, human-figure-shaped wormwood-weaved headwear or human-figure-shaped silk headwear.

Among the ornaments, the "Evil-driving & Blessing" coins (made by the folks——for playing only, with no denomination) might embody the perfect integration of evil-driving and blessing. According to Mr. Xu Jiahua (a collector), of his two collected "Evil-driving & Blessing" coins, one (an antique coin cast perhaps in the late Ming Dynasty) is a round brass coin with a round hole in the center. On the front side of the coin, there are bat patterns (in Chinese, 蝙蝠——bat is the homonym to blessing) and four traditional full-form Chinese characters " 驱邪降福 " ("evil-driving & blessing") in regular script; and on the reverse, there are patterns of snake, gecko, toad, spider and tiger and some characters like " 钟馗驱五毒 " (Zhong Kui drives away "Wudu").

Another "Evil-driving & Blessing" coin might be cast during the period of Republic of China (1912—1949 AD), a red copper coin for hanging on the wall. On the front side, there is an image of Zhong Kui (with a sword lifted high in one hand and a yellow flag in another) and four characters " 驱邪降福 " in simplified form; while on the reverse, there is an image of Taoist Master Zhang (with a sword in one hand and a talisman in another) and four characters" 诸 神 回 避 " (Master Zhang is here and other gods go away). By integrating the functions of cord ornament and "poison-driving" ornament, such "Evil-driving & Blessing" coins could roll the folk belief in ghost and Taoist religious belief in ghost-chasing into one, epitomizing the folks' living philosophy——evil-driving and disaster-avoiding.

3.4 Auspicious perfume pouches

Perfume pouch embroidering was also an important needlework for the females in the past. Early before the arrival of the Dragon Boat Festival, in a big family, the daughters and daughters-in-law would prepare for stitching perfume pouches. During the process of making such perfume pouches (usu. made of cotton cloth or silk cloth), exquisite craft was indispensable: careful cutting, stitching, mending, pasting and winding. With their talents and skills fully shown in the boudoirs, once the delicate works were finished, these happy females would demonstrate their pouches and present them mutually."In the boudoirs, girlfriends show their own magic stitches in the needlework and present their newly-embroidered pouches mutually."

There were different perfume pouches of various shapes: rectangle, square, triangle, diamond, heart, edge, hod, crescent, sector, etc. There were auspicious patterns embroidered on the pouches—— the twelve Chinese zodiac animals, lion, double fishes, flat peach, flower & grass, worm & bird, lucky beast, vegetable, fruit and Luohan coin etc. Inside the pouches, the fillers could be realgar, cinnabar or herbal medicines like Chinese atractylode and vanilla. By different-shaped cord locks made of five-colored silk threads, several small pouches could be linked as a string, with exquisite styles and lovely looking. When these perfume pouches or realgar pouches were carried, they could not only add festive atmosphere, but also drive away plagues with their faint scent.

On the Dragon Boat Festival, whether old or young, all people for peace-praying would wear perfume pouches with especially great variety: some pouches were embroidered with

Auspicious perfume pouches

a single object or pattern, some with several Chinese characters like 福禄寿喜 (luck, salary, longevity and happiness) and
some several auspicious patterns. The auspicious connotations
implied in those shapes and patterns of the pouches were somewhat intriguing.

4. Home-decorating Cultures of the Dragon Boat Festival

When the most fierce and hottest month (the fifth lunar
month) is coming, how could we forget home-decorating,
another important way of avoiding disaster and evils? Look:
Every household will hang wormwood and calamus on the
door and paste the Master charms and portraits of Zhongkui,
for the sword-like calamus could drive away the evil ghosts and
Zhongkui could dispel the evils and protect his followers.

4.1 Hanging wormwood to avoid evils and eating it to live long

When Summer Solstice came during the Dragon Boat
Festival, the medicinal properties of calamus and wormwood
would reach their best state and the folks would collect them
for hanging on the doors to avoid evils. In the regions south of
the Yangtze River, on the Dragon Boat Festival, after binding a
bundle of calamus and wormwood with red paper or making a
figure of man with calamus leaves, the locals would hang it on
the doors together with peach peduncles and garlic to dispel
ghosts and disasters and keep healthy. In Shanghai, "bundles
of calamus and wormwood were hung on the doors, with
garlic and colored talisman added." In Taicang, Suzhou, "the
locals would hang wormwood, calamus, chinaberry and garlic
on the doors." In Hangzhou, Zhejiang, "calamus swords and
wormwood-weaved tigers were hung on the doors, with peach
twigs inserted."According to "Qing Jia Lu" (a book recording

the customs and tour sights in Suzhou), "the locals would hang calamus swords and strafes (plus peach peduncles and garlic) on the doors to dispel ghosts."

Why are calamus, wormwood and garlic hung on\over the door on the Dragon Boat Festival? The folks firmly held that the sword-shaped calamus and strafe-shaped wormwood, plus the peculiar smell of the wormwood and garlic, would drive the genies and ghosts away. There is a proverb in Shanghai dialect——"Ghost touches the garlic head", which means someone gets muddle-headed and does something wrong. Calamus is one kind of aquatic herbage. In the book "Tao Te Ching——Calamus", calamus is regarded as "the essence of waterweeds and panacea of immortals" and the method of calamus picking, processing and taking is also introduced in detail. When it comes to the medicinal properties of calamus, "Shen Nong's Herbal Classic"——the first medicine book in ancient China which is still extant——ranks it as the top grade: Calamus, owning pungent smell and warmth-stimulating effect, could mainly cure cold, numbness and cough, and help to refresh your mind, nourish the five internal organs, sharpen your eyesight and hearing, get nine orifices unblocked and regain the lost voice. Long-time taking of calamus will keep your body fitter, your mind sober and your life longer. Li Shizhen also added some medicinal effects of calamus in his masterpiece "Compendium of Materia Medica": "When one's limbs are numb and unable to move, or a child gets malaria and feels hot, he could bathe in hot 'calamus' water. Calamus could also cure ear-ringing, head-wind, tear-dropping, pathogenic factor, skin ulcer and kill parasites. Meanwhile, it could relieve rheumatic pains and asthma, reinforce the memory, eliminate worry or chest/stomach pains. Additionally, cholera and earache could be relieved if the patient eats the fried calamus minces while they are hot." It is clear that calamus has long been highly related to man's health in the real life. The great poet Li Bai (in the Tang Dynasty) once composed one poem "Calamus Picker in Mount Song"——"I come here for calamus picking and I'll take it for life-prolonging." Due to their limited scientific knowledge, the common ancient people believed that all diseases resulted from ghosts and evils, so they would naturally hang the calamus with medicinal effects on the "fierce" double-fifth day to avoid evils and pray for a peaceful and healthy life.

Meanwhile, highly praised by the alchemists and scholars, calamus has long been endowed with the connotations of righteousness, justice and valiance. Calamus owns another name Yao chive, whose long and straight leaves look like swords——able to "slay demons" as epitome of justice. According to "Classics", "in Emperor Yao period (about 23rd century BC), the essence of the heaven fell onto the court and was converted into chive, and finally turned into calamus by absorbing 'yinqi' (nutrient in the soil and air). That's why it was also called 'Yao chive'." Qu Yuan, the representative historical figure commemorated on the Dragon Boat Festival, mentioned and praised calamus repeatedly in his masterpiece "Chuci"——"Elegies of The South" ("The Songs of Chu"). For example, in his poem "Shaosming" (name of the goddess guarding the children) he asked, "why are you still sad while their children are under guard?" In the Song Dynasty, the great poet Sushi also thought highly of this plant: "If soaked in a basin of clean water, calamus will keep green for dozens of years with scarce leaves but strong burls and intertwined root hairs, standing erect on the table... Content with placidity, it could endure cold and bitterness, accompanied with clear spring and pure stone." One calamus sword of

Duanwu could just symbolize integrity and nobility——never yielding to vicious power. In ancient Japan, since calamus (し ょ う ぶ) was a homophony to warrior (し ょ う ぶ), apart from hanging calamus on the doors, the Japanese boys would play the game of "calamus-fight", wear calamus knives, play calamus swords, drink calamus wine and bathe with calamus water. We could say that the connotation of calamus has long transcended "driving evils and avoiding disasters", and calamus itself has been endowed with good wishes for the healthy growth, unyielding strength and remarkable success of the children.

4.2 Taoist Master Zhang to keep the house intact and Zhong Kui to catch ghosts

On the Dragon Boat Festival, everywhere around China (esp. in the regions south of the Yangtze River), each household

Portrait of Zhong Kui

would hang the portraits of Taoist Master Zhang or paste Master charms in the central hall and such portraits or charms would stay there for a whole month. According to "Qing Jia Lu—— Master charms", "on the first day of the fifth lunar month, each household would paste Master charms granted by the Taoist temples in the central hall for evil-awing, all kowtowing and burning incense.

Till the first day of the sixth lunar month, the charms would be burnt to send off Taoist Master Zhang." In Hangzhou, "people would cut calamus or ricepaper into the shape of Master Zhang riding a tiger and place this handicraft on a plate, encircled by some five-colored calamus threads or leather-cut insects. They would also weave scripture cones or charm satchels with calamus threads, wormwood leaves or colored woolen threads mixed with gold threads, presenting them mutually." Custom of hanging portraits of Taoist Master Zhang on the doors could be found in Wei Yuanlv's Ci: "Hang the portrait of Master riding a wormwood-weaved tiger, goggling eyes looking down! The lingering ghosts are scared away, while some faraway genies dare to come, only to be caught right away!" We could see the awing posture of Taoist Master Zhang who is guarding the door of each household and scaring the ghosts away, riding a wormwood-weaved tiger with his goggling eyes staring ahead.

Apart from portraits of Taoist Master Zhang, some other "Master charms" (with no portrait but only two carved or written characters ——" 天 师 "——Taoist Master) could also be used. In the preface of "Customs and Festivals in Yangtze River Delta", Wu Manyun pointed out that on the Dragon Boat Festival, "In Hangzhou, the Taoists would present charms on which two characters should be added——天师——Taoist Master, for only such charms were able to scare the ghosts away." According to a survey made in 1929, there were two kinds of pictures of Master charms in Guangzhou, Guangdong Province: one was the portrait of Taoist Master Zhang, the other was Taiji——Eight Trigrams. Added to both were the same words: "Decree——on the double-fifth day, all slanders and lawsuits will be avoided and all poisonous creatures will be dispelled" in the middle, with "Calamus sword to kill evils" and

175

"wormwood flag to greet blessings" on each side.

To worship Taoist Master Zhang involved inviting him to awe the evils and prevent diseases. Then, in the late Qing Dynasty, the people living in the regions south of the Yangtze River began to hang the portraits of Zhong Kui. They usually hung his portraits in the central hall for evil/demon-dispelling for a whole month. Li Fu once wrote a poem——"Portrait of Zhong Kui": "With fierce looking but fearless heart, Zhong Kui sits beside the rose willow and green calamus. We all count on you to wipe out all evils, for we are tortured by the fake ghost catchers." Lu Yusong (in the Three Kingdoms period, 208-280 AD) also described this ghost-catcher: "Standing beside the red pomegranate flowers and green calamus, Zhong Kui looks pure-minded in the picture. Wearing green gown and buck leather boots, he must come from Mount Zhongnan. He has pitch-dark eyes and ragged hair, with crimson lips and red beards. Seeing through all the base souls, he eats nothing but the evil souls. When will he leave his trail in the world? On Duanwu he shall dispel plagues in the world. Alas! Although there are countless evil spirits, none could flee under his sharp sight! Counting on his millions of avatars, we all hopefully see him dispel all the evil spirits!" Originally, Zhong Kui was able to kill five goblins and these goblins in the legend gradually evolved into five bats (symbolizing five blessings) in the mind of the folks.

On the Dragon Boat Festival, each household would paste or hang the portraits of Zhong Kui, in which he maintains the posture of fencing and killing 'Wudu' (poisonous creatures). On the portraits characters like "Divine Judge" would be stamped and "Wulei" charm (able to drive away ghosts) would be pasted. The small-sized portraits would be hung on the doors, while the large-scrolled portraits would be hung in the central halls. Some households would paint red the eyes of Zhong Kui and the seven stars on his sword with cinnabar, holding that the portraits could be endowed with supernatural power then. Worshiped in the regions south of the Yangtze River and all over China, Zhong Kui even has played an important part in the folk beliefs of ancient Japanese. Printed in 1838, "Customs and Festival of Edo" recorded the customs and festivals during the Edo period (1603-1867 AD). In this book, there was an illustration portraying the street view of Edo (present-day Tokyo) on the Dragon Boat Festival: a flag with the portrait of Zhong Kui is waving in the breeze.

4.3 Charms & pictures to dispel evils

Apart from the portraits of Taoist Master Zhang and Zhong Kui hung or pasted on the Dragon Boat Festival, charms and pictures were also used to dispel evils during the festival. The charms to avoid evils first appeared in the Han Dynasty. It was recorded in "Book of the Late Han——Etiquettes" as follows: on the double-fifth day, red cords and five-color printing charms are hung on the doors as decorations to dispel evils. In the Qing Dynasty, in the regions south of the Yangtze River, the poor would paste five-colored peach charms to avoid evils: "The poor will paste five-colored peach charms, on which portrait of Jiang Ziya or God of wealth or picture of cornucopia is painted."

The custom of carving image of the Door God with peach wood originated from the ancient's worship for peach. According to "Mencius", Peng Meng, the servant of Archer Hou Yi (who shot down nine suns in the legend), once smashed the sun-shooting hero dead with a big peach stick. Legend has it that due to his contribution to the world, Hou Yi was apothe-

177

osized as Zongbu God in charge of the ghosts and goblins in the hell. Since Hou Yi——the lord of hell could be stricken dead by a peach stick, the folks believed that peach wood could also awe the evil spirits. Hence, the ancient Chinese apotheosized the peach wood as a soul-endowed object, calling it "immortal wood".

Apart from peach charms, many other charms were also used to avoid evil spirits. In some Taoist temples, the Taoists would paint charms on the yellow core papers ("Taoist Master Papers") and present or sell them to those regular donors, who would paste such charms on the doors for evil-dispelling. "Some Buddhist temples would paint charms on the red, yellow or white core papers and present them to each household on the Dragon Boat Festival. Of course, theirs were not Taoist Master charms, for only the Buddhism-believers would paste them on the doors." On the papers, with cinnabar-inked brushes some official households would write such sentences: "on the double-fifth day, all the malicious slanders shall be stopped!" Then, such charms for evil-dispelling would be pasted on the doors.

Besides charms, there was another kind of evil-dispelling picture pasted or hung on the Dragon Boat Festival. For example, paper-cut "Wudu" pictures would be pasted on the doors and windows in the regions south of Yangtze River. "Wudu" referred to five poisonous creatures——scorpion, centipede, gecko, toad and snake (different creatures in different places perhaps). "The nuns will cut five-colored threads into the shape of the toad, the lizard, the spider, the snake and the tortoise and present them to their donors for pasting on the door heads or in the bedrooms, which are called 'Wudu' charms to dispel the poisonous creatures." Paper-painted or paper-cut "Wudu" pictures would also be hung on the doors. People pasted the

"Wudu" pictures on the walls for the purpose of "setting a thief to catch a thief". Some households would sting the "Wudu" charms or "Wudu" pictures with needles, which involved that the poisonous creatures were stung dead and the evil spirits could be prevented from striking the people then.

Further reading

Preserving and inheriting celebration cultures of the Dragon Boat Festival in China

In May 2006, the Dragon Boat Festival was listed as one of the first National Intangible Cultural Heritages by the State Council of China. In 2008, the Dragon Boat Festival was declared as a public holiday in China. In September 2009, the Dragon Boat Festival was listed as the World Intangible Cultural Heritage by the United Nations Educational, Scientific and Cultural Organization, the first one prior to other listed Chinese festivals.

We are delighted to find it a trend to cherish the intangible cultural heritages now. As for the Dragon Boat Festival, it is preserved and inherited in many places by means of exhibitions and performances. Every year, apart from the four places (Zigui, Huangshi, Miluo and Suzhou) which first jointly applied for the "list" , many other places around China will also hold colorful festive activities like dragon—boat races and bustling fairs, which attract the local masses.

Inheritance of the Dragon Boat Festival can never go far without the efforts of those inheritors. It is wood—carving inheritors in Zigui County (Hubei Province), paper—cutting inheritors in Zigong (Sichuan Province) or folk culture inheritors in Laiwu (Shandong Province), who by all means make beauty stay once and for all in their masterpieces.

In recent years, intangible cultural heritages have stepped into class—rooms and our teenagers could easily sense the charisma of these cultural treasures at close range. When festive exhibitions and performances of Duanwu are demonstrated, many parents with their children are invited to watch, which makes our next generation more proud of their traditional cultures and, therefore, makes possible the inheritance and continuance of such cultural treasures.

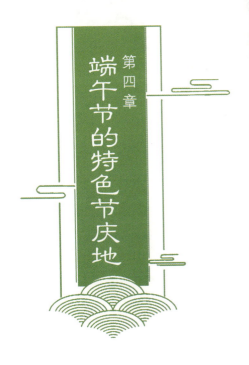

第四章 端午节的特色节庆地

　　端午节流传至今，已经成为老百姓生活中一直践行的节庆活动了。随着越来越丰富的节庆习俗，中国的端午节成功申报世界非物质文化遗产，成为目前我国非物质文化遗产中唯一传统节日。它包括由湖北秭归县的"屈原故里端午习俗"、黄石市的"西塞神舟会"及湖南汨罗市的"汨罗江畔端午习俗"、江苏苏州市的"苏州端午习俗"四部分内容组成，这三省四市的端午习俗集中体现了中国端午节的特色。本章将着重介绍这三省四市的特色节庆。此外本章还选取了江苏省盐城陈家港镇的端午节作为特色节庆予以介绍。

一、
屈原故里秭归的端午节

　　每年的五月，在秭归堪称"端午月"。这个月有三个端午节：五月初五过"大端阳"（亦称头端阳），五月十五过"小端阳"，五月二十五过"末端阳"。秭归端午风俗源远流长，也形成了独特的端午文化，其内涵丰富多彩。2009 年，秭归端午习俗被列入世界非物质文化遗产名录。

（一）龙舟文化

　　秭归是屈原的故乡，秭归龙舟文化以纪念伟大的爱国主义诗人屈原为主题，经过 2200 余年沉淀，意义丰富，久盛不衰。南朝梁人宗懔《荆楚岁时记》曰："五月五日竞渡，俗为屈原投汨罗日，伤其死，故并命舟楫以拯之。"《隋书·地理志》亦载："其迅楫齐驰，掉歌乱响，喧振水陆，观者如云，诸地皆然，而南郡尤甚。"

　　秭归的龙舟竞渡独具风采，龙舟式样色彩缤纷，竞赛水域惊险刺激，祭祀程序庄重肃然，竞赛场面震天动地。特别是吊唁屈原的"招魂"仪式，悲壮婉转，如泣如诉，感人肺腑。颜色各异的龙舟都竖起"魂兮归来"的招魂幡，以白龙为首在江中缓行环游，峡谷中则回响起荡气回肠的《招魂曲》：

我哥哟，回哟嗬，听我说哟，嘿嗬哟！天不可上啊，上有黑云万里，地不可下啊，下有九关八极。东不可往啊，东有旋流无底，南不可去啊，南有豺狼狐狸。西不可向啊，西有流沙千里，北不可游啊，

○屈原故里赛龙舟

○三峡大坝平湖竞渡活动

北有冰雪盖地。唯愿我大夫，快快回故里，衣食无须问，楚国好天地……

秭归龙舟竞渡历史悠久，至今不仅已形成了系统的俗规和完整的唱腔、乐调，而且均在宽阔的长江水域进行。三峡水利枢纽工程兴建后，竞渡水域又选在三峡大坝一公里之上的秭归新县城边长江水域。龙舟竞渡与移民新县城、三峡大坝、长江风光等景观融为一体，其秀丽景观，壮观场面，更是无与伦比。2004年7月，秭归被国家体育总局授予"中国龙舟运动基地——中国全民健身著名景观"，确定该县为全国唯一的龙舟基地和全国十大体育景观之一。

秭归龙舟都用杉木或柏木打造而成。龙头上，用玻璃球镶嵌眼珠或雕刻龙眼，用彩丝制成须髯。舟身涂抹质量上乘的桐油后，再用红、蓝、黄、白等色油漆绘成鱼鳞形的"龙甲"。其中白龙被称为"孝龙"，特指屈原故乡后裔为纪念诗祖屈原尽忠尽孝。龙舟底涂上猪油或牛麻藤汁，专供竞渡之用。秭归工匠打造的10米长龙舟，被确定为全国龙舟竞渡标准龙舟。另外有一种"雕画龙舟"，专门用于乘载观看竞渡的嘉宾贵客。舟上雕梁画栋，有飞龙走兽、鸟虫花草等彩绘浮雕。龙舟下水时，都要选择良辰吉日，并烧香拜佛，以求平安。

○秭归屈原故里旅游线路图

（二）饮食文化

秭归端午饮食文化五彩纷呈，意蕴浓厚。南朝梁人吴均《续齐谐记》载：“原以五月五日投汨罗，楚人哀之，每至此日，以筒贮米祭，今市俗置米于新竹筒中蒸食之，谓之装筒。其遗事，亦曰筒粽。”晋代周处《风土记》载："仲夏端午，端，初也。以菰叶裹粘米，以栗枣灰汁煮之令熟，节日吱，取阴阳尚包裹之象，亦日因屈原也。"秭归作粽讲究，在米粽中置一粒红枣，因此流传有（粽子歌）："有棱有角，有心有肝。一身洁白，半世煎熬。"

○秭归粽子

秭归端午包粽子，一是节日食用，二是投水祭奠屈原，三是作为时令佳品，当作礼物相互馈赠。《本草纲目·谷部》释粽曰："今俗五月五日以为节物，相馈送。或言祭屈原，作此投江以饲蛟龙。"意谓以粽子饲蛟龙，避免投江的屈原尸首被蛟龙伤害。

除了包粽子外，当地还有蒸面馍、饮雄黄酒、食盐蛋的习俗。蒸面馍俗语叫作蒸粑粑，即用上等面粉制作发酵的面馍，再放入垫有芭蕉叶的锅或蒸笼中蒸熟，与粽子一起作为端午节食品，或作为礼物相送，或招待客人。端午节吃面馍，祈求风调雨顺，五谷丰登。农历四月中下旬，几乎家家户户将新鲜鸡蛋或鸭蛋用食盐裹拌后置

○秭归市民包粽子过端午

于空坛中腌制，到端午节时，与糯米粽子一起蒸煮食用。将熟热的盐蛋置于幼儿肚脐周围反复揉动，可以治疗消化不良症状。除以上饮食风俗之外，还有吃大蒜、吃卤面等。

（三）祭祀文化

每逢五月初五，秭归人聚于县城的屈原祠或乐平里的屈原庙，搭设祭坛，开展祭祀屈原的活动。祭祀仪式内容包括：咏屈原诗作，唱招魂曲，挂招魂幡，敬三牲果品，献香花草木，向屈原塑像烧香叩拜，痛诵《公祭祝文》，或默哀，或叩首，或鞠躬等。唐代归州刺使王茂元曾在屈原祠举行公祭屈原活动，从此以后，祭祀活动频繁。自20世纪80年代以来，秭归已连续举办六届"端午文化节"，祭吊屈原的活动则是端午文化节的主要内容。秭归祭祀屈原多在大端午进行，或民间自发举办小型祭祀，或政府主持大型公祭。

在龙舟竞渡前，要举行祭龙舟仪式，亦称"龙头祭"。人们将龙舟头抬进屈原祠，设置祭台。首先将红带或红布披挂于龙头上，称之为"上红"。然后焚香烧纸，唱祭辞，点龙睛（亦称"开光"），放

○为龙头披红

187

鞭炮，祈祷平安。祭祀龙首后，才能将龙舟抬下水开始竞渡。

端午节期间，凡出嫁的姑娘都要回娘家祭拜先祖，看望父母。清代潘荣陛《帝京岁时纪胜·五月端阳》载："已嫁之女亦各归宁，呼时曰为女儿节。"晋代袁山松《宜都山川记》曰："屈原有贤姊，闻原放逐，亦来归，喻令自宽，全乡人冀其见从，因名曰秭归。"秭归人沿袭"贤姊"的美德，出嫁的姑娘在端午节携带着粽子等礼物回娘家省亲，探望父母、兄弟姊妹及侄儿侄女，到娘家祖坟插青挂蟠，祀先灵。

（四）佩饰文化

端午节期间，秭归人们既注重自身装扮，又特别讲究饰物的佩戴，形成了别具一格的端午佩饰文化。主要佩饰有以下几种：

一是系彩丝。屈原故里端午系彩丝的方式有两种：一是作粽时缠丝。《襄阳风俗记》载："屈原五月五日投汨罗江，其妻每投食于水以祭之。原通梦告妻，所祭食皆为蛟龙所夺。龙畏五色丝及竹，故妻以竹为粽，以五色丝缠之。"作粽缠丝是为了屈原投江后的尸首免遭蛟龙劫食。秭归端午龙舟竞渡时，必向江中抛撒缠丝的米粽。二是手臂系丝。东汉应劭《风俗通》记："五月五日，以五彩丝系臂者，辟兵及鬼，令人不病瘟。亦因屈原。"秭归女性及儿童用五彩丝织品系于臂，既起着妆饰和避邪的作用，又意在怀念屈原。

○香囊

二是佩香袋。香袋亦称荷包，形状有梭形、圆形、方形、心形等，图案有虎、猫、鱼、鸟、香草植物等，缝缀严密，形象逼真。秭归人用五色丝线绣成各式各样的香袋，佩挂胸前。

屈原在其作品中有特殊的"香草"情结，如《离骚》："昔三后之纯粹兮，固众芳之所在。杂申椒与菌桂兮，岂维纫夫蕙茝。"这里的椒，指花椒；桂，指桂树；蕙，与兰草同类的香草；茝，指白芷。皆为"众芳"的香草植物。"纫夫蕙茝"，指缝制成的装有蕙茝的香袋。

秭归人为承袭屈子文风及其精神，将香袋中装上桂皮、花椒、丁香、茴香、山柰，或装上白芷、雄黄、花椒、细辛、苍术，称为"五香"。这些香草植物均是屈原在其作品中所颂扬的。民间有"香包身上带，份儿逗人爱"的俗语。传说孩童佩戴香袋既可祛邪避凶，又可强身健体。

三是戴艾虎。《荆楚岁时记》五月五日注："今人以艾为虎形，或剪彩为小虎，粘艾叶以戴之。"东汉应劭《风俗通》记载："虎者阳物，百兽之长也，能噬食鬼魅……亦辟恶也。"说明艾与虎结合，可以辟邪除秽，驱魔逐鬼。少女或少妇用艾叶作虎形钗饰，或剪彩绸为虎形再贴艾叶，戴在鬓边，既能散发出清香，又别具情趣。

（五）禳疫文化

五月正值春末夏初，气温升高，多雨潮湿，各种病原微生物大量繁殖，毒虫滋生，传染病进入高发季节。因此，端午节不少习俗都旨在保健防病。

采露水艾。《荆楚岁时记》载："荆楚人以五月五日并蹋百草，采艾以为人，悬于门户，以禳毒气。"又说："常以五月五日鸡未鸣时采艾……用灸有验。"《本草纲目》曰："艾叶气芳香，能通九窍，灸疾病。"每年的五月初五凌晨，乐平里人家家户户采割"露水艾"，在门头、窗上悬挂一束束用红纸条扎成的白艾。有的熏制艾绒，不仅醒脑提神，而且驱虫治病。还有用阴干的艾叶熬水洗澡或洗脚。

悬艾草的另一种说法是，屈原视艾为恶草，影射楚王朝廷奸党邪人。乐平里的人们为表达对屈原的热爱和对昏君奸臣的痛恨，故悬艾草于门楣，意将奸臣邪人悬于门上示众。

○挂艾草

洗菖蒲澡。《本草纲目》载："菖蒲主治风寒湿痹，咳逆上气，开心孔，补五脏，通九窍，明耳目，出声音。久服轻身，不忘不迷，延年。益心智，高志不老。"秭归端午节期间，以菖蒲叶或根熬制药汤用于沐浴，或泡制菖蒲酒饮用。

洒雄黄酒。民间又认为，将雄黄酒洒到居室墙角、床头等处，既驱蚊蝇和虫蚁，又祛邪避瘟。有的用雄黄酒在小孩的额头画"王"字，或点吉祥痣，或涂抹于耳、鼻等处，以求祛病疫，保平安。

○湖北秭归县，一位老人将雄黄酒涂在一个男孩脸上，这是当地端午节期间的一个习俗，希望孩子们不受蛇虫的伤害。

多彩中国节

端午节

（六）信仰文化

秭归民间信仰纷繁，但其端午习俗形成独具一格的端午信仰文化。

供奉屈原。乐平里流传的"八怪"中的一怪就是"屈原当作神仙拜"——将屈原当作神灵一样对待。屈原祠内存放的石雕文物中，有一尊明代嘉靖十六年（1537）百姓捐赠镌刻的屈原石雕像，原供奉于小青滩白狗峡屈大夫庙内，是国内今存最早的屈原石雕像。像侧铭文曰："荆州府归州桐油沱信人曹端福，善同妻朱氏四子，发心舍造屈原相公一尊，人于白狗峡庙中。永镇此方，保安家犬。"至今，屈原祠及乐平里屈原庙内均供奉着屈原塑像，秭归人有的在端午节时专程前往烧香敬拜，有的家中还供奉着屈原木雕像或画像。

○湖北秭归屈原祠

挂菖蒲剑。据秭归民间传说，秦兵欲挖掘秭归屈原祠的屈原衣冠冢时，神仙托梦告知百姓，家家户户于门旁悬挂菖蒲剑，并在屈原衣冠冢上遍插菖蒲剑。秦兵见遍地皆剑，知晓百姓对屈原有深厚的感情，不敢贸然动手。此后，秭归便形成了端午节于门户上悬挂菖蒲剑的习俗，纪念屈原。

送端阳符。《秭归县志》记载，每遇五月初五头端阳，乐平里屈

191

原庙的守庙人始到周围农户家中送"端阳符"，讨善款、求喜钱、祝平安。画符中的图画均是趋吉避凶、吉祥如意等内容，有时配有"祛邪扫瘟"的红色字画，贴于各户神完之下，三个端阳后将其焚烧。

送瘟船。亦称"送神船"。秭归长江两岸或溪河边的农户，在末端午节当天扎制纸船，并在纸船内放入油捻或短小的蜡烛，傍晚时分点亮油捻或蜡烛后，将纸船放置水面让其随波逐流。此俗意在送走瘟神，驱除瘟疫，以保全家安宁。

旅游小贴士

屈原故里——秭归

秭归县位于中国湖北省西部，地处川鄂咽喉，长江西陵峡两岸。秭归为三峡工程坝上库首，是伟大爱国诗人屈原的故里，也是历史上四大美女之一的王昭君的故乡，楚文化发祥地之一。

秭归山川秀丽，风景如画，名胜古迹有乐平里屈原故里、屈原庙、读书洞、照面镜、兵书宝剑峡、香溪河、崆岭峡、九畹溪探险漂流、道教五指山、昭君故里等多处，每年为纪念屈原的龙舟竞渡、民俗歌舞等也极具当地特色，吸引众多游人前来。

屈原故里景区位于秭归县新县城，高峡平湖美景尽收眼底，同时以屈原祠、江渎庙为代表的24处峡江地面文物集中搬迁于此，2006年5月被国务院公布为第六批全国重点文物保护单位。其保护区主要内容包括以屈原祠为主的屈原纪念景区，以新滩古民居、峡江石刻、峡江古桥等为重点的三峡古民居区，以及屈原文化艺术中心、

多彩中国节

端午节

滨水景观带等景点。

在屈原故里还有一奇值得一提。这里的耕牛不穿绳，却能听从指挥。相传屈 原从楚都回家，快到家门口时，侍者挑书简的绳子断了，一老农当即把牛鼻绳解下来给他。从此以后，这里的牛就不再用牛鼻绳了。

交通：

公共汽车：在宜昌火车东站右侧的宜昌客运中心站有直达秭归（茅坪）的大巴车及旅游专线，流动发车，抵达秭归县城后，可步行或者乘坐出租车抵达景区门口。

自驾游：可以直接从宜昌市区走三峡翻坝高速抵达秭归县城景区门口。

三峡大坝景区至屈原故里景区乘车可以坐景区的专线车或者坐宜昌至秭归的公共汽车，抵达秭归县城后乘坐出租车抵达景区。

二、
西塞神舟会

唐代张忠和诗云："西塞山前白鹭飞，桃花流水鳜鱼肥"。宋代苏轼词曰："西塞山前白鹭飞，散花洲外片帆微。"这便是美丽的西塞山，

193

传承了一千多年的端午禳疫民俗活动——神舟会流传于长江南岸西塞山脚下的道仕袱村（原属大冶地区）。这是道士袱村民在端午时节自愿捐资举办的传统盛会，主要活动有扎制神舟、祭祀、巡游、唱大戏、恭送神舟下水等。

每年农历正月初一，神舟会会员（活动组织者）都要开会，对前一年的活动组织情况进行总结，对本年的活动作出计划安排。农历四月初八佛祖诞生之日，举行扎制神舟（龙舟）的开工仪式。自此，拉开了为期40天的盛会序幕。神舟是整个活动的载体，须在五月初四之前扎制完成。

整个神舟长近9米，宽1.4米。龙头高2.8米，龙尾高2.1米。船体上置牌坊及楼阁，其中牌坊高2.6m，阁楼高1.4米，凉亭高2.6米，从船底到桅杆顶端共高7米。船体为木制结构，用粗制篾席包裹，然后覆上红布，其他部分均为竹制纸扎。亭台楼阁的每个飞檐都饰以龙形。在楼阁窗户处，绘有花鸟及各式戏曲人物。龙舟上安放纸扎人物共103个。作为祭祀活动的载体，龙舟的体量无疑是宏大的；作为民间美术作品，龙舟给人的视觉冲击也无疑是令人震撼的。

农历五月初五子时由道士主持仪式，为龙舟及菩萨开光。被置于庙堂中央的高低座架上供奉着屈原、张元柏等40尊纸扎神像，屈原塑像与观音像分置两侧。菩萨前放置香案，盛满稻米的斗被供奉在香案之上，这便是开光之前的"拜斗米"仪式。道士诵经念咒，人们则肃穆站立并双手合十，在心中默默许愿，祈求风调雨顺。然后道士杀雄鸡取血，或将鸡血涂于菩萨脸上，或绕龙舟一周将鸡血洒于龙舟之上，谓之"开光"。道士一边念经一边相继将12盏油灯点燃，开光仪式便宣告结束。开光之后龙舟与菩萨也就被赋予了人们心目中所能想象得到的神秘色彩，龙舟就成为真正意义上的神舟了。

开光后，虔诚的人们随时都可以恭请道士为其打醮，满足消灾、祛病和求平安的心理。与此同时，活动主办方也开始接受人们自愿捐资办会的资金，并以红榜公之于众。

农历五月十五（大端午）子时由道士主持仪式开始"上登"。所谓"上登"，即恭请各位菩萨依次登上神舟。每请一位（或一组）菩萨之前要打卦，阴卦或阳卦皆不可，只有阴阳并现才行。阴阳卦难以并现时，打卦人及神舟会主要负责人便虔诚下跪而求之。据说可以根据打卦上登顺利与否来预测当年年成的好坏。

随着打卦仪式的不断进行，菩萨也依次登上神舟。菩萨上灯（登）顺序依次为：杨泗、伞师、千里眼、顺风耳、五方（5名）、鸡鸭虎马（4名）、皂班（4名）、四洲和尚、刀手（2名）、框阜、京锣、都天、铳手、大夫、圣母、彩女（1对）、武中军、文中军、老少太监（1对）、土地、舵公、排希（4名）、张元柏（伯）、忠孝王、水手（24）。

农历五月十五至十八日是神舟会的正式会期。这个盛会也是当地一年中难得的一次庙会。盛会期间，四乡八岭的群众纷纷赶来向神舟敬香禀祝，或还愿，或求财，或求子，或求平安，并将自制的纸衣、纸鞋置于神舟内。有人将自带的茶、米洒于神舟内，祈求五谷丰登；也有人将神舟上的茶、米带回家，以求好运。此外，屈原宫前搭好了戏台，当地剧团纷纷登台献艺。屈原宫周围也形成了一个集贸市场，人们在进香看戏之余，还可买些日用品，会会亲朋好友。正是有这样一举多得的效果，当地群众才热心捐资办盛会。

农历五月十六上午八点，神舟由16名青壮小伙抬着出宫巡游，在村内绕行一周。只见华盖簇拥、旗幡导引、金锣开道、鼓乐齐鸣，场面宏大蔚为壮观。所到之处，家家户户都要在门边悬菖蒲挂艾草，在门口设香案、燃香烛，摆上酒、茶、米、水果等供品恭迎神舟到来。每到一家，都要放鞭迎接，撒茶米、祭拜，并燃烧艾草，恭迎神舟并送走邪气与不祥。

农历五月十七晚，神舟底下点亮48盏长明灯，村民通宵请道士打醮并守夜。

农历五月十八日上午十点神舟出宫，由道士主祭，杀鸡取血书写天师符置于神舟的龙口和龙尾。祭祀完毕，道士和神舟会全体成员共同为神舟开路，由16名青壮小伙抬着神舟恭送入江。此时江上众多渔民在船头摆香设案、齐鸣鞭炮、绕神舟三圈，以示送行。来自十里八乡的人们云集在西塞山下，目送神舟入江。他们双手合十、虔诚跪拜，祈求神舟带走瘟疫和灾难，祈盼吉祥与安康。神舟下水之后，切忌停靠或调头，故神舟所流经的下游各地为防止神舟停靠本土，纷纷组织"打龙舟"的活动。

○西塞神舟带着人们的祝福在阵阵爆竹声中准时下水

之所以说神舟会是送瘟神的盛会，是因为神舟上有位叫作张元柏的重要菩萨，他是我国民间传说中司瘟疫的瘟神。《中国道教》说："瘟神又称五瘟使者。中国古代民间信奉的司瘟疫之神。即春瘟张元伯（柏），夏瘟刘元达，秋瘟赵公明，冬瘟钟仕贵，总管中瘟史文业。"张元柏作为五瘟之首，被请上神舟送入长江，神舟便成了名副其实运载瘟神的瘟船。

从每年的农历四月初八扎制神舟，到农历五月十八大端午恭送神舟下水，神舟会历时40天。这样规模之大、时间之长、参与人数之多的民俗活动在我国较为罕见。神州会在上千年的传承过程中，逐步融入了端午纪念屈原的传说，使其祭祀活动与祭吊屈原结合在一起，这对弘扬民族精神，促进民族文化认同产生了深远影响。

西塞神舟会之所以能流传这么多年，还因为有详尽的文字图片史料。在扎制神舟的纸扎艺人手里保存着代代相传的神舟样式手绘本，有两个版本——清光绪八年版和民国二十四年版。其中民国二十四年版为手绘线装本，封面有"龙舟绘图杂志民国二十四年蒲月吉日 游新亭订"字样。本子内容含盖节符神咒、神舟样式、幡旌旗华盖样式、满船物件名称及张元柏等各路菩萨的名称，是整个神舟会的图式指南。

从汉唐直到元、明、清，道仕袄一直是繁华的政治、经济、文化中心城镇。但从东汉末年到新中国成立前，发生在西塞山的战争达一百多次。由于常年战乱，人们只有通过神舟送瘟神这一活动来表达对幸福安康生活的祈盼。从"拜斗米""撒茶米"等祭祀活动到祭祀场所标语"神舟诸尊菩萨显灵""有求必应有应必争"，以及人们对神舟的顶礼膜拜等行为可以看出，人们企盼风调雨顺、五谷丰登，达到祈祥纳福的心愿。

旅游小贴士

黄石西塞山

西塞山风景区位于湖北省黄石市城区东部长江南岸，规划总面积 0.495 平方公里，区内以西塞山险峻秀丽的自然景观和纷呈的胜迹为实物主体，有道仕袄、古黄石城等著名景点，旅游资源非常丰富，景点众多。黄石西塞山风景区海拔 176.5 米，周长 18.5 公里，历史上就以其吴头楚尾的地理位置和险峻的地形集古战场和风景名胜于一身。

从东汉末年到新中国成立前，发生在西塞山的战争达一百多次，文人雅士观赏西塞山晨曦暮色述志言情而吟诗填词近百篇，并在悬崖陡壁上留下不少摩崖石刻。市园林部门从 1985 年 5 月起，在西塞山着手进行游览小道、长廊、上观亭、桃花亭、沿江铁链护栏和桃花古洞、古钓鱼台的维修建设，景点不断得到开发利用。

　　地址： 黄石大道 654 号附近。

三、

汨罗江畔的端午习俗

　　汨罗地处湘东北，西临洞庭湖，汨罗江自东向西流贯全市，注入洞庭湖，是楚文化的发源地之一。汨罗江畔端午节习俗含盖了屈原文化、龙舟文化、节庆文化等多重内容，一条名江（汨罗江）、一位名人（屈原）、一座古祠（屈子祠）将它们紧紧连为一体，并衍生出一项与祭屈相关的龙舟竞渡活动。

　　汨罗端午习俗主要有：

1. 造龙舟

　　汨罗的龙舟多以自然村或姓氏家族为单位打造，一般在古历四月中旬即开始。造舟前大家推举出三至五位德高望重的人组成龙舟会，其经费都是村民们自愿募捐的。造舟场地一般选在祠堂的大厅或临时搭建的工棚。四周围得严严实实，不准女人和小孩接近。因为女人属阴，"阴"有翻船之虑；小孩口无遮拦，恐说出不吉利的话。请来菩萨问卦择黄道吉日开工，在主筋木前摆一张小方桌，桌上摆上香烛，一阵鞭炮过后，"掌墨师"（即为主的木匠师傅）拿公鸡一只，割鸡冠血抹在筋木上，念上一大段祭词，祭祀之后，掌墨师砍下第一斧，谓之"发木"。造船工程正式开始。雕龙头则在另一间屋内进行，闲杂人等不得擅入，雕成后请老匠人开光（点睛），亦要举行隆重的祭龙头仪式，谓之"关头"，然后日日香烛供奉。龙舟造成后还要大摆筵席俗称龙舟宴以示庆贺方能下水。

○第七届中国汨罗江国际龙舟赛场上6只参赛队伍进行激烈角逐

2. 上红

龙舟下水既是娱乐也是操练。沿江如有此条龙舟所在地的至亲好友，其亲友必备上一两条香烟，一两瓶酒，一条红绸，一挂鞭炮，将红绸系在竹竿上，来到江边，举起竹竿一边摇晃一边呼喊本族龙舟，并燃放鞭炮。被呼唤的龙舟则奋力划向岸边，待龙舟靠岸后，岸上持盘者面对龙舟念上一段赞词。龙舟上的头儿，一般是摧桡（指挥）或扶招（舵手）者上岸，接过礼品互换位置回诵一段赞词，然后将红绸系于龙角上，仪式告毕。

3. 朝庙

农历五月初四前，汨罗江两岸的龙舟都要陆续划到屈子祠所在的玉笥山下江边，由头头扛着龙头。划手们扛着桡子——划船用的桨，排着整齐的队伍，敲锣打鼓来到屈子祠内屈原神龛前，将龙头放到香案上，摆上供品（古时要求用太牢之礼即整猪整牛整羊），敲钟擂鼓，管弦同奏，铳炮齐鸣，主祭者长袍马褂，净手正冠。诵祭文，展祭联，器乐三引，香、果、酒三献，众三叩首，反复三次，是为三跪九叩。因屈子祠古称汨罗庙，故其仪式称"朝庙"，实际是祭祀屈原。仪式结束，为首者扛起龙头，率众绕神龛一周，在鼓乐鞭炮声中步出屈子祠，飞奔下山，冲入汨罗江中，五沉五浮，谓之给龙头洗澡，再把龙头安上船首，就可以参加竞渡了。

4. 扯龙须

龙头的胡须一般用苎麻染色制成，在龙头朝完庙或抢红靠岸的瞬间，观众中有眼明手快者，扯下一两根龙须系在小孩的手腕上，俗信可保小孩一年平安。

○道县端午龙舟启程

5. 竞渡

众龙舟在江面上悠闲地划过，非竞赛时前后各四桡将桡子立于胸前，随船俯仰。当两条船划至并列的位置时，往往一条

多彩中国节

端午节

船上的人就向另一条船上的人发出挑战："拼一船好啵。"另一条船上的人当然不示弱，应声"好讪"。随着一声刺耳的令哨，锣鼓大震，前后各四位划手立即将桡子扦入水中拼力划起来，江面上顿时水花飞溅。两船相拼必有输赢，有时快者还从慢者的船头包抄过去，称之为"包头"，这是竞渡之大忌，往往因此引发械斗。划输的船发誓来年一定要划赢。到了第二年，他们早早地重新造船，早早地操练，抛田荒地也在所不惜。因此汨罗江畔流行"宁可种输一年田，不能划输一年船"的说法。划赢了的要大摆筵席，搭台唱戏以示庆贺。

6. 草划子竞渡

汨罗江一带的村民们每到春天都要到洞庭湖湖洲上打青草，用一种狭长的小船运回来沤到田里做肥料。这种小船就叫"草划子"，就是平时捕鱼的鱼划子。造不起龙舟的地方，年轻人又想热闹，便将这种草划子中间竖起将军柱，系上缆绳，挂上彩旗，用桨做"招"（即舵），钉上几把桡子，也敲锣打鼓地划起来。他们不与正规的龙舟竞赛，只与草划子竞赛或自娱自乐。

7. 收龙舟

相传，屈原五月五日投江，五月十五日才被打捞上来，故此汨罗江一带的乡民在五月十五还要举行一次龙舟竞赛，名曰过"大端阳"。过完大端阳才将龙舟洗净，燃放鞭炮，点上香烛，祭祀一番再将龙舟收起来，意为"谢龙"。公举一户大家都信得过的人家，恭恭敬敬将龙头送到他家楼上，安放在事先准备好的小方桌上。这户人家要负责在每月的初一、十五给龙头燃烛、上香、作揖，直到来年端午节。

8. 饮雄黄酒与插菖艾

在酒里掺上雄黄，称雄黄酒，大人喝酒，并将酒抹在小孩的额头上，可避蚊虫侵扰。很多人家还将雄黄酒洒在房前屋后，墙角旮旯，防蛇蝎等五毒侵入。端午节前夕各家各户都要采菖蒲、艾株，扎束悬挂于门窗两旁，并用黄纸条写上"五月五日午，屈原骑艾虎，手持菖蒲剑，驱魔归地府"贴在门上。还要刈回一些收藏待用。

9. 包粽子

粽子是祭典必备的祭品。端午前后，各家各户都要包大量的粽子，按配方分类有肉馅粽、果馅粽、豆馅粽、酱菜馅粽和纯糯米粽，按形制有九凤朝阳九子粽、屈原八仙粽、屈子艾香粽、屈子珍塔粽等。

10. 抢龙水

○汨罗市旅游交通图

202

端午节这天天刚亮时，沿江居住的人家都要抢先到汨罗江挑回一担江水倒到家里的水缸内，人们笃信，这时龙已经出游，喝了龙沐浴过的水可以强身健体。

11. 踏青

端午节清晨，人们光着脚或穿上新布鞋，奔向江畔草地，往复踩踏，让露珠尽沾双脚，以祈健身。

12. 洗端午澡

端午节这天，会游泳的人都要跳到汨罗江洗一次澡。俗信，洗了端阳澡可祛病除灾。

13. 挂香荷包

古历四月中旬开始，人们将一些中草药和头年收藏的干艾叶，拌上冰片等香料。用各色碎布缝成粽子、桃子、枕头、小锁等形状，系上五色彩线，挂在小孩的脖子上，以避灾除病，戴到大端阳才扔掉，名为"扔灾"。

14. 调节

端午节前数日，已出嫁的女儿必定要准备一份礼品，包括粽子数十个、酒两瓶、鲜猪肉一块、蒲扇若干把（如娘家有未出嫁的小姨子则用折扇），偕同夫君送给娘家，谓之"调节"。端午节这天丈母娘必定要接女婿、女儿、外孙回娘家。有儿歌曰："汨罗江长又长，外婆接我过端阳。一不要你的饼，二不要你的糖，只要你的黄壳粽子给我尝。"

15. 歇端阳

端午节这天必定要休息。汨罗江一带有"牛歇谷雨马歇社（方言读 sha），人不歇端阳惹人骂"之说。

延伸知识

汨罗江畔"四大活动"闹端午

每年端午节，汨罗江畔都要举办大型的国际龙舟节。按照《"我们的节日·端午"——2015 第十一届中国汨罗江国际龙舟节主题活动方案》，端午期间汨罗江畔举办了民间龙舟邀请赛、音乐帐篷节、快乐戏迷、摄影大赛四大活动，体现"民间·民俗·民族情"主题。

活动一："龙瑞罗城"汨罗江民间龙舟邀请赛，于 6 月 19 日下午至 20 日上午在汨罗江国际龙舟竞渡中心举行；活动由 200 米、500 米直道预决赛组成，20 支来自汨罗本地的龙舟队参加当天的比赛。

活动二："狂欢端阳"汨罗江国家湿地公园音乐帐篷节，于 6 月 19~20 日在汨罗江国际龙舟竞渡中心两侧湿地公园举行；活动内容包括"感受端午情、浓浓粽子香"包粽子比赛，"爸爸妈妈咱去哪？"亲子活动，怒放摇滚英雄演唱会，拔河比赛，角斗士比赛，篝火晚会，龙舟体验 7 大项。

活动三：第三届湖南省快乐戏迷岳阳赛区海选专场（汨罗），于 6 月 19 日上午在汨罗江国际龙舟竞渡中心举行。评选环节包括简短唱段清唱和伴奏演唱两部分。

活动四：中国（汨罗）首届"端午源头"国际摄影大展，从 6

月 20 日开始，邀请国内知名摄影家赴汨罗，进行摄影采风创作，发掘汨罗江端午文化，展现汨罗生态、人文、旅游风光及端午习俗。评选出一批优秀作品，进行巡展、网上展览、编辑出版等，并在 2016年龙舟节举行颁奖仪式。

四、
苏州端午节

在苏州，端午节曾经是民间最为隆盛的传统节日之一。

五月五日天未燠，南门城外龙船作。
龙船作，人头簇，衣香扇影摇波绿。
龙船之高高于谷，龙船之长长十拓。
船头船尾台高盖，俊儿上驾青丝络。

清人石方洛这首题为《龙船》的诗，生动地描写了吴地端午龙舟竞渡的盛况。

苏州的龙舟竞渡，主要集中在胥江。此外，山塘、枫桥水滨及太湖等地也是竞渡的好地方。

205

竞渡时，船上结彩张旗，勇士们奋力划船。这时，锣鼓喧天，鞭炮齐鸣，河边观者如云，万人喝彩，气氛热烈。龙舟竞渡的沿岸，常扎起许多牌楼，搭起许多凉棚，还有人设了酒席，坐在那儿边吃边看。龙舟过牌楼时，便燃放鞭炮，这时龙舟又会起劲地表演一番。

苏州的竞渡，颇有特色。据《乾隆吴县志》记载："端午为龙舟竞渡，游船聚集，男女喧哗，管弦杂沓。投鸭于河，龙舟之人争入水相夺以为娱乐。"将鹅、鸭之属引入竞渡之中，是苏州人的创举。在商品经济特别发达的苏州，竟还发展成了"放标"之嬉。即商家们叫人在稻草或蛋壳里放上彩券掷于水面，龙舟上的健儿们见了便跳入水中去争夺——在龙舟竞渡的同时又展开了一场游泳比赛，顿时浪花四溅，观众及同舟伙伴齐声呼喊，促其加劲，鼓励他夺标而返。彩券上写有奖品名称，夺得者即可到指定商号领奖。奖品大多是糕饼、糖果、粽子等吃食或折扇、毛巾等日常用品。这也可谓是商家参与赛事，利用赛事做商业广告的最早尝试。

粽子是苏州人端午不可或缺的食品。苏州人还用它来祭祀祖先并互相馈赠。端午节一早，家家户户的厨房就会飘出粽子箬叶的阵阵清香。

○苏州市民展示包好的小脚粽

旧时的苏州人在这一天有很多禁忌，如忌晒床上的席子，忌用茅草盖房子等。为了化解这一天的不吉利，人们想出了不少办法。过去未满周岁的孩子，端午这一天都要到外婆家去过，称为"躲午"；端午节，家长还要给孩子戴老虎头帽子，穿老虎头鞋子；端午节，家家还都要挂出钟馗像。据说钟馗有捉鬼的本领，挂上了钟馗像自然就能够驱鬼避邪了。信佛、道的人家，还会通过做佛事、用朱墨画韦陀像，或到道观去请一张"天师符"贴到厅堂里等方法，来达到"镇恶"的目的。饮雄黄酒、带香包也是苏州端午驱毒习俗。苏州人给七岁以下的小孩子穿上印有老虎图案的"五毒衣"。

○虎头鞋

禳解端午之毒的方法还有很多。人们将艾叶做成人形，将菖蒲做成宝剑的样子，把蓬条做成鞭子，杂以蒜头，挂于门首，避邪驱鬼。同时，人们点燃苍术、白芷等中草药，烟熏室内，并用艾叶、菖蒲烧汤沐浴。

○五彩绳

207

还有的人家以"五色桃印为门户饰，以止恶气"。

苏州女子，心灵手巧，端午节令，更是她们"露一手"的难得机会。端午前数日，她们就开始缝制一种形似荷包的绣花袋，里面放上雄黄、苍术、香草等中草药，小巧可爱，香气扑鼻，所以称为"香包"或"雄黄荷包"，带在身上以驱瘟散毒。袋子外面用丝线绣上花卉、鸟兽等图案，十分漂亮，惹人喜爱。

兰汤沐浴也是一种寓意健康的习俗。每到端午节，人们都会用艾草、菖蒲等几十种花草和药材，泡制后用汤水沐浴，洗过之后据说可以达到蚊虫不侵的效果。这一习俗在全国各地都有，但只有在江南一带，才被称为"兰汤沐浴"，体现出一种江南地区更为精致的文化特点。

○苏州端午粽子

○雄黄酒

苏州人在端午节一直有"吃五黄"的习俗。所谓"五黄"，是指黄鱼、黄鳝、黄瓜、黄泥咸鸭蛋黄和雄黄酒。黄鱼、黄鳝等都是时令食物，很有滋补功效，而雄黄酒则是有杀菌杀虫，使蚊虫不侵的功效。

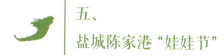

五、
盐城陈家港"娃娃节"

江苏省盐城市响水县陈家港镇的端午节，以自然形态出现于每家每户的生活中。陈家港镇是居于灌河入海口的海港小镇，其端午节又称为"娃娃节"。过端午的时候以孩子为中心，除了插艾、吃粽子、系五彩线、佩香包以外，还要煮蛋、用青草汤沐浴、吃雄黄酒腌制的黄瓜，小孩子还要穿新衣服。这里的人们对端午很重视，几乎家家都过节（即使没有孩子的家庭也是如此）。陈家港镇的端午节习俗可以分为两个方面来记述，一是节前准备；二是节中行事。

（一）节前的准备

陈家港的居民对端午有着别样的情怀，离端午还有几日的时间便开始准备过节了。端午节前，街上随处可见售卖端午用品的摊子。大姑娘小媳妇结伴上街，各自挑选着心仪的物品。人们通常会先采买穿戴的东西，主要有五彩丝线、香包和衣服。五彩丝线，其实并不止五种色彩，除了白色以外，其他颜色基本都有。以前的丝线都是绣花线，现在出现了开司米线，甚至有的直接编制成了手链，上面还缀有合金或者银质的小铃铛、花生、花朵等饰物，精致可爱，让小姑娘们爱不释手。香包也是种类繁多，花鸟造型、生肖图案的各式香包令人目不暇接。端午节的香包以前都是由手巧的女子自己缝制，多缝制为心形，里面放上自己采的香草或制作的干花瓣。现在街上卖的香包多是机器绣花，香料的种类也增加很多。此外，服装店也是门庭若市，因为这里还有小孩穿新衣的习俗，家长们都希望把家里的孩子打扮得焕然一新，迎接端午的到来。

　　除了穿戴物品以外，还有许多其他物品需要购买，主要有用来包粽子的芦苇叶（当地称为柴叶）、糯米、白糖、红枣及其他干果，此外还有艾草、菖蒲、矾块、雄黄等。芦苇叶是包粽子所不可缺少的，为了端午早上吃粽子，人们通常提前一天把粽子包好并煮熟。除了买穿戴用品和包粽子以外，还有其他东西要提前准备，不过也有人会在端午当天碰运气去获取——捉一只癞蛤蟆，个儿越大越好。捉癞蛤蟆说容易也不容易，逢上雨天倒是很容易见到的，但是若碰到连续的晴天便有些困难了。所幸这癞蛤蟆也不是家家都要准备的，一般有老人在的家庭才会去捉。

（二）节中的习俗

　　这里端午的习俗主要体现在上午和正午两个时段，上午主要是插艾、吃粽子和蛋，然后是吃午餐。正午要更忙碌一些，除了沐浴、吃雄黄酒腌制的黄瓜、系五彩线、佩香包以外，还要腌制黄瓜矾和蛤蟆矾等。除此之外，还有几个人们最重视的习俗：

　　第一，插艾草菖蒲。镇上老人说，以前人们是农历五月初一的时候插艾草和菖蒲用以辟邪。传说古时候有一种妖怪，会在五月来临的时候突然出现，见人便咬，有的时候还吃人，人们为此恐惧不已。

后来有一天来了一个游方道人，告诉人们在门上插上艾草和菖蒲，这样妖怪就不敢出来了。人们依法行之，果然妖怪不敢再犯，后来插艾草菖蒲这一习俗便慢慢流传了下来。现在很多人习惯在端午的早上插艾草和菖蒲，不过也有人在端午节前几天便插上。艾草主要是插在各屋的门檐和窗檐角上，艾草的数量也不一而足，有的是直接插一根，有的喜欢取几根捆成一束再插。有的人家喜欢在门檐和窗檐的一侧（左右都有）插艾，也有两边都插上的。当地有句

○端午节街头卖艾草的老人

俗语：“五月五蚊虫出。”艾草和菖蒲能发出蚊虫害怕的香气，当地人重视艾草超过菖蒲，有“端午不插艾，死后变成大白菜”的说法。

第二是早饭要吃蛋。端午这一日，主妇们会很早起床，尤其是家里有小孩子的。她们早上要做的第一件事是到青草多的地方采摘最嫩的青草头，最好是在露水还没干的时候采来。采完草头再回到家里做早餐，主妇们会将事先煮好的粽子放到锅里煮，此外还要在同一个锅里煮上鸡蛋、鸭蛋或鹅蛋。这样一锅煮熟了以后，蛋也有了粽叶的清香味，别有一番滋味。大人们喜欢直接吃粽子，而小孩子则喜欢将粽壳剥掉，将里面白胖软糯的粽仁放到碗里，蘸着白糖吃。孩子们喜欢带上家里煮的蛋到学校和同学“斗蛋”，比一比谁家的蛋更坚硬，赢了的人会很开心。当地还有“三鸡四鸭治晕病”的说法，也就是端午这天吃上三个鸡蛋和四个鸭蛋，便可治疗眩晕。

第三是沐浴穿新衣。吃过午饭以后，主妇们会取早上采摘的青草头煮上一锅水，水色呈淡绿，看起来清爽莹澈。至正午时分，将这水混些凉水弄成温水，给家里的小孩子沐浴。据说这天用青草头

211

煮的水给小孩沐浴，可以祛除湿疹，治疗一些皮肤疾病。等到洗完，大人会取来雄黄和酒按比例调制成糊糊，并用手将其抹在孩子的耳朵、肚脐、肛门等处。此外，还要吃上一片雄黄和酒腌制的黄瓜片。这一系列活动结束以后，孩子们便可以穿上家长给准备的新衣服了。

第四是系丝线佩香包，当地人称之为"扣丝线"。也就是将丝线扣在手腕、脚腕抑或是指头关节处。系丝线一般是长辈给晚辈系。取来均匀配好的丝线，从中间绕着手腕一圈，丝线两端一寸长短，然后打个半结，并将结拉紧使之不至于松脱，比对垂下的流苏，拿剪刀剪齐。小孩子一般手腕脚腕都会系上，年纪大些的只系一个手腕。所谓"男左女右"，系丝线也遵循这一规则。汉代应劭《风俗通义》说："五月五日，赐五色续命丝，俗说以益人命。"南朝梁代宗懔的《荆楚岁时记》中也有记载："以五彩丝系臂，名曰辟兵，令人不病瘟。"这些说法都以五彩线为长命缕或辟邪物，但是小镇的说法有所不同，认为系上五彩丝线，手脚便不会抽筋。也有人是哪里容易抽筋便将丝线系在哪里，因而除了系手腕外，脚腕、指头等处皆可以系。

香包也是由丝线作索，系在脖颈之上，有祛除晦气的说法。五彩丝线一旦系上，不到农历六月六不能随意剪掉，否则便不灵验了。这一说法源于牛郎织女的传说。当地人认为在六月六这日将五彩线剪下扔到房顶上，等到七月七的时候便会被喜鹊衔走用来搭桥，这样牛郎织女才能相会。若是丝线被喜鹊衔走，七月七日的晚上，躲在葡萄架下，便可以听到牛郎织女说的悄悄话。

第五是制矾。许多人家要在端午这日的正午腌制黄瓜矾和蛤蟆矾，这也是事先要准备好一只癞蛤蟆的原因。所谓的黄瓜矾，便是用黄瓜、雄黄和矾做成。首先取半截黄瓜，将其瓜瓤掏干净，然后在黄瓜内侧抹上一层雄黄，再将块较小的矾块塞进去，最后拿线从两边穿孔，悬挂在屋檐。这样经过十多天的风吹日晒，黄瓜的皮已经是干巴巴的，它的水分和雄黄便进入矾块。这时，将其中的矾块取下便可以用了。癞蛤蟆矾的做法源于"以毒攻毒"的说法，人们认为癞蛤蟆皮肤上是有毒的，因而可以用来治疗一些病痛。当地人治疗"牙痛"有个小偏方，便是用癞蛤蟆皮肤上的浆汁抹在疼的部位，若是有龋齿，直接将蛤蟆的浆滴入，便可止疼。俗语说"越老越毒"，人们之所以喜欢用大的蛤蟆，除了这个原因以外，还由于大的蛤蟆含的浆容量比较大。不过制作癞蛤蟆矾的方法比较残忍，人们直接将矾块从活蛤蟆的嘴巴塞进去，直到蛤蟆的肚子再盛不下为止，然后也依样吊在屋檐下。蛤蟆矾制作的时间相对要长一些，一般要二十天到一个月左右，等蛤蟆完全风干再取出其体内的矾块。之所以选择端午做黄瓜矾和蛤蟆矾自然是有原因的，人们认为五月五的阳光是至阳的，可以杀菌，正午太阳光能量是平时的百倍，吸收了阳光的矾块消炎效果也会加倍。家里若是有人生了口疮什么的，只需要取些矾块（轻微的可用黄瓜矾，严重些的可用蛤蟆矾，但是并没有明确区分）将其化开，用矾水漱口，很快便可以消去，这便是矾块

○五月端午节娃娃们最开心

的妙用。过了正午，腌制完矾块以后便也没有其他的活动了，端午也就算是结束了。

这里的端午节又是"娃娃节"，孩子们有新衣穿，还有好吃的，所以会格外开心。青年男女也很喜欢过端午，他们也像孩子一样穿新衣服系丝线，玩得不亦乐乎。主妇们尤其注重端午了，若是自己的吃食比别人做得好，孩子打扮得比别人的漂亮，那她们会觉得很有面子。老人很喜欢热闹，看着儿孙满堂的热闹景象就欣慰不已。

（三）年年过端午

小镇的居民之所以格外重视端午，是因为人们相信五月初五是特别的一天，端午阳光杀菌的功效很强，特别是正午的阳光对治疗疾病有独特的功效，到了端午便意味着真正进入了夏季。小镇沿海，这一段时期的海产品不仅种类多而且个大味美，是品尝美食的好时机，而那些依靠贩卖海鲜为生的居民则可以比平日挣更多的钱。而如果端午这天不是晴天也无妨，这里有句俗语"端午下雨长海蜇"，这一天下雨则意味着丰收。这个"长"是长得很快、很多的意思。海蜇多了，表示当年会大丰收。

总之，不管是晴天还是下雨，对人们来说这一天都是吉祥。

盐城市陈家港镇

陈家港镇是江苏省百家名镇，隶属江苏省盐城市北部城镇，分属响水县。陈家港镇位于响水县东北部，被誉为"苏北黄浦江"——灌河的入海口处。全镇下辖 13 个村、6 个居委会，辖区面积 151.6 平方公里，总人口 6.8 万人。陈家港镇东濒黄海，北依灌河，原名"蛏架港"。1929 年建镇，物产丰富，四鳃鲈鱼蜚声海内外，风光旖旎，灌河八景和开山岛别具特色，是一个现代化的港口城镇，经济强镇、军事重镇和旅游大镇。

交通：

飞机：陈家港镇距盐城、连云港两市机场和火车站分别为 1 小时、40 分钟车程。

火车：盐连铁路正在建设之中。

汽车：乘汽车经高速公路到上海 3.5 小时车程，到南京、苏州、无锡、常州均为 3 个小时以内车程，到南通 1.5 小时、盐城 1 小时、连云港 40 分钟车程。

气候与游季：

陈家港镇属于温带大陆性气候，冬暖夏凉，冬天温度较低。最佳的旅游时间每年的 5~10 月。端午节前后是最好的旅游季节。

Chapter Four
Unique Celebrations in Five Places

The traditional customs of the Dragon Boat Festival have been handed down up till now and are still favored by the Chinese people. Owing to its more and more colorful festivities, in 2009, "Chinese Dragon Boat Festival" was successfully listed as the World Intangible Cultural Heritage by UNESCO, being the exclusive Chinese traditional festival in the UNESCO intangible cultural heritage lists (the 24 Solar Terms is listed this year, but not as a festival). "Chinese Dragon Boat Festival" which is listed as a whole consisting of four parts— "Duanwu Customs of Zigui—Qu Yuan's Hometown" (preserved in Zigui County, Hubei Province), "Xisai/Western Pass Divine Boat Festival" (celebrated in Huangshi City, Hubei province), "Duanwu Customs of the Miluo River" (preserved in Miluo County, Hunan Province) and "Duanwu Customs of Suzhou" (preserved in Suzhou City, Jiangsu Province). We may say that the four parts mentioned above could epitomize the main characters of Chinese Dragon Boat Festival. In addition, we will also introduce the characteristic festive activities of Chenjiagang Town (Yancheng City, Jiangsu Province), hoping to show the

readers the festivities of the Dragon Boat Festival in some other places with no grand rituals.

1. Duanwu Customs of Zigui——Qu Yuan's Hometown

In Zigui County, the fifth lunar month is called "Duanwu Month". It is interesting that there are three Dragon Boat Festivals here: the double-fifth day is called "Big Duanyang" or "Beginning Duanyang", the fifteenth day "Small Duanyang" and the twenty-fifth day "End of Duanyang". With a long history, Duanwu customs of Zigui County are famous for their unique festive culture and colorful connotations. In 2009, Duanwu customs of Zigui were listed as the World Intangible Cultural Heritage by UNESCO.

1.1 Dragon Boat Culture

As the hometown of the great patriotic poet Qu Yuan, Zigui County has witnessed the evolvement of the Qu Yuan-themed Dragon Boat culture for more than 2,200 years, whose rich connotations have never died. Zongtan (living in the 6th century) recorded such a festivity in his book "Records of

Dragon Boat Race

217

Customs and Festivals in the Chu Region": "The locals hold dragon boat race on the double-fifth day when Qu Yuan was said to throw himself into the Miluo River. Mourning for his death, the racers will row the boats to 'save' him." In "Book of Sui——Geographic Chronicle" we could find the following record: "When the dragon boats dash ahead, the earth-shattering boat songs quaked both land and water, echoed by the cheers of the beholders on both riverbanks. Such a scene is seen everywhere, particularly more common in the southern prefectures."

Zigui County belonged to the South Prefecture (territory of the former State of Chu) in the Qin Dynasty. The boat race in Zigui owned unique features: colorful racing boats of variety, thrilling boat race, solemn sacrificial rituals and earth-shattering competitive scene. The most eye-catching was the Evocation Rite to "call back" the spirit of Qu Yuan who left his hometown for good. The solemn and touching rite would deeply move every spectator present: On each colored boat erected a "spirit flag"——"May your spirit come back!" and headed by the "white dragon boat", all the boats would flow slowly down the river. Impressive spirit-calling "Requiem" would resound in the gorge.

"Alas! May you come back, our Minister! Here are our words, our Minister! Never go to the heaven for it's heavy! Never go to the hell for it's bumpy! Never go to the East for the torrent will swallow you! Never go to the South for the wolf may tear you! Never go to the West for the drift sand will trap you! Never go to the North for the snow may freeze you! Alas! May our Minister come home right away and never stray, for you will be treated warmly in our beautiful homeland!"

With the systematic regulations established and the integrated singing style and melody unchanged so far, the time-honored Zigui boat race has long been held on the broad Yangtze River. Since the construction of the Three Gorges Water-control Project, Zigui boat race has been held in the water area near the new town of Zigui County which is only about one kilometer upstream of Three Gorges Dam. With the new town of migrants, Three Gorges Dam and the beautiful scenery of the Yangtze River as the background, the Zigui boat race is extraordinarily spectacular! In July of 2004, General Administration of Sport of China granted Zigui County the title of "National Dragon Boat Sports Base——Famous Human Landscape for National Fitness", designating it as the exclusive dragon boat sports base nationwide and one of the ten human landscapes for national fitness.

Zigui dragon boats are all made of fir wood or cypress wood. On the dragon "head", dragon eyes are the inlaid glass balls or the carved ones, and his whiskers are made of colored threads. Smeared with quality tung oil, the dragon "body" will be painted with red, blue, yellow and white paints in the shape of scaly "dragon armors". Among the boats, the white boat is called the "Filial Dragon", involving that the descendants of Qu Yuan's hometown commemorate this patriotic poet with great loyalty. On the bottom, lard or evergreen Mucuna juice is smeared. Used only in the boat race, the 10-meter dragon boats made by the craftsmen of Zigui County are designated as the standard race boats nationwide. In addition, there is another kind of boat——"carved & painted dragon boat"——for carrying the honorable guests watching the boat race. On the boat, there are "carved beams and painted rafters", on which images of dragons, beasts, birds or plants are carved or painted. A new boat is usually built or launched on a lucky day, when the craftsmen will burn scents and pray to Buddha for safety.

1.2 Food Culture

The food culture of the Dragon Boat Festival of Zigui County is much colorful and meaningful. According to Wu Jun's "Collection of Mythical Stories——Sequel" (in the Southern Dynasties), "Qu Yuan threw himself into the Miluo River on the double-fifth day. In honor of him, on this very day, the Chu people later would worship him with rice filled in the bamboo tubes. Nowadays, the folks will fill rice into the new bamboo tubes and steam it for eating, which is called 'filling tubes', with the steamed rice called 'tube zongzi'." Zhou Chu (in the Jin Dynasty) recorded another custom in his book "Records of Customs": "What does Duanwu in midsummer mean? The character Duan (端) means the beginning. On the Dragon Boat Festival, the locals here will wrap glutinous rice with reed leaves and boil them in the water blended with chestnut/date soda lye. They eat such food on the festival for wrapping of zongzi could symbolize Yin and Yang. And they wrap zongzi also for worshiping Qu Yuan." The locals living in Zigui would wrap zongzi in a unique way——placing a red date inside the

Zong Zi

glutinous rice. Hence, there spread a folk song about zongzi: "With edges and angles, it has heart and liver. With pure white body, it suffers half a life. "

On the Dragon Boat Festival, the locals of Zigui wrapped zongzi for eating and worshiping Qu Yuan (via throwing them into the river). Meanwhile, as a seasonal delicacy zongzi was presented among the relatives and friends mutually. Li Shizhen also explained the custom of wrapping zongzi in his masterpiece "Compendium of Materia Medica——Cereal": "On the double-fifth day, as a festive delicacy zongzi is presented among the relatives and friends mutually. Zongzi is also believed to be sacrificed for worshiping Qu Yuan——the locals here throw it into the river to feed the flood dragon, hoping the satiated beast will not hurt the poet's body."

Apart from wrapping zongzi, there are some other customs like steaming buns, drinking realgar wine and eating salty eggs. Steaming buns is also known as steaming "baba" (paste)——making yeasty pastes with quality flour and placing them into the banana leaf-padded pots or steamers. Together with zongzi, such snack could be eaten as festive food or presented as a gift. The locals eat such food on the Dragon Boat Festival to pray for favorable weather and harvest. In mid/late fourth lunar month every year, after mixing fresh eggs or duck eggs with salt and stirring them together, nearly every household here would preserve salty eggs in the empty earthen jars. On the Dragon Boat Festival, these salty eggs would be steamed together with zongzi. The hot salty eggs could be laid around the babies' navels and rolled to and fro to cure indigestion. Besides the customs mentioned above, the locals here would eat garlic and sauced noodles.

1.3 Sacrifice Culture

On the double-fifth day, the locals of Zigui would crowd into Qu Yuan Temple (in Zigui County or Lepingli Town——where he was born), setting up alter and worshiping this great poet. The sacrificial rites might include chanting his poems, singing spirit-calling requiems, hanging 'spirit flags', offering sacrifices like livestock and fruits, dedicating flowers and herbs and burning incense and kowtowing before his statue. When the "public sacrificial essay" was chanted, all would stand in silent tribute, kowtow or bow down. In the Tang Dynasty, Wang Maoyuan, the governor of Guizhou Prefecture, once hosted the sacrificial ritual in Qu Yuan Temple. From then on, sacrificial ritual has been frequently held. Since 1980s, six sessions of "Duanwu Cultural Festival" have been held successively, with the sacrificial ritual as the essential festive activity. In Zigui County, sacrificial ritual was always held on "Big Duanwu"——the double fifth day, with the small-sized held by the folks or the grand-scaled by the local government.

The descendants of Qu Yuan are hosting dragon head saerifice cenemong at Zigui county, Hubei Province

Before the dragon boat race, a boat-sacrifice would be held, which was also called "Dragon Head Sacrifice". Carrying the "dragon head" of the boat into Qu Yuan Temple and setting up the altar, the locals would hang red ribbon or cloth on the dragon head, a rite called "hanging red". Then they would burn incense and pilgrim papers, chant the sacrificial essay, paint the dragon eyes red (to "bring dragon to life") and set off firecrackers, praying for safety. Only the boat-sacrifice was over could the dragon boats be carried down to the river for the boat race.

During the festival, the married daughters would return to their natal homes, worshiping their ancestors and visiting their parents. In the Qing Dynasty, such a custom was once recorded in Pan Rongbi's book "Customs and Festivals of the Capital——Duanyang in the Fifth Lunar Month": "The married daughters will return to their natal homes on Duanyang, which is also called 'Daughters' Day'." In the Jin Dynasty, Yuan Shansong described the custom in his book "Mountains and Rivers of Yichang": "Hearing the exile of Qu Yuan, his elder sister——a virtuous woman——also returned home and consoled the poet. The villagers all hoped other girls would follow her good deeds, so they called it 'return of sister'." Having inherited the virtue of Qu's virtuous sister, the married daughters of Zigui would carry gifts such as zongzi and return to their natal homes, visiting their natal family members and worshiping their ancestors before their graves by hanging green streamers.

1.4 Ornament Culture

During the Dragon Boat Festival, the locals of Zigui not only cared about their appearances, but also were particular about their ornament wearing, thus forming a peculiar ornament culture. Their ornaments included the followings:

Tying colored threads

There were two ways of tying colored threads in Zigui. The first was tying threads around the zongzi. According to "Customs of Xiangyang", "Qu Yuan threw himself into the Miluo River on the double-fifth day, so his wife would worship him by throwing food into the river on this very day. One day, Qu told his wife in her dream that the sacrifice was all snatched by the flood dragon. Since the beast feared five-colored threads and bamboo, his wife made zongzi with bamboo tubes and tied five-colored threads around them…" From then on, the locals would throw zongzi tied with colored threads into the river to scare the dragon away, thus keeping the poet's body intact. Such zongzi was also a must to be thrown when the dragon boat race was held on the Dragon Boat Festival in Zigui. Such custom was also recorded in the book "Overview of Customs" (written by Ying Shao): "⋯⋯ on the double-fifth day, the five-colored threads are tied around the arms⋯⋯to avoid the war disasters or ghosts and keep the folks from diseases. Minister Qu Yuan is said to be commemorated too on this very day⋯⋯" Women and children of Zigui tied five-colored threads around their arms in order to adorn themselves and avoid evils on the one hand, and commemorate Qu Yuan the patriotic poet on the other.

Wearing perfume pouches

Perfume pouches here were usually weaved in the shape of spindle, circle, square and heart, with life-like patterns like tiger, cat, fish, bird and vanilla tightly stitched. The locals here would wear various perfume pouches on their chests embroidered with five-colored threads.

Qu Yuan had a specific vanilla "complex" in his works. For example, he wrote the following lines in his masterpiece Li Sao——"Sorrow of Departure": "With their flawless virtues, the three ancient sage-kings gathered all the talents; like the lenient kings, I wish perfume pouches should contain vanillas such as pepper and laurel, not only orchids and angelica roots!" In the poem, like the perfume pouches which could contain all vanillas, the poet wished that King Chu-huai could tolerate all talents (apart from his favored ones——orchids and angelica roots), as those crowded-out were also fragrant vanillas after all.

To inherit Qu Yuan's writing style and noble spirit, the locals of Zigui would fill the perfume pouches with cinnamon, pepper, clove, fennel and sand-ginger or angelica root, realgar, pepper, asarum and atractylodes lancea, which were called "five spices", as these vanilla herbs were all lauded by Qu Yuan in his po-

Perfume Sachets

ems. There was an old saying that "wear perfume pouch on his body, and the baby will look much lovely". Legend has it that wearing perfume pouches may help the children to avoid evils and keep fit.

Wearing wormwood-weaved tigers

Such a custom was recorded in "Records of Customs and Festivals in the Chu Region" (written by Zongtan in the 6th century): "On the double-fifth day, the locals here will weave wormwood tigers or cut colored papers into cubs, then paste them with wormwood leaves for hanging." Ying Shao described another custom in the book "Overview of Customs": "As the king of the beasts, the strong tiger can settle the disputes and swallow the demons……It also could drive away the evils." According to their descriptions, we may say that the integration of wormwood and tiger could drive away evils and dispel demons. Meanwhile, when the girls or young ladies wore tiger-shaped wormwood hairpins in the hair or colored silk-cut tigers pasted with wormwood leaves beside their temples, the faint-scented wormwood tigers looked much funny.

225

1.5 Plague-avoiding Culture

When the fifth lunar month arrived, it was just late spring and early summer, with high temperature and humid rainy weather. Due to the mass propagation of pathogenic microorganisms and poisonous insects, epidemic diseases would meet their seasonal peak. As a result, various Duanwu customs of health-keeping and disease-preventing emerged.

For example, there was a custom called "picking dewed wormwood". According to "Records of Customs and Festivals in the Chu Region", "the people of Chu will tread the grass on the double-fifth day and weave human-shaped ornaments with the newly picked wormwood for hanging on the doors to avoid evils...and they usually go to pick wormwood before the crowing of the cock on the double-fifth day, as it is believed that such wormwood is effective in the fuming therapy." Wormwood's medicinal effects were also recorded in Li Shizhen's "Compendium of Materia Medica": "The aromatic wormwood could unblock nine orifices and the burning wormwood may cure some diseases." In the early morning of the double-fifth day, every household of Lepingli Town would pick the dewed wormwood and hang on the doors or window panes bundles of wormwood bound with red paper tapes. Some families would burn moxa for refreshing their mind and curing diseases. And some others would boil water blended with dried wormwood for washing bodies or feet.

There was another story about wormwood-hanging. In Qu Yuan's "Sorrow of Departure", there is a line "why the once fragrant grass is crowded out by the withered wormwood now?" In his eyes, wormwood was "wicked" plant alluding to those treacherous officials in the court. To express their deep love for the loyal minister and profound hatred for the fatuous monarch and treacherous officials, they would hang wormwood——"the treacherous men" on the doors.

The locals here would have "calamus bath". "Compendium of Materia Medica" once recorded the medicinal effects of calamus: "Calamus could mainly cure cold, numbness and cough, and help to refresh your mind, nourish the five internal organs, unblock nine orifices, sharpen your eyesight and hearing, and regain the lost voice. Long-time taking of calamus will keep your body fitter, your mind sober and your life longer. It also does good to the mental health, making the old sober-minded." During the Dragon Boat Festival, the locals of Zigui would boil water blended with calamus leaves or roots for washing bodies, or drink calamus wine.

Spraying realgar wine was also a festive must. According to the folk belief, spraying realgar wine onto the corners of the bedroom or the bedhead would dispel the flies or mosquitoes and prevent plagues as well. With realgar wine, some would paint a Chinese character "王" (king) on a child's forehead or a "lucky" mole on his cheeks, or smear the wine on his ears or nose, hoping to avoid diseases and pray for safety.

1.6 Belief Culture

Among the varied folk beliefs of the locals of Zigui, their beliefs in the Dragon Boat Festival have always been unique.

1.6.1 Worshiping Qu Yuan.

There were "Eight Strange Customs" of Lepingli Town, one of which was to "worship the immortalized Qu Yuan"—— taking him as a god. Among the stone carvings collected in the Qu Yuan Temple, one is the statue of Qu donated by one local family of Guizhou County in the 16th year (1537 AD) of Jiajing reign period of the Ming Dynasty. This relic was formerly enshrined in the Minister Temple located in the "White-Dog

(Baigou) Gorge", which is the oldest stone statue of Qu Yuan extant. On its one side there is the epigraph: "Cao Duanfu, a pious follower coming from Guizhou County, Jingzhou Prefecture, together with his wife (Lady Zhu) and four sons, dedicates the statue of Qu Yuan the Minister and enshrines it in the Baigou Gorge Temple to bless all the folks here!" To this day, the statue of Qu Yuan is still respectively enshrined in Qu Yuan Temple in Zigui County and Qu Yuan Temple in Lepingli Town, and most of the locals will go there to worship him during the Dragon Boat Festival, with wood-carved or painted images of the patriotic poet enshrined in some homes.

1.6.2 Hanging calamus sword.

One foot or even a few feet long, the calamus leaf looks like a sword, so the locals of Zigui have long called it "calamus sword". According to a folklore of Zigui, when the army of Qin intended to dig Qu Yuan's cenotaph located in Qu Yuan Temple after they conquered the state of Chu, immortals "informed" the locals of the tragic news beforehand in their dreams. As a result, every household hung calamus swords on the doors and also infixed such "swords" into the cenotaph. Seeing the calamus swords hung everywhere, the soldiers of Qin got to know the locals' deep love for this righteous minister, so they withdrew. From then on, to commemorate him, the locals of Zigui have preserved the custom of hanging calamus swords on the Dragon Boat Festival.

1.6.3 Sending Duanyang charms.

According to "Zigui Annals", on the double-fifth day ("Beginning Duanyang"), the monks of Qu Yuan Temple in Leliping Town would send "Duanyang charms" to the neighboring peasants, collecting donations and sending blessings. With auspicious/evil-dispelling patterns or four characters 祛邪扫瘟

（dispel evils and plagues）sometimes, these charms would be hung under the images of gods and burnt after the three "Duanyangs".

1.6.4 Sending away the "plague-boat".

This custom was also called sending away the "plague-god boat". On the "End of Duanyang", the peasants of Zigui living along the banks of the Yangtze River or those streams would make paper boats, in which oil kindling or smallish candle was placed. In the late afternoon, when the oil kindling or smallish candle was ignited, the paper boat would be placed on the water, drifting downstream. Such a custom involved sending away god of plague and plagues as well, thus the whole family would be protected.

Tips for Tourism

Zigui County: Qu Yuan Hometown

A vital district connecting Sichuan Province and Hubei Province, Zigui County lies in the west of Hubei, stretching on both sides of Xiling Gorge (one part of Three Gorges along the Yangtze River). Alongside the upper reaches of the reservoir of Three Gorges Project, Zigui County, as one of the birthplaces of Chu cultures, is the very hometown of Qu Yuan——the great patriotic poet and Wang Zhaojun——one of the Four Beauties in ancient China.

Along with the picturesque mountains and rivers here, those scenic spots and historical sites will also delight the eyes of the travelers. They can visit Lepingli Town——hometown of Qu Yuan, the Qu Yuan Temple, the Study Cave (a cave where little Qu Yuan read books after school), the Face-reflecting Well, the Military Book and Sword Gorge, Xiangxi River (fragrant stream), the Lingkong (steep cliff) Gorge, the Jiuwan Stream (to enjoy rafting), the Five-finger Hill (a Taoist retreat) and the hometown of Wang Zhaojun. Doubtlessly speaking, the dragon—boat races and folk songs and dances to commemorate Qu Yuan will attract the travelers most.

Qu Yuan Hometown Scenic Area is located in the newly—built city of Zigui County, where the beautiful scenery of "wide—and—calm river passing by steep cliffs" comes into view. Among these 24 relics (once—to—be—drowned) relocated here, Qu Yuan Temple and Jiangdu Temple (to worship the god of river) could be regarded as the representative cultural symbols. In May 2006, all these relics as a whole were approved by the State Council as the "Important Museum Under the State Protection". In this scenic area under protection , the travelers could visit Qu Yuan Temple (the core of the memorial scenic spot) and the ancient dwellings in Three Gorges District (including the ancient dwellings in Xintan Town, the stone—carving art on the cliffs and those old bridges). Qu Yuan Culture and Art Center and the new landscape belt along the banks are also worth visiting.

There is another anecdote worth telling. The farm oxen here are al—ways docile even without ox ropes tied. Legend has it that Qu Yuan once came back from the capital of Ying and he was approaching home when the rope tied around the books carried by the attendant suddenly broke. Seeing their embarrassment, a kind—hearted old farmer untied his ox rope in no time and did them a favor. From then on, the oxen here got free from rope—tying.

By coach: At the Yichang Centre Bus Station (on the right side of the Yichang Railway Station), the travelers can take nonstop shuttle coaches (departing in turn in a short time) to get to Maoping Station. After reach—ing Zigui, they could take taxis to get to the scenic area or just go there on foot.

For self—driving: After leaving Yichang City, the drivers could first cross the Three Gorges Dam via the Fanba (surmount the dam) Expressway and get to Zigui scenic area directly.

If the travelers start off from the Three Gorges Dam, there are shuttle buses for them to get to the Zigui scenic area.

Ticket for the scenic area: ¥90.

2. Xisai/Western Pass Divine Boat Festival

Zhang Zhonghe (a poet in Tang Dynasty) once praised the beautiful scenery of Mount Xisai/ (Western Pass): "Over the Mount Xisai the carefree egrets are flying, in the rapids the fat mandarin fish are swimming." In the Song Dynasty, the great poet Su Shi also described its beauty: "Over the Mount Xisai the carefree egrets are flying, out of the Sanhua Isle the lonely sailboat is floating." Just at the foot of beautiful Mount Xisai, the unique festivity of the Dragon Boat Festival——Xisai Devine Dragon Boat Festival for plague-driving has been inherited for more than 1,000 years, which is still held in Daoshifu Village (formerly administered by Daye Prefecture, Hubei Province). Via holding such age-old folk celebration, the locals here have long expressed their strong wishes for evil-dispelling and happy-life-enjoying. It is also a traditional grand festival donated by the locals of Daoshifu Village, mainly consisting of making paper boat, worshiping, cruising, playing local operas and launching the divine paper-made boat.

In the past, on the first day of the first lunar month, the organizers of the divine Dragon Boat Festival would gather, summarizing their work in the previous year and scheduling the festive activity in the coming year. On the eighth day of the fourth lunar month (the birth date of Buddha), the opening ceremony for paper boat making would be held, which marked the beginning of the 40-day grand festival. As the carrier of the whole boat festival, the divine paper boat should be finished before the fourth day of the fifth lunar month.

With a 2.8-meter dragon head and a 2.1-meter dragon tail,

231

the boat would be 9 meters long, 1.4 meters wide and 7 meters high (from the bottom to the top of the mast), in which a 2.6-meter memorial archway, a 1.4-meter attic and a 2.6-meter pavilion would be placed. The boat body was made of wood, wrapped by bamboo mats and covered by red cloths, with other parts all made of paper (that's why it was called paper boat). Every cornice of the attic or pavilion was made in the shape of dragon. As decorations, the paper-cut patterns were widely pasted to beautify every part of the divine boat; on the windows of the attic and pavilion pictures of flowers, birds and opera figures would be painted. In the boat, 103 paper-made figures would be placed. As the carrier of the sacrificial ritual, this paper dragon boat was undoubtedly very big in terms of volume; and as a folk artwork, it was also visually shocking.

In the midnight of the double-fifth day, Taoists would host the opening ceremony for the boat festival and "open the light" for the divine boat and Bodhisattva. In the middle of Qu Yuan Temple, on the high-low stand were enshrined the paper-made

Dragon Boat Race

images of Qu Yuan and other gods, with the statue of the poet and Avalokitesvara (Guanyin) placed on each side. In front of the statue of Avalokitesvara, people placed an incense table on which a hodful of rice was offered, which was just the "rice-hod worship" rite before the "light-opening" ceremony. When the Taoists chanted scriptures, with their palms put together devoutly, the locals would stand in silence, making wishes and praying for favorable weather. Then, Taoists would kill a rooster and hold the "light-opening" ceremony——smear the rooster's blood on the face of Bodhisattva, or spray the blood onto the dragon boat while walking around the boat. When chanting scriptures, Taoists would ignite 12 oil lamps one by one, and then the ceremony was over. Only after such ceremony could the dragon boat and Bodhisattva be endowed with mysterious color as people imagined and the dragon boat become a divine boat "virtually".

After the "light-opening" ceremony, the pious locals could respectfully request the Taoists to tell fortunes, praying for disaster-avoiding, disease-preventing and peace-seeking. Meanwhile, the organizers of the boat festival would accept the money donated voluntarily by the locals, making the donations public on the honor roll.

In the midnight of the fifteenth day ("Big Duanwu"), Tao-ists would hold "Embarking" Rite——respectfully invite all the gods to embark on the divine boat. Before every god or every group of gods embarked, divination should be practiced——Yin diagram or Yang diagram alone was neither good, only a bal-anced Yin-Yang diagram was expected. When such a balanced Yin-Yang diagram didn't appear, the diviner and the organizers would kneel down to plead for it piously. It is said that whether the rite of "Embarking" or Divination went on smoothly or not could predict the yield of that very year, which also reflected the age-old witchcraft and divination of the ancient Chu.

With the divination rite going on, gods would embark on the divine boat in turn: Yangsi (dragon-slaughtering general), Master Umbrella (Vaisravana), god of Thousand-mile Eye and Wind-accompanying Ear, gods of Five Directions (5), gods of rooster, duck, tiger and horse (4), 4 yamen runners, Monk Sizhou, 2 executioners, Kuangfu, a gong player, Dutian, a blunderbuss carrier, Qu Yuan, Goddess, 2 maids, a general, an official, young and old eunuchs (a pair), lord of the land, a helmsman, Zhang Yuanbo (god of plague in charge of plagues in the spring), Loyal Duke and 24 sailors.

The real divine boat festival would start on the double-fifth day and end on the eighteenth day, which was also an annual grand fair locally. During the boat festival, the neighboring villagers would flood into Daoshifu Village to worship the divine boat, burning incense, redeeming former wishes, asking for fortune or offspring, or praying for safety. They would place their home-made paper clothes and shoes into the divine boat, or throw their own tea or rice into it, praying for a harvest. Some would carry tea or rice in the divine boat back home for luck-seeking. In addition, a stage was already set up in front of the Qu Yuan Temple and the local opera troupes would perform there. Around the temple, a temporary peddlers' market was formed, where the locals could buy some groceries or meet their relatives & friends while burning incense and watching operas. Just due to the multiple functions of this grand fair, the locals were always ardent to donate.

At eight sharp on the morning of the sixteenth day, 16 strong fellows would carry the divine boat out of the temple and parade around the village. Circled by gorgeous canopies

Dragon Boat Race

and guided by colored flags, the divine boat "cruised" with the sound of gongs and drums heard far away. What a spectacular scene! When the divine boat passed by each household, they would hang calamus and wormwood on the doors and at the doorway set up an incense table, on which they burnt incense and placed wine, tea, rice and fruits to greet the boat. Meanwhile, each household would set off firecrackers, throw tea and rice, worship the divine boat and burn the wormwood leaves, hoping that the boat would take away evils and bad luck.

On the evening of the seventeenth day, 48 altar lamps were ignited under the boat and Taoists were invited to chant prayers and keep watch the whole night.

The divine boat was carried out of the temple for "drifting" at ten sharp on the morning of the eighteenth day. The Taoist hosting the ritual would write Master charms with rooster blood and paste them on the mouth and tail of the dragon. Sacrificial ritual over, the Taoist and the organizers of the festival would walk ahead, opening a way for the divine boat. 16

235

strong fellows would carry the boat all the way till they reached the riverbank, reverently placing the boat on the river. The fishers then would set incense tables on the bows and set off firecrackers, circling the divine boat three times to "see it off". The neighboring villagers would gather at the foot of beautiful Mount Xisai, watching the divine boat enter the river slowly. With their palms put together, they would kneel down devoutly, hoping that the divine boat could take away the plagues and disasters and bring luck and peace. After the divine boat entered the water, any stopping or U-turn of the boat was tabooed. Therefore, when the boat drifted downstream, the activity of "striking dragon boat" was held to shove it away in case that it might stop.

The divine Dragon Boat Festival was also held to "send away god of plague", as there was an important Bodhisattva——Zhang Yuanbo enshrined in the boat, the god of plague in charge of plagues in Chinese folklores. According to the "Chinese Taoism Journal", "In the folk beliefs of the ancient Chinese, gods of plague are also called five-plague envoys in charge of all the plagues in the world, including Zhang Yuanbo (in charge of plagues in the spring), Liu Yuanda (in charge of plagues in the summer), Zhao Gongming (in charge of plagues in the autumn), Zhong Shigui (in charge of plagues in the winter) and Shi Wenye (in charge of all plagues)." Since Zhang Yuanbbai (God of plague listed as the first of the five envoys) was "invited" and "sent away" on the Yangtze River, so the divine boat turned out a real "plague-boat".

From the eighth day of the fourth lunar month to the eighteenth day of the fifth lunar month, the Xisai Divine Dragon Boat Festival as a whole (from boat making to boat sending) would last 40 days, which was rarely seen in ancient

China for its large scale and attendance. In its 1,000 years of cultural inheriting, the divine boat festival absorbed the legend of worshiping Qu Yuan on Duanwu step by step, and at last the two sacrificial rituals were rolled into one, which imposed far-reaching influence on the promotion of national spirit and ethnical cultural identity.

Why could the divine boat festival have lasted for so long? Besides the pious beliefs of the villagers of Daoshifu Village, the well-preserved historical data (words or pictures) also contributed much. In the hands of those paper-boat-making craftsmen, we still can find two age-old editions of hand-illustrated manuals for paper-boat making: one was printed in the 8th year of Guangxu reign period (in 1882 AD), the other was printed in the 24th year of Republic of China period (in 1936 AD). The latter is a thread-bound edition, on whose cover a sentence is printed: "Hand-illustrated manual for dragon-boat making——printed on the lucky day of the fifth lunar month in the 24th year of Republic of China period and bound by You Xinting". This manual covers the pattern of divine boat, various patterns of festive charms, banners, flags and canopies, specific names of all the articles or parts of the boat and the names of each Bodhisattva as well. It could be called a comprehensive hand-illustrated guidebook for the whole process of the divine Dragon Boat Festival.

Ever since the Han, the Tang, the Yuan, the Ming and the Qing Dynasty, Daoshifu has long been a political, economic and cultural center town in Hubei. But from the late Eastern Han Dynasty to the establishment of People's Republic of China (1949 AD), more than 100 wars/battles have taken place in Mount Xisai District. Under the shade of war, the locals here had to convey their wishes for peace via the divine boat to "send away plagues". From the rites of "worshiping rice-hod" and "throwing tea and rice", those banners like "May all the gods in the divine boat appear and bless us" and "Grant us whatever is requested", and their pious worship for the divine boat, we may see the locals held such ritual simply to pray for favorable weather, harvest and peaceful life. That also accounts for why this divine boat festival has been inherited for 1,000 years.

Tips for Tourism

Mount Xisai/ (Western Pass) in Huangshi

With its planning area over 0.495 km², Mount. Xisai/ Western Pass Scenic Area is located on the southern bank of Changjiang River to the east of Huangshi City, Hubei Province. It is home to many tourism resources, since there are precipitous yet magnificent landscapes and varied historical sites. The travelers can visit numerous scenic spots like the Daoshifu Village and the Old Town. With 176.5m above the sea level and a perimeter of 18.5km, Mount Xisai has long been integrated as both an ancient battlefield and a scenic spot due to its unique geographical position (on the border between the State of Wu and Chu) and precipitous terrain.

From the late Eastern Han Dynasty (25−220 AD) to the founding (1949) of new China, there have off and on appeared battles more than one hundred times here. Meanwhile, when totally lost in the first ray of the rising sun and the last ray of the setting sun, many literati could not help but voice their feelings in nearly 100 poems, some of which were preserved via stone inscriptions carved on those steep cliffs and huge rocks. Early in May 1985, the local Bureau of Gardening and Greening started to renovate the touring paths uphill, the Long Corridor, the Shangguan Pavilion, the Peach Blossom Pavilion, the Peach Blossom Cave, the iron−chained railings along the river and the ancient Fishing Platform.

Address: 654 Huangshi Avenue

Tel: 0714−6402825

Bus No.10 and No.19 are available.

Ticket for the scenic area: ¥20

3. Duanwu Customs Along the Riversides of Miluo River

Located in the northeast of Hunan Province, Miluo City——one of the cradles of Chu Culture——lies to the east of the Dongting Lake, with the Miluo River running through from east to west and merging into the Dongting Lake. Duanwu customs along the riversides of the Miluo River are featured by Qu Yuan-related culture, dragon boat culture and festivity culture, which are closely united as one by a river (the Miluo River), a great man (Qu Yuan of course) and an old temple (Qu Yuan Temple), with the derivation of dragon boat race to commemorate the poet.

The Duanwu customs of Miluo mainly include the followings:

3.1 Making dragon boats

In Miluo, dragon boats were usually made by a village or a big family and the work would start from the middle of the fourth lunar month. Before the boat-making, three to five reverend old men were elected to organize the boat race, which was sponsored by the villagers. The ancestral temple or a makeshift work shed was usually chosen as the boat-making site, where was enclosed tightly to keep any women or children from approaching: on the one hand, women belonged to "Yin" (opposite to "Yang"——the powerful dragon here) which could mean "overturning the boat"; and on the other, the rash children might speak out some inauspicious words. A Bodhisattva would be invited to "divine" a lucky day for the star work.

Before the reinforcing-bar a small square table was set, on which joss sticks and candles were placed. Firecrackers set off, the "ink-marker" master (the chief carpenter) would cut the cockscomb and smear the rooster blood onto the reinforcing-bar. Chanting prayers in his mouth and worshiping the gods, the chief carpenter would start the first stroke of axe——called "beginning of woodwork", then the boat-making would start formally. The carving of dragon head was conducted in another room where only the carvers could enter. When carving was over, an old craftsman was invited to "open the light" (paint the eyes of dragon to make it animated). A solemn "dragon-head worshiping" rite would also be held and joss sticks and candles would be offered every day from then on. After the boat-making was over, a feast ("dragon boat banquet") was made to celebrate the launching of the boat.

3.2 Tying red-silk ribbon

When the dragon boat was placed on the Miluo River, the rowers would row the boat upstream and downstream, training hard for the boat race and seeking fun as well. On the riversides, the rowers' relatives and friends would prepare one or two bars of cigarette, one or two bottles of liquor, a red-silk ribbon and a string of firecrackers, waiting for the boat. When the boat drew near, they would lift a bamboo pole tied with that red-silk ribbon and swing it in the air, yelling out the name of their clan and setting off firecrackers. The "called" boat would dash to the riverside and stop there. The clan member holding the gift plate would utter praise for the dragon boat, and the headman of the boat (usu. the chief rower or helmsman) would take the gift and chant praise for the boat in return. When the red-silk ribbon was tied around the dragon's horns, the boat-greeting rite was over.

3. Worshiping Qu Yuan in the temple

Before the fourth day of the fifth lunar month, all the dragon boats along the riversides of the Miluo River would in succession gather at the foot of the Yusi Hill (jade bamboo basket) where Qu Yuan Temple was located. The headman of the boat carrying the dragon head and the rowers with oars on their shoulders would in a line climb up the stairs until they reached the temple, gongs and drums beating all the way. Then before the shrine to Qu Yuan, they placed the dragon head on the incense table and offered sacrifices (in ancient time, sacrifices consisting of an ox, a sheep and a pig were required, which was called "Tailao" gift), with bells ringing, drums beating, strings playing and blunderbuss firing. With his hands washed and his crest righted, the officiant wearing long gown and mandarin jacket would chant the eulogy and demonstrate the couplets. With the instrumental music played thrice and the incense, fruits and wine offered thrice, the pious racers would kowtow thrice and repeat twice, which was called "kneeling thrice and bowing nine times". Since Qu Yuan Temple was once called the Miluo Temple in ancient time, this ritual was originally called "worshiping the temple", but virtually it was held to commemorate Qu Yuan, the great patriotic poet. The ritual over, raising the dragon head over his head, the headman would lead his team to walk around the shrine once. Accompanied by the drums and firecrackers, they ran down the hill and dashed into the river, sinking and floating five times to "wash the dragon head". Then, the dragon head was installed on the bow of the dragon boat and the boat could attend the boat race now.

3.4 Pulling dragon whiskers

The whiskers of the dragon were generally dyed with ramie. Right after the ritual of "tying red-silk ribbon" and "worshiping the temple", some "nimble" spectators would pull one or two dragon whiskers and tie them around the kids' wrists, holding that their kids would be protected in a whole year.

3.5 Dragon boat race

The rowers rowed dragon boats leisurely on the Miluo River. When two boats drew near and became parallel to each other, the rowers in one boat used to "challenge" the rowers in another, "Come on, will you?" The "challenged" rowers certainly would take up the glove, "Why not!" With an ear-piercing whistle and noisy beating of gongs and drums, the rowers (4 sitting in the front and 4 in the back, who generally pitched and lifted the oars to their chests before the boat race) would quickly thrust the oars into the water and row hard, water splashing joyfully. Boat race was certainly a win-loss game. To defeat the rival, sometimes one boat would pass over the bow of another boat, which was a tabooed maneuver in the race and could cause clash easily. The loser would undauntedly swear to win the next year and they really kept their promise——they would build the boat and start training much early the next year, even at the cost of giving up farming. That's why there was once a saying spread in the Miluo River area——"We'd rather give up farming than lose the race." The winner would entertain the villagers with feast and local operas to celebrate.

3.6 Fishing boat race

When spring came, the villagers living in the Miluo River area would mow grass on some isles in the Dongting Lake and take the grass back home in their narrow canoes for fertilizing the field. Such "grass-carrying canoes" were in fact the small fishing boats. Unable to build their own dragon boats but eager to seek fun during the Dragon Boat Festival, some poor young men would hold a fishing boat race: Amidships erecting a color-flag pole fixed by the mooring rope, they used one oar as the helm and made several oars fixed by nails. With beating of gongs and drums, they would compete with other fishing boats (not the formal dragon boats of course) for fun-seeking.

3.7 Retrieving the dragon boat

Legend has it that Qu Yuan threw himself into the Miuo River on the double-fifth day and his body was salvaged on the fifteenth day of the fifth lunar month, so the villagers living along the Miluo River would hold another boat race on the fifteenth day to celebrate the "Big Duanyang Day". The boat race over, after washing the dragon boat clean, they would set off firecrackers and burn joss sticks to worship the boat and retrieve the boat——a rite to "thank dragon". They would elect a credible family and respectfully carry the dragon head to the attic of that family, placing it on the small square table prepared beforehand. On the first and fifteenth day of each lunar month, the elected family was supposed to burn incense & joss sticks and bow before the dragon head, a rite lasting till the next Dragon Boat Festival.

3.8 Drinking relagar wine and hanging calamus & wormwood

The locals would drink realgar wine and smear it on the kids' foreheads to avoid mosquitoes and gnats. They would also spray the realgar wine around their houses or into the corners indoors to prevent the poisonous snakes and insects. Before the Dragon Boat Festival, every household would pick calamus and wormwood and hang these bundled grasses on the doors or beside the windows. Meanwhile, on the doors the locals would paste straw-papered charms, on which some words were written——like "on the double-fifth day, with a calamus sword in his hand, Minister Qu Yuan rides a wormwood tiger to dispel all the demons back to the hell!" They also gathered some used charms for use in the next year.

3.9 Wrapping zongzi

Zongzi was a must for the sacrificial ritual. Around the Dragon Boat Festival, every household would wrap a large amount, which could be classified as meat stuffing, fruit stuffing, bean paste, pickle stuffing and glutinous rice zongzi in terms of ingredients, or nine-offspring, eight-immortal, wormwood and pearl-pagoda zongzi according to the types and shapes.

3.10 "Scrambling" to fetch dragon-blessed water

Just at daybreak of the Dragon Boat Festival, the local villagers flooding to the Miluo River would "scramble" to fetch a load of water and return home hurrily, pouring it into the water vat, for they held the dragon had emerged before daybreak and the "dragon-blessed" water could keep them healthy and strong.

3.11 Treading grass

On the early morning of the Dragon Boat Festival, barefooted or in new shoes, the locals would run to the grassland beside the Miluo River and tread the fresh grass to and fro with their feet wet with dewdrops, hoping to keep healthy.

3.12 Bathing on the Dragon Boat Festival

On the double-fifth day, whoever was able to swim would jump into the Miluo River and have a bath merrily, for they believed that bathing that day could help to dispel diseases and disasters.

3.13 Hanging perfume pouches

Just ever since the middle of the fourth lunar month, the locals here would mix spices like borneol with some medicinal herbs and the dried wormwood leaves collected the previous year. Then, with colored cloth scraps they would sew pouches in the shape of zongzi, peach, pillow and tiny lock, tied with five-color threads. They would hang these spice-filled perfume pouches around the kids' necks to avoid disasters and diseases. Only on "Big Duanyang Day" could the kids throw away these pouches, which was called "throwing away disasters".

3.14 Visiting parents

Several days before the Dragon Boat Festival, the married daughter would prepare some gifts for her natal family—— dozens of zongzi, two bottles of wine, a piece of fresh pork and several calamus fans (or folding fans for her unmarried sisters) and visit her parents together with her husband. It was a custom for the mother-in-law to take her daughter, son-in-law and grandchild (granddaughter or grandson) back home on the Dragon Boat Festival. There once was a nursery rhyme here: "The long Miluo River runs along and my granny will take me back home. I want neither cakes nor candies, for I only like the bamboo-leaved zongzi!"

3.15 Resting on the Dragon Boat Festival

The locals here would rest on the Dragon Boat Festival of course. There once was an old saying: "Even the ox and horse will rest on Grain Rain Day, so he is to be blamed who works on Double-fifth Day!"

Further reading

Four Festivities of Duanwu on the Banks of Miluo River

On the Dragon Boat Festival every year, the large—scaled international dragon boat race will be held on the Miluo River. Many local boat teams will join the invitational dragon boat race (another one for the amateur). In addition, festivities like "Tent Music Festival" , "Happy Opera Fans" and "Photo Contest " are also held. These four festivities are much en—

joyed by the masses for they are so close to them.

The Miluo River Invitational Dragon Boat Race is held in the Wet-land Park beside the Miluo River International Dragon Boat Race Center. About 20 local dragon boat teams contend in the 200-meter-straight-lane pre-finals and 500-meter-straight-lane pre-finals.

"Duanyang Carnival"—— Miluo River National Wetland Park Tent Music Festival, is also held in the Wetland Park with 7 interesting activities: the game of "Zongzi-Wrapping"——to feel bustling Duanwu and taste sweet zongzi, the family activity "Where are we going, Mom and Dad?", "Rock Heroes Concert——Life in Blossom", the game of "Tug of War", the game of "Foot-knee Fighting", the bonfire party and "Experiencing Dragon-boats".

"Happy Opera Fans" is held in the Miluo River International Dragon Boat Race Center. The contestants will sing a short aria of one opera accompanied by music or no music at all.

"Origin of the Dragon Boat Festival——Miluo Duanwu Photo Contest" invites well-known photographers to take photos on the spot. Their works will greatly explore cultures of the Dragon Boat Festival originated from Miluo, painting a panoramic picture of Miluo——its ecological status quo, local cultures, tourism resources and landscapes and local customs of the Dragon Boat Festival. Some carefully selected photos will be awarded after they are exhibited and published in print.

4. The Dragon Boat Festival in Suzhou City

The Dragon Boat Festival was once one of the biggest festivals celebrated in Suzhou City.

It is not hot yet on the Double-fifth Day,
but beyond Southern Gate the dragon boats have already set off.
As the boats draw near the crowd cluster,

reflections of scented dresses and jolting fans flutter on the green waves.

The boats are as tall as the grain heap and as long as 60 feet.

Pavilions erect on both the bows and sterns,
lovely costumed kids playing on the swings...

The above poem titled "Dragon Boats" (written by Shi Fangluo, the Qing Dynasty) vividly presents us the grand dragon boat race held in ancient Wu district.

In Suzhou, the dragon boat race was mainly held on the Xu River. Additionally, there were some other suitable places like the Tai Lake or waterways passing through the Shantang Street or running under the Feng (Maple) Bridge.

During the boat race, the rowers strived to row ahead the festoon-decorated dragon boats with waving flags. Meanwhile, with the beating gongs and drums and the cracking fire-crackers, the crowd clustered along the riverbanks, cheering and laughing, all lost in the noisy boat race. Along the

Zong Zi

riverbanks, some pavilions and shade-sheds were built, under which the rich could make feasts and sit there, enjoying the boat race and the delicious food as well. When the boats passed by the pavilions, firecrackers would be set off, and the rowers were inspired to show their talents again when hearing the banging.

The dragon boat race held in Suzhou was also featured by its "prize-winning", which was once recorded in the "Local Chronicle of Wu County in Qianlong Reign Period": "When the dragon boat race is held on the Dragon Boat Festival, apart from the race boats, other pleasure boats will gather on which merry people cheer and laugh, accompanied by the noisy strings. When ducks (the prize for the boat race) are thrown into the river, the dragon boat rowers will jump into the water to snatch them for fun." It was an innovative idea for the locals in Suzhou to introduce goose or duck into the dragon boat race. In Suzhou——a highly commercialized city once, the boat race was evolved into a "prize-winning" game somewhat. The merchants here would have the attendants place "lotteries" into the straw bundles or eggshells and throw such "prizes" onto the water for the stout rowers to snatch. The boat race then became a swimming match——the cheering spectators and the fellow rowers encouraged the prize-contenders to snatch the prizes in the water splashes. Specific names of the prizes were written on the lotteries and in the designated shops could the prize-winners get the corresponding prizes like cakes, candies, folding fans and towels. Such a "sales promotion" could be taken as the earliest attempt of the Chinese merchants to advertise their goods anyhow via sponsoring sports matches.

In Suzhou, zongzi was always the indispensable food on the Dragon Boat Festival. The locals would not only eat zongzi but also worship their ancestors with it and present it mutually. Early on the morning of the Dragon Boat Festival, faint fragrance of bamboo leaves would "float" out of every household.

In Suzhou, there used to be many taboos this day. For example, it was a taboo to hang the mattress in the sun or build a house with thatch. To dispel all sinisterness, the locals figured out quite a few tricks. On the Double-fifth Day, babies less than one year old would be sent back to their maternal grandmothers' home, a custom called "Duanwu Escaping"; parents would ask the children to wear tiger-shaped caps or tigerhead-shaped shoes; every household would hang the portraits of Zhongkui——it was believed that hanging the portrait of this ghost-catcher could dispel any demons. In order to awe or overwhelm the evils, locals who believed in Buddhism or Taoism would request monks to practice Buddhist services and draw portraits of Bodhisattva Wei Tuo (who is able to dispel ghosts) with cinnabar ink, or go to the Taoist temples to get a Master charm and paste it in the central halls. There was another important custom in Suzhou——to clothe the kids under the age of 7 with tiger-patterned "Wudu" (five poisonous creatures) vests.

There were also some other tricks to dispel "Wudu". The locals would weave wormwood into a human-figure-shaped talisman and make a calamus sword or a rattan whip, then hang them together with garlic on the doors to avoid evils. Meanwhile, they would burn some medicinal herbs like atractylodes and angelica root to get the rooms fumigated and bathe with hot water blended with wormwood leaves and calamus. Some households would "decorate the doors with five-color peach charms to dispel evils".

Clever-minded and nimble-fingered, girls in Suzhou would never miss the talent-showing chance on the Dragon Boat Festival. Several days before the festival, they would start to stitch embroidered pouches, inside which medicinal herbs like realgar, atractylodes and vanilla were stuffed. Looking exquisite and smelling fragrant, such lovely ornaments were called perfume pouches or realgar pouches, which could dispel plagues and viruses when worn. On the surfaces of these pouches patterns like flowers and birds and beasts were embroidered with silk threads, pretty beautiful and endearing.

249

Like wearing "Wudu" vests, having an "orchid bath" was also a health-keeping custom. On the Dragon Boat Festival, people here would soak dozens of herbs and medicines like wormwood and calamus in the water and boil the water for a bath, for it was said that having such a bath could drive away all mosquitoes. Bathing custom was seen all over ancient China, but only in regions south of the Yangtze River, could it be called "orchid bath", reflecting the more sophisticated aspect of Duanwu culture here.

In Suzhou, the locals have preserved the custom of eating "Five Huang"(五 黄)——huangyu (yellow croaker), huangshan (ricefield eel), huanggua (cucumber), yadanhuang (salted duck egg yolk) and xionghuang (realgar) wine. (in Chinese, 黄—— huang could mean yellow) Yellow croakers and eels are both seasonal food with high tonic effects, and realgar could sterilize and kill pests.

5. "Children's Day"——the Dragon Boat Festival in Chenjiagang Town

When the locals living in Chenjiagang Town (Yancheng City, Jiangsu Province) celebrate the Dragon Boat Festival, the Duanwu customs appear in their natural forms in the life of every household. In Chenjiagang Town, a small port located at the mouth of the sea where the Guan River merges into the sea, the Dragon Boat Festival celebrated here is also called "Children's Day", since children will become the primary concern of the festival. Apart from hanging wormwood, eating zongzi, tying five-color threads and wearing perfume pouches, other customs like boiling eggs, bathing with hot water boiled with green grass and eating cucumbers pickled in realgar wine are still preserved. The children will wear new clothes of course.

The locals take much count of Duanwu and every household will celebrate it (even those childless families will do so). Duanwu customs in Chenjiagang Town can be described from the following two aspects: preparations before the festival and festivities during the festival.

5.1 Preparations before the Festival

With their special love for the Dragon Boat Festival, the locals here will make preparations several days before this red-letter day. They will go shopping together and prepare some food for the festival. Before the Dragon Boat Festival, on the streets the stands selling festive goods are placed everywhere. Girls or daughters-in-law will choose their favorite articles——wearings first of course: five-colored threads, perfume pouches and dresses. In fact, except white threads, many other colored ones (more than five colors) can be found, among which customers can choose any (whether pure-colored or motley), with one strand costing one yuan usually. In the past, only embroidery threads were sold, but now cashmere threads are also welcome. Such threads are also weaved into bracelets, on which alloyed or silver ornaments in shape of petty bells, walnuts and flowers are embellished. Those girls will always lay their hands on such exquisite and lovely bracelets. Perfume pouches are also of great variety——flower/bird/zodiac animal-patterned pouches might dazzle your eyes. Those nimble-fingered girls used to stitch heart-shaped perfume pouches on their own, into which they would put vanilla or dried flowers. And nowadays, perfume pouches on sale are usually machine-embroidered with more variety of spices stuffed. Additionally, clothing shops are also much visited, as parents all hope to dress up their children with new clothes to greet the Dragon Boat Festival.

Apart from wearings, many other goods need to be pur-

251

chased: reed leaves, glutinous rice, sugar, red dates, dried fruits, wormwood, calamus, alum cakes and realgar. Reed leaves are indispensable for wrapping zongzi. To be able to eat zongzi in time in the morning of the Dragon Boat Festival, the locals will wrap zongzi and boil them till soft just one day ahead of the festival. In the past, it was unadvisable to wrap zongzi too early, since they would easily go bad without the help of freezers in the scorching summer.

Besides buying wearings and wrapping zongzi, the locals have some other customs. For example, some will seek fortune on the very day of Duanwu——try to catch a toad, the bigger the better. Catching a toad is no easy work in fact, for toads are is easily found in a rainy day but hardly seen in shiny days in succession. Fortunately, toad is not a must for every household and only when there are old people in a family will the young go out catching.

5.2 Festivities during the Festival

In Chenjiagang Town, festivities during the festival mainly take place in the morning and at noon. In the morning, locals here will hang wormwood and eat zongzi and eggs. After lunch at noon, they will bathe, eat cucumbers soaked in realgar wine, tie five-color threads and wear perfume pouches. Meanwhile, they will preserve "cucumber alum cake" and "toad alum cake". The following customs are what the

An old man who sells multicolored wire

252

locals value most.

The first custom is hanging wormwood & calamus.

In the light of the old, the people here in the past would hang wormwood & calamus on the first day of the fifth lunar month to avoid evils. Legend has it that long long ago, when the fifth lunar month dawned a nameless genie would pop up and bite (or even eat) the residents here, scaring them so much. One day, a wandering Taoist came and told the people to hang wormwood & calamus on the doors, which could drive the genie away. His instruction turned out effective and the genie never appeared again. Later custom of hanging wormwood & calamus was handed on. Today, many locals are used to hanging wormwood & calamus in the morning of the Dragon Boat Festival, while many others will do so several days before the festival. Wormwood leaves are usually hung on the door canopies and window hoods, with varied amount——either a piece or a bundle is acceptable. Some families will hang wormwood on one side (or both sides) of the door canopies and window hoods. Every household will hang wormwood, but hanging calamus is just optional. There is a local saying: "Mosquitoes and gnats will appear on Double-fifth Day." Wormwood & calamus may release some kind of aromatic scent to drive away the mosquitoes and gnats, so people hang them for the sake of health-keeping. The locals here value wormwood more than calamus anyhow, perhaps because they are influenced by a local saying that "whoever hangs no wormwood on the double-fifth day will turn into a cabbage on his dying day".

The second custom is eating eggs in the morning.

On the double-fifth day, ladies (esp. mothers) will get up early, not to make breakfast, but to pick the most tender dewy green grass in the grassland. When returning home, they will

253

make breakfast——boil zongzi (cooked the previous day) and eggs (chicken eggs, duck eggs or goose eggs whatsoever) in the pot. When cooked, the eggs will release unique fresh scent of reed leaves, much pleasing to the palate. Adults like to eat zongzi directly, while the kids prefer to dip the soft and glutinous paste in the sugar and eat the sugar-coated zongzi. When going to school, the kids will take their boiled eggs to "contest" with other classmates——make two eggs crack against each other. The owner of harder-shelled eggs will win, much delighted. There is another local saying that "three chicken eggs and four duck eggs will cure dizziness"——if you eat three chicken eggs and four duck eggs on the Dragon Boat Festival, you won't feel dizzy any more.

Another custom is bathing and wearing new clothes.

Locals here will have lunch earlier than usual with richer dishes——pork and fish are indispensable! Delicious food is always prepared to go with wine——even the kids are allowed to drink a little on the Dragon Boat Festival. After lunch, women will boil a pot of water added with the grass picked in the morning. The boiled water looks light-green and crystal-clear. At noon, they will add some cold water into the pot and bathe the kids with the much cooler water. It is said that bathing the kids with such water could help to cure eczema and some other skin diseases. Bath over, parents will mix some realgar with a little wine and churn them until the mixture becomes paste, then smear it on the kids' ears, navels and anuses. Meanwhile, they will also eat a piece of realgar-wine-soaked cucumber. The locals like to lie on the ground for cooling bodies in the hot summer, so they smear the realgar paste to prevent the snakes and poisonous insects. All the above festive activities over, the kids now can put on the new clothes prepared by their parents.

The fourth custom is tying silk threads and wearing perfume pouches.

Such a custom is also called "making a knot" with silk threads——usually the elder will tie silk threads around the junior's wrist, ankle or even knuckle. Well-matched colored silk threads are tied around the wrist and a half-knock is made with the one-inch ends of threads. The half-knock is tightly strained in case it is easily untied, while the uneven tassels are scissored neat. Silk threads are usually tied around both the kid's wrist and ankle, but only the wrist of much older teenager——"around the boy's left wrist (ankle) and the girl's right wrist (ankle)", a common festive custom. Once Ying Shao (in the East Han Dynasty) wrote in his book "Overview of Customs"——"On the double-fifth day, the five-color longevity cords are tied to prolong the kids' life." Zongtan (in the 6th century, the Southern Dynasties) also pointed out in his book "Records of Customs and Festivals in the Chu Region"　——"On the double-fifth day, the custom of tying five-color threads around the kids' arms is called 'war-avoiding' to prevent diseases and plagues." According to them, the five-color threads were taken as longevity cords or talismans. However, different from their views, the locals in Chenjiagang Town hold that tying five-color threads will prevent the cramping of hands and feet. Some others will tie the threads around anywhere that is apt to cramp——the wrist, ankle and even the knuckle as well.

Silk-thread-tied perfume pouches are hung under the necks to prevent bad luck. Once tied, the five-color threads should be worn until the sixth day of the sixth lunar month, otherwise the kids could not be blessed. Such custom derives from the age-old story——"Meeting of Cowherd and Weaving Maid". On the sixth day of the sixth lunar month, if you scissor the five-color threads and throw them up onto the roof, on the seventh day of the seventh lunar month the magpies will come and take them away in their mouths to build a bridge, on which Cowherd and his beloved wife Zhinv——Weaving Maid could meet after one year's sorrowful departure. If your silk threads are really taken away by the magpies, you hide under the grape trellis on the evening of the seventh day of the seventh lunar month (Qixi Day——Chinese Lover's Day), and chances are that you will "hear" the two lovers' soft and sweet talk.

The fifth custom is preparing alum cakes in the Dragon Boat Festival.

At noon of the Dragon Boat Festival, many households will prepare (pickle) "cucumber alum cake" and "toadalum cake", that's why a toad should be caught beforehand as mentioned. "Cucumber alum cake" as such, is made of cucumber, realgar and alum. Hollowing out half a cucumber, the locals will smear realagr on its inside wall and put a piece of alum cake into the cavity. Then, they will pierce both the ends of the cucumber with a needle (with thread) and hang it under the eave. After ten days' exposure to the weather, the skin of the cucumber is sundried, while its moisture and the smeared realgar are absorbed by the alum cake. Now, this alum cake can be taken out for use. The making of "toadalum cake" derives from the age-old idea "Set a thief to catch a thief": people think the poisonous skin of toad can cure some ailments. Here is one folk remedy to cope with toothache: Smear the secretion of toad's skin on the aching part or drip it directly into the hole of the decayed tooth to stop ache. As the saying goes that "the older a toad is, the more poisonous it is", the locals like to use the bigger (older) toad to make alum cake; meanwhile, they also prefer its larger capacity——making of larger alum cake is possible.

However, making of "toad alum cake" is more or less cruel: the locals will directly stuff the alum cakes into the belly of a living toad through its mouth until none else can be stuffed, and then hang the dying toad under the eave. It will take much longer to make "toad alum cake"——up to 20 days or one month, and only when the toad is totally sundried can the alum cake be taken out. The locals think it's advisable to make "cucumber alum cake" and "toad alum cake" on the double-fifth day, for they hold that on that day (the summer solstice), the hottest sunshine in a year could easily kill viruses and the alum cake absorbing the strongest solar heat at noon could diminish inflammation with doubled effect. If one suffers from mouth ulcer or the like, he only needs to take some alum cakes ("Cucumber alum cakes" could be used for the mild symptoms while "toad alum cakes" the severe, with no clear differences.) and make them melt in the water. Rinsing the mouth with such "alum" water could ease tooth pains soon——a unique medical effect of the alum cake. Apart from sterilizing with the alum cakes, the locals also warm their feet with the sundried pebbles to remove dampness or soak the feet with sundried bittern to cure foot-cracking. Noon over, when the locals finish making the alum cakes, they will have no other festive activities and the Dragon Boat Festival will come to an end.

In Chenjiagang Town, the Dragon Boat Festival celebrated here is also called "Children's Day", and the children are especially joyful as they will enjoy new clothes and delicious food. The young also look forward to this festival, for they will wear new clothes and silk threads as the kids do, much delighted too. The busy mothers value the holiday most——seeing their children dressed beautifully (the better if more beautifully than other kids) and their prepared food better than others', they will feel much flattered. The senior male, usually unable to lend a hand, has no special activities, but relishes the festival air and his big family vibrant with life.

5.3 A Festival every year

Locals here particularly think highly of the Dragon Boat Festival because they believe the double-fifth day is a special day, when the midday sunlight with its strong sterilizing efficacy could help to cure some ailments. Duanwu involves the real coming of summer, when along the coast of this small town, it is a good timing for the gourmets to enjoy those big and tasty seafoods of great variety and the seafood vendors to earn more money than usual. If it happens to rain on the Dragon Boat Festival, that doesn't matter, for there is a local saying that "the jellyfish will grow bigger and faster if it happens to rain on Duanwu"——rain is a symbol of harvest. Meanwhile, the increasing number of jellyfish also involves a harvest this year. All in all, rain or shine, the double-fifth day is always lucky for the locals here.

Tips for Tourism

Chenjiagang Town, Yancheng City

Chenjiagang Town, a member of the "One Hundred Famous Towns" in Jiangsu Province, lies to the north of Yancheng City. Located at the mouth of the sea where the Guan River (also called "Huangpu River in Northern Jiangsu") merges into the sea, this town is administered by Xiangshui County and itself administers 13 villages and 6 neighborhood committees (communities), with its area of over 151.6 km² and a population of 68,000. Lying to the west of the Yellow Sea and to the south of the Guan River, Chenjiagang Town was founded in 1929 (originally called "Razor-Clam Airing Stand Port" ,with the pronunciation similar to

Chenjiagang in Chinese). It has long been famous for its abundant natural resources and the four—gill bass growing here is especially well—known both at home and abroad. The "Eight Scenes of Guan River" and Kai—shan Isle make here more beautiful. At present, Chenjiagang (used to be a small town) has developed into a modernized well—off port town rich in tourism resources.

After reaching Yancheng and Lianyungang by air or by train, the travelers could go to Chenjiagang by taking coaches. This short trip will take an hour (from Yancheng) or 40 minutes (from Lianyungang) respec—tively.

By expressway, the travelers could get to Shanghai in 3.5 hours, Nan—jing, Suzhou, Wuxi and Changzhou in 3 hours, Nantong in 1.5 hours, Yancheng in 1 hour and Lianyungang in 40 minutes.

Influenced by the temperate continental climate, it is cool in summer and warm in winter here, with the temperature somewhat low in winter. The best tourist season starts in May and ends in October, with the Drag—on Boat Festival the best of the best.

259

附　录 Appendix

关于端午节食品、装饰、玩具制作的三个小技巧
The Making Process of Festive Food, Ornament and Toy

　　为了便于中外读者深入了解和体验中国端午节的习俗，本书特辑录三个端午标志物（粽子、香包、小龙舟）的制作方法和技巧，以飨读者。

In order to facilitate our readers' in-depth understanding and better experiencing of the customs of Chinese Dragon Boat Festival, we have collected some tips for making three symbolic items (namely zongzi, perfume pouches and little paper dragon boat).

一、"粽子"的制作方法
Tips for Making Zongzi

　　粽子又称"角黍""筒粽"，由粽叶包裹糯米蒸制而成，是中华民族传统节庆食物之一。其制作步骤如下：

Zongzi, also called "jiaoshu" (horn-shaped) and "tongzong" (tube-shaped), is one of the most common traditional Chinese festive foods. It is usually made of glutinous rice wrapped by reed leaves. Here are some tips for making and cooking.

制作步骤 /Procedures

1. 选择当年、新鲜的优质糯米，把大片竹叶放水里浸泡，用清水洗净。
Choose quality glutinous rice (fresh rice of the year best), then soak big reed leaves in the water and clean them.

2. 选择两张粽叶，将粽叶反面相叠，窝成一个漏斗形。
Choose two pieces of reed leaves and fold them from the back sides (one leaf halfly covering the other) to make it funnel-shaped.

3. 依次在粽叶里填入糯米，肉等料，将粽叶翻转封住馅心，然后用粽绳捆紧。一定要包紧，尤其是绳子要扎牢。
Fill the "funnel" with glutinous rice and meat, then overturn the sticking-out part of the leaves to cover the fillings and tie the "half-made" zongzi with a string of reed-made rope. Bear it in mind that the ropes must be tied tight!

4. 在锅中倒入水，沸腾后把裹好的肉粽放入锅中煮熟。同时，锅内的水要浸没粽子，不要让粽子露出。
Pour water into the pot and put the wrapped zongzi into the water after it is boiled. Remember that zongzi must be totally drowned by the water!

5. 粽子起锅即可剥去竹叶食用。
After zongzi are cooked, you may enjoy them when they are unwrapped.

二、"香包"挂件的制作方法
Tips for Making an Ornament——Perfume Pouch

香包，又称香囊、香袋、香缨、佩帏，用绸布制成，内装雄黄、熏草、艾叶等香料。它是古代汉族劳动妇女创造的一种民间刺绣工艺品，也是以男耕女织为标志的古代汉族农耕文化的产物。据说香包可以避邪，端午节时多会配挂香包。

With other names like perfume purse, perfume bag, perfume tassel and perfume pouch for wearing, perfume pouch is usually made of silk inside which spices like realgar, melilot and mugwort leaves are filled. Traditionally, it not only was one folk embroidery handcraft created by the Han workwomen, but also witnessed the men-plough-and-women-weave family-working pattern which symbolized the farming culture of the Han people. It is said that perfume pouch could drive away evils, so on the Dragon Boat Festival it was worn everywhere.

制作步骤 /Procedures

1. 准备材料：白卡纸或挂历纸、彩色荧光笔或毛线、吊坠、细铁丝。
Prepare materials needed——ivory board paper or calendar paper, colored
fluorescent pens or colored woolen threads, one tassel and a short thin iron wire.

2. 将白卡纸裁剪成一溜儿大小的纸条。
Cut the board paper into several pieces of smaller slips of the same size

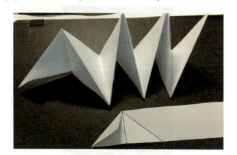

3. 将纸条按照三角形对折，然后拆开叠成菱形。
Fold the paper slips in the shape of a triangle and then unfold these triangles to make
them diamond-like.

4. 将吊坠串在细铁丝或粗线上，从菱形粽子香包中间穿过。

Fix one end of the the thin iron wire or thick thread with the tassel and then make the other end go through the diamond–shaped paper "zongzi" (perfume pouch).

5. 以此继续折大小不等的菱形粽子香包，再一一串起来。

Go on folding diamond–shaped paper "zongzi" (perfume pouches) in different sizes and bunch them together.

6. 用荧光笔上色，也可以用各色丝线缠绕在表面。

Color the pouches with florescent pens or twine the colored threads around the surfaces.

三、"小型龙舟"的手工制作方法
Tips for Making a Paper Dragon Boat

龙舟是船上画着龙的形状或做成龙的形状的船。赛龙舟是端午节的传统水上体育娱乐项目，多人集体划桨竞赛，是我国悠久历史文化继承性和集体主义精神的充分体现。

The Dragon boat refers to the boat that is drawn or made in the shape of a dragon. Dragon boat races are traditional folk water sports on the Dragon Boat Festival. The dragon boat races, which could be finished only by teams of rowers, have always fully embodied the inheritance of Chinese long history and brilliant cultures and demonstrated the long-geld teamwork spirit of Chinese people.

制作步骤 /Procedures

1. 准备材料：废弃的牛奶包装盒、牛皮信封、牙签、荧光笔、一次性筷子。
Prepare materials needed——one used milk packing carton, one brown envelop, several toothpicks, florescent pens and one disposable chopstick.

2. 将牛奶盒对半剪开，将其中一半作为船舱，另一半用来绘制龙头和龙尾。
Cut the milk carbon in half from the middle, with one half for making the cabin and the other the "head" and "tail" of the dragon.

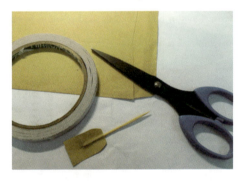

3. 用牛皮纸信封和牙签制作船桨。
Make oars with the brown paper and toothpicks.

4. 将制作好的船桨插入船舱两侧。
Make oars go through both sides of the boat.

5. 将剩下的牛皮纸信封制作成船帆，并用一次性筷子串起来，毛线作为纤绳，并上色。

Make the sail with the brown paper unused and use the disposable chopstick as the mast. Make oars go through both sides of the boat. Colored threads (you may also paint them as you like) could be used as the "fixing cables".

丛书后记

上下五千年的悠久历史孕育了灿烂辉煌的中华文化。我国地域辽阔，民族众多，节庆活动丰富多彩，而如此众多的节庆活动就是一座座珍贵丰富的旅游资源宝藏。在中华民族漫长的历史长河中，春节、清明、端午、中秋等传统节日和少数民族节日，是中华民族优秀传统文化的历史积淀，是中华民族精神和情感传承的重要载体，是维系祖国统一、民族团结、文化认同、社会和谐的精神纽带，是中华民族生生不息的不竭动力。

春节以正月为岁首，贴门神、朝贺礼；元宵节张灯、观灯；清明节扫墓、踏青、郊游、赏牡丹；端午节赛龙舟、包粽子；上巳节祓禊；七夕节乞巧，牛郎会织女；中秋节赏月、食月饼；节日间的皮影戏、长安鼓乐；少数民族的节日赶圩、歌舞美食……这一桩桩有趣的节日习俗，是联络华人、华侨亲情、乡情、民族情的纽带，是中国非物质文化遗产的"活化石"。

为了传播中华民族优秀传统文化，推进中外文化交流，中国人类学民族学研究会民族节庆专业委员会与安徽人民出版社合作，继成功出版《中国节庆文化》丛书之后，再次推出《多彩中国节》丛书。为此，民族节庆专委会专门成立了编纂委员会，邀请了国际节庆协会（IFEA）主席兼首席执行官史蒂文·施迈德先生、中国文联原执行副主席冯骥才先生、第十一届全国政协民族和宗教委员会副主任周明甫先生等担任顾问，由《中外节庆网》总编辑彭新良博士担任主编，16 位知名学者组成编委会，负责丛书的组织策划、选题确定、体例拟定和作者的甄选。

出版《多彩中国节》丛书，是民族节庆专业委员会和安徽人民出版社合作的结晶。安徽人民出版社是安徽省最早的出版社，有60余年的建社历史，在对外传播方面走在全国出版社的前列；民族节庆专业委员会是我国节庆研究领域唯一的国家级社团，拥有丰富的专家资源和地方节庆资源。这套丛书的出版，实现了双方优势资源的整合。丛书的面世，若能对推动中国文化的对外传播、促进传统民族文化的传承与保护、展示中华民族的文化魅力、塑造节庆的品牌与形象有所裨益，我们将甚感欣慰。

掩卷沉思，这套丛书凝聚着诸位作者的智慧，倾注着编纂者的心血，也诠释着中华民族文化的灿烂与辉煌。在此，真诚感谢各位编委会成员、丛书作者、译者以及出版社工作人员付出的辛劳，以及各界朋友对丛书编纂工作的鼎力支持！希望各位读者对丛书多提宝贵意见，以便我们进一步完善后续作品，将更加璀璨的节庆文化呈现在世界面前。

为了向中外读者更加形象地展示各民族的节庆文化，本丛书选用了大量图片。这些图片，既有来自于丛书作者的亲自拍摄，也有的来自民族节庆专委会图片库（由各地方节庆组织、节庆主办单位报送并授权使用），还有部分图片是由编委会从专业图片库购买，或从新闻媒体中转载。由于时间关系，无法与原作者一一取得联系，请有关作者与本书编委会联系（邮箱：pxl@jieqing365.com），我们将按相关规定支付稿酬。特此致谢。

《多彩中国节》丛书编委会

2018 年 3 月

丛书后记

Series Postscript

China has developed its splendid and profound culture during its long history of 5000 years. It has a vast territory, numerous nationalities as well as the colorful festivals. The rich festival activities have become the invaluable tourism resources. The traditional festivals, such as the Spring Festival, the Tomb-Sweeping Festival, the Dragon Boat Festival, the Mid-Autumn Festival as well as the festivals of ethnic minorities, represent the excellent traditional culture of China and have become an important carrier bearing the spirits and emotions of Chinese people, a spirit tie for the national reunification, national unity, cultural identity and social harmony, and an inexhaustible motive force for the development of Chinese nation.

The Spring Festival starts with Chinese lunar January, when people post pictures of the Door Gods and exchange gifts and wishes cheerfully. At the Lantern Festival a splendid light show is to be held and enjoyed. On the Tomb-Sweeping Festival, men and women will worship their ancestors by sweeping the tombs, going for a walk in the country and watching the peony. And then the Dragon Boat Festival witnesses a wonderful boat race and the making of zongzi. Equally interesting is the needling celebration on the Double Seventh Festival related to a touching love story of a cowboy and his fairy bride. While the Mid-Autumn Festival is characterized by moon-cake eating and moon watching. Besides all these, people can also enjoy shadow puppet shows, Chang'an drum performance, along with celebration fairs, songs and dances and delicious snacks for ethic groups. A variety of festival entertainment and celebrations have formed a bond among all Chinese, at home or abroad, and they are regarded as the "living fossil" of Chinese intangible cultural heritage.

In order to spread the excellent traditional culture of China, and promote the folk festival brand for our country, the Folk Festival Commission of the China Union of Anthropological and Ethnological Science (CUAES) has worked with the Anhui People's Publishing House to publish *The Colorful Chinese Festivals Series*. For this purpose, the Folk Festival Commission has established the editorial board of *The Colorful Chinese Festivals Series*, by inviting Mr. Steven Wood Schmader, president and CEO of the International Festival And Events Association (IFEA); Mr. Feng Jicai, former executive vice-president of China Federation of Literary and Art Circles(CFLAC); Mr. Zhou Mingfu, deputy director of the Eleventh National and Religious Committee of the CPPCC as consultants; Dr. Peng Xinliang, editor-in-chief of the Chinese and foreign Festival Website as the chief editor; and 16 famous scholars as the members to organize, plan, select and determine the topics and the authors.

This series is the product of the cooperation between the Folk Festival Commission and Anhui People's Publishing House. Anhui People's Publishing House is the first publishing house in Anhui Province, which has a history of over 60 years, and has been in the leading position in terms of foreign transmission. The Folk Festival Commission is the only organization of national level in the field of research of the Chinese festivals, which has experts and rich local festival resources. The series has integrated the advantageous resources of both parties. We will be delighted and gratified to see that the series could promote the foreign transmission of the Chinese culture, promote the inheritance and preservation of the traditional and folk cultures, express the cultural charms of China and build the festival brand and image of China.

The Colorful Chinese Festivals Series is bearing the wisdoms and knowledge of all of its authors and the great efforts of the editors, and explaining the splendid cultures of the Chinese nation. We hereby sincerely express our gratitude to the members of the board, the authors, the translators and the personnel in the publishing house for their great efforts and to all friends from all walks of the society for their supports. We hope you can provide your invaluable opinions for us to further promote the following works so as to show the world our excellent festival culture.

This series uses a large number of pictures in order to unfold the festive cultures in a vivid way to readers at home and abroad. Some of them are shot by the authors themselves, some of them come from the picture database of the Folk Festival Commission (contributed and authorized by the local folk festival organizations or organizers of local festival celebrations), and some of them are bought from Saitu Website or taken from the news media. Because of the limit of time, we can't contact the contributors one by one. Please don't hesitate about contacting the editorial board of this series (e-mail: pxl@jieqing365.com) if you're the contributor. We'll pay you by conforming to the state stipulations.

Editorial Committee of *The Colorful Chinese Festivals Series*
March, 2018